Consumption, Cities and States

Consumption, Cities and States

Comparing Singapore with Asian and Western Cities

Ann Brooks and Lionel Wee

ANTHEM PRESS
LONDON · NEW YORK · DELHI

Anthem Press
An imprint of Wimbledon Publishing Company
www.anthempress.com

This edition first published in UK and USA 2015
by ANTHEM PRESS
75–76 Blackfriars Road, London SE1 8HA, UK
or PO Box 9779, London SW19 7ZG, UK
and
244 Madison Ave #116, New York, NY 10016, USA

First published in hardback by Anthem Press in 2014

British Library Cataloguing-in-Publication Data
A catalogue record for this book is available from the British Library.

Library of Congress Cataloging-in-Publication Data
The Library of Congress has cataloged the hardcover edition as follows:
Brooks, Ann (Professor)
Consumption, cities, and states: comparing Singapore with Asian and western cities /
Ann Brooks and Lionel Wee.
pages cm. – (Key issues in modern sociology)
Includes bibliographical references and index.
ISBN 978-1-78308-226-1 (hardcover : alk. paper)
1. Singapore–Economic conditions. 2. Asia–Economic conditions. 3. Western
countries–Economic conditions. 4. Citizenship–Singapore. 5. Citizenship–Asia. 6.
Citizenship–Western countries. I. Wee, Lionel, 1963- II. Title.
HC445.8.B76 2014
339.4'7–dc23
2014011572

ISBN-13: 978 1 78308 426 5 (Pbk)
ISBN-10: 1 78308 426 X (Pbk)

Cover photo: aphotostory/Shutterstock.com

This title is also available as an ebook.

TABLE OF CONTENTS

ACKNOWLEDGMENTS

The authors would like to acknowledge the support of a number of individuals in this project. Ann Brooks was supported by a six-month Asia Research Institute (ARI) senior visiting research fellowship at the National University of Singapore (NUS) and Lionel Wee and Ann Brooks were supported by a grant from the NUS toward the production of the book. Both authors are immensely grateful for this support, without which the book would not have been possible. We would particularly like to thank Professor Prasenjit Duara, director of the ARI and Raffles professor of humanities and director of research for humanities and social sciences in the Faculty of Arts and Social Sciences at the NUS, for his immense support of the project. We would also like to acknowledge the support of the migration cluster leader and dean of the Faculty of Arts and Social Sciences, Professor Brenda Yeoh. In addition the entire administrative team at the ARI were immensely supportive. A special thanks to Jonathan Lee from the ARI team for his assistance in designing the front cover of the book. Both authors wish to acknowledge the encouragement of Bryan Turner in suggesting Anthem Press to us. At Anthem our editor Rob Reddick and the entire team at Anthem have been excellent and made the production process effortless.

INTRODUCTION

In this book we analyze the intersection of consumption and rights within the context of different states and cities in Asia and the West. We focus on the concept of the global city and consider a range of contested understandings within this concept.

We are interested in the cultural economy and political economy of the global city set in the context of globalization. Stevenson (2013, 38) notes, 'In "wealthy nations" such as Japan, Australia, and those of North America and Western Europe, between 72 and 95 percent of the population lives in cities, whereas in Africa and Asia, the percentage is 38 and 41, respectively.' Despite the figure for Asia, what is clear is that global cities are becoming the hallmark of growth in Asia. A key factor in the growth of cities globally in late modernity is neoliberalism. Theoretical debates around neoliberalism are thus explored in the chapters of this book. Stevenson observes that 'Neoliberalism is also implicated in the increasing spatial division and fragmentation that is evident in cities around the world. Of significance is a deepening of the inequitable distribution of urban resources, which although taking a number of forms, is perhaps most highly visible in residential segregation' (Stevenson 2013, 26).

Different cities offer different insights, and we draw on the Asian city-state of Singapore as an exemplar of an aspiring global city. Singapore is of particular interest because it also serves as a model for many other cities and states with aspirations toward global city status (see Chua 2011). To provide a more comprehensive analysis we also draw on a range of cities in Asia and in the West to highlight parallels and divergences. Secondly, cities also exist as part of states. This then raises the further question of whether it might be at all feasible to attempt an exploration of the politics of global city aspirations without taking into account the relationships between cities and states. In this introductory chapter we briefly outline our thoughts on these issues in order to provide some background to the book.

Ranking Cities

Cities have long been the subject of rankings. A report in the 1990s by the London Planning Advisory Committee maintained that only London, Tokyo, New York and Paris could legitimately claim to be world-class cities, while other world cities such as Milan, Frankfurt, Berlin and Hong Kong could be considered as being in the process of pursuing this elite label. There are a number of other reports that have also produced contemporary rankings of global cities. The Globalization and World Cities Research Network, based in Loughborough University in the United Kingdom (http://www.lboro.ac.uk/gawc/projects/projec71.html, accessed 18 July 2013), 'has developed an influential classificatory system that ranks cities in groups. […] According to the criteria employed, two cities (London and New York) receive the highest Alpha++ rating with eight (Beijing, Shanghai, Singapore, Tokyo, Sydney, Milan, Hong Kong and Paris) being ranked as Alpha+' (Stevenson 2013, 124). An Asian research institute (the Institute for Urban Strategies) in Japan has produced another kind of ranking model called the Global Power City Index, which 'ranks major cities of the world according to their comprehensive power to attract creative people and excellent companies from around the world amidst an environment of increasingly strong urban competition worldwide' (Institute for Urban Strategies 2010, 1). Based on this index, the top four cities globally in rank order are New York, London, Paris and Tokyo. What is becoming clear from a range of surveys is a marked shift in global economic power from West to East. This is confirmed by the Knight Frank Global Cities Survey (2011), which predicts that 'New York and London will continue to occupy the top two spots on the list but Paris will drop to ninth and the "gap" between the two top cities and the rest will close considerably. And where the 2010 survey has two Asian cities (Tokyo and Beijing) in the top ten, there are six in the 2020 forecast (Tokyo, Beijing, Shanghai, Mumbai, Hong Kong and Singapore)' (Stevenson 2013, 125).

States and Cities

The emergence of the concept of the global city is linked in economic terms with the move from an international to a global economy (see Amin and Thrift 1992, 2008). As Stevenson (2013, 123) indicates and as we show below, 'In this respect, Saskia Sassen's (1991) characterization of global cities as the "command centers" of the global economy and the associated empirical focus on transnational networks of business and finance have been influential in setting the research agenda.'

In this book we draw on Singapore as a benchmark for global city aspirations, while also making a number of comparisons with other cities and states. This is motivated by various considerations. Singapore represents a particularly clear and explicit example of a state that is responding to globalization by aggressively attempting to transform into a 'global' or 'cosmopolitan' city. The state uses these terms interchangeably, and these therefore represent exactly the aspirational categories that need to be distinguished from Sassen's own use of 'global city', which is intended as part of an analytical model for understanding the flow of finance and related services in the context of the global economy (2001, 8). These two uses of 'global city' – the more academic and the more political/populist – are of course related since Sassen's influential study is no doubt a contributory factor in Singapore's desire to appropriate the label for itself. However, the measures that the state undertakes to effect this transformation do not always sit easily with its attempts to also maintain Singapore's identity as an Asian nation-state, and managing the potential conflicts between the 'global city' and the 'Asian nation-state' narratives leads a variety of negotiations between state and society. In this regard, a focus on Singapore promises to throw up a host of interesting insights into the problems and issues that may need to be faced as cities aim to be seen as global cities.

However, this book is also concerned with the relationship between cities and states. Thus Singapore also stands out in that it is both a city as well as a state. Singapore's political status as a city-state gives its political leaders a fair amount of leeway in introducing policy initiatives that are intended to transform Singapore into a global city, certainly more so than the political leaders of cities that are not city-states (and conversely leaders of states that are not coextensive with cities). Thus, a focus on Singapore brings into relief certain affordances and advantages that other cities and states may not necessarily enjoy. This is where a comparative orientation becomes useful. By comparing the data from Singapore with other states and cities, it becomes easier to both understand and also extract some generalizations concerning the social politics behind global city transformations. As Stevenson (2013, 123) notes, 'Increasingly in political and economic terms it is global cities rather than nation states that have international hegemony.' In this book, then, we make comparisons – in varying degrees of detail – with other cities in Asia and the West, such as Sydney, Hong Kong, Kuala Lumpur and San Francisco, among others.

Dimensions of Consumption: Reflexivity, Cosmopolitanism and Citizenship

We are interested in how the phenomenon of consumption is managed in the context of cities and states. Because of this, we find it necessary to situate our discussion of consumption in relation to institutional reflexivity, cosmopolitanism and citizenship. This section elaborates on our reasoning.

Global cities are an aspect of late modernity. The latter's theoretical underpinnings have been captured in debates around reflexivity and within sociological theory, including debates around 'reflexive modernization' (Beck 1992, 1994, 2000; Beck et al. 1992, 1994; Giddens 1991, 1992). Thus, as regards the issue of thematic focus, we think it is important to give particular attention to the notion of reflexivity. This is because aspirations of any sort implicate identity work: they point to how the aspiring entity sees and evaluates itself, as well as what the entity would like itself to be. Global city aspirations are no different in this respect.

But while reflexivity represents a theme of major sociological interest, discussions and explorations about reflexivity have often tended to be focused at the level of the individual. Questions then arise about the extent to which such reflexivity might or might not lead to greater individual agency (Adkins 2003; Giddens 1991, 1992; Kennedy 2001). Sustained exploration of reflexivity has also led to intersections with other significant sociological themes, such as cosmopolitanism, consumption and citizenship (Beck 2000, 2006; Ellison 1997; Wee and Brooks 2010).

In our view, while this focus on the individual is warranted, it has also rather unfortunately resulted in a tendency to underplay the reflexivity of institutions. We grant that institutional reflexivity is ultimately enacted by individuals, but when individuals do so in their capacities as institutional agents, they are faced with rather different kinds of constraints arising from the fact that institutions qua highly public entities are entrusted to pursue specific programs or causes. So, when individuals holding key institutional positions (the president of a university, a government minister, the CEO of a corporation) start revisiting and re-evaluating these programs or causes – especially in consultation with relevant advisory boards or shareholders, or via public referendums – the unavoidable result is a set of reflective negotiations about institutional priorities and the strategies for realizing them. But in the context of global city aspirations, the notion of institutional reflexivity itself becomes inextricably linked to other sociological themes, such as cosmopolitanism, citizenship and consumption. What is needed, then, is a sufficiently comprehensive approach that provides a theoretical articulation of both individual and institutional reflexivity, while connecting these to a consistent empirical base that not only allows for sociological themes such as cosmopolitanism, citizenship and consumption to be highlighted, but also allows the analysis to address the interrelationships between them.

This book aims to do exactly this. We develop an analytical framework for approaching reflexivity that acknowledges its manifestation as an institutional as well as individual phenomenon, while also acknowledging reflexivity's transformative potential and thus its relationship to agency. In addition we examine the construction of the cosmopolitan, and the positioning of the 'citizen-consumer'. We show that the analysis of negotiated responses involving the state can be usefully viewed through the lens of sociological themes such as cosmopolitanism, citizenship and consumption, which therefore provide the rubrics by which we organize our discussion in the book. In the case of cosmopolitanism, it is common to raise questions about the ability of the state to serve as a framework for community membership. We also focus on the relationship between citizenship rights, consumption and reflexivity. We do this by drawing particularly on data from the US and Singapore. The issue of consumption is a focus of the debates around how to govern the 'citizen-consumer'. Consumption is also relevant because the state in Singapore has realized that, if it is to enhance its reputation as a global city, there must be sufficient 'buzz' to make it attractive to mobile and affluent individuals. This has led the Singapore state to reconsider its long-time ban on casinos. Thus an analysis of the reflexivity of the state vis-à-vis consumption on issues such as casinos is also the subject of a discussion of the citizen-consumer. Comparisons are made with other casino cultures including Macau and Las Vegas, to name a few. We draw on Ritzer's (2010) concept of 'cathedrals of consumption' to understand a global model of consumption which extends beyond casinos.

A second dimension that focuses on the reflexivity of the Singapore state is the response to the consumption potential of the 'pink dollar' and attitudes toward the gay community. This issue is considered in some detail via a comparison between San Francisco and Singapore. When consumption activities raise the specter of gambling addiction or are potentially at odds with more conservative sexual mores, reflexivity enters the picture because one of the ways in which the state aims to regulate consumer activity is by calling for consumer self-discipline (in the case of gambling) and consumer discretion (in the case of the gay community). These two dimensions provide interesting local and global examples of both consumption and reflexivity.

Organization of the Book

The theoretical underpinnings of the book provide an important framework for both conceptual development and understanding the relevance of examples. Chapter 1 of this book, 'Consumption, Reflexivity and Citizenship in Global Cities', illustrates the sociological significance of reflexivity with reference to three themes that together form the central theoretical dimensions of this book: cosmopolitanism, citizenship and consumption, even though our key interest is in the latter. As mentioned above, there has been a tendency to focus on reflexivity at the level of the individual, to the extent where reflexivity at the level of the institution appears to have been neglected. We demonstrate this lacuna in Chapter 1, and our discussion will then set the stage for the theoretical framework that we present in Chapter 2.

In Chapter 2, 'Orders of Reflexivity', we develop an analytical framework for approaching reflexivity that acknowledges both its institutional as well as individual manifestations. We do this by drawing on Bohman's (1999) reworking of the Bourdieusian habitus, the latter having been criticized for being overly deterministic. Bohman's reworking of Bourdieu starts with the position that reflexive practices that encourage deliberations and debates can in fact lead to transformative second-order desires, such as the desire to be a certain kind of individual/institution, or the desire to have certain kinds of goals and not others. In our discussion of Bohman's rehabilitation of Bourdieu, we also explain how the notion of a habitus benefits from greater attention being given to the mediating roles of reflexivity and ambivalence. Our argument is that where second-order desires result from deliberations and public debates, transformations in identity conceptions can and do emerge.

The main postulates of our framework are as follows:

(i)   Ambivalence represents a first-order conflict, arising from the need to resolve conflicting values as a result of participation in multiple markets. Ambivalence is pervasive because no individual or institution ever occupies only a single market.
(ii) Agency is to be construed as the balancing of available resources arising from the inevitable membership in different markets.
(iii) Second order reflexivity is especially relevant in late modernity in order to resolve first-order conflicts.

This emphasis on second-order reflexivity and deliberation motivates our choice of data, which is drawn from public speeches, newspaper reports, survey results and internet forums, among others, in order to track the developing discursive trajectories as states, cities and citizens negotiate the various initiatives and implications that arise from global city aspirations.

A major impetus for state initiatives comes from the changing relationship between a modernist state and the late modern conditions of existence. One such manifestation of this changing relationship is the relationship of the global city to the state. Chapter 3, 'Rescaling for Competitiveness', examines the relationship between Singapore as an Asian state and Singapore as a global city. This chapter raises the question of why Singapore is so keen on acquiring the status as a global city. To do this, we provide a brief historical description of Singapore's emergence as an independent nation-state in 1965. We show how the state has changed its narrative to gradually emphasize the need for Singapore to transform – in this case, rescale – itself into a global city. Our examination closes with a discussion of the concomitants of rescaling, where we give specific attention to the issues of temporality and competitiveness. A number of issues arising from our discussion of rescaling are pursued in greater detail in subsequent chapters. We make comparisons with other cities such as Kuala Lumpur and Sydney in order to understand whether Singapore shows any unique characteristics in its pursuit of global city status.

Chapter 4, 'The Dynamics of State–Society Negotiations', applies the framework developed in Chapter 2 to provide a broad-based understanding of the dynamic nature of state–society negotiations in Singapore. Even in a society that is as reputedly authoritarian as Singapore, the state has to explain and defend its policies in order to ensure that these gain traction among the general population. Here, we focus on the various ways in which public engagement is manifested. These include the National Day Rally speeches, various feedback mechanisms installed by the state, the state's initiation of 'Our Singapore Conversation', and its organization of 'Singapore Day'. We show that the state is very much concerned with consistently spelling out the rationales behind various policy initiatives. In doing so, we throw into relief the ongoing public discussions on what kind of society Singapore is or ought to be, and thus we also bring out the highly reflexive nature of the state. But such discussions, of course, also have implications for what kinds of individuals Singaporeans ought to be. The second-order reflexivity of the state then is in dialectical relation with that of its citizens.

Chapter 5, '(De-)Regulating Asian Identities: Comparing Asian Cities and States', takes up this issue of the dialectics between cities and states by comparing Singapore with Malaysia and Hong Kong. We begin with an explanation for our decision to focus on Asia, drawing specific attention to the fact that many states and cities in Asia have strong religious or other cultural commitments that might conflict with issues of sexual, ethnic and cultural diversity. Unlike Singapore, which is both a city and a state (a city-state), Malaysia represents a state that is unable to plausibly descale into a city, and Hong Kong represents a city that has (since the handover in 1997 to China) been co-opted back into a state. We develop our discussion in a comparative perspective with data from Malaysia and Hong Kong, providing a more nuanced appreciation of the relationship between cities and states (and the issues involved in any attempt to effect a global city transformation).

Chapter 6, 'Citizenship, Reflexivity and the State: Investigating "Defensive Engagement in a City-State"', gives specific attention to the relationship between citizenship, reflexivity and the state. As mentioned above, one of the most interesting issues regarding the study of citizenship has to do with

the relationship between a modernist state and the late modern conditions
of existence, and because of this, the chapter considers the various initiatives
undertaken by the state of Singapore in its attempts to reinvent itself in
varying contexts of rapid transformation, and how such attempts are received
by the populace (Brooks and Wee 2008; Ong 1999, 2006; Sassen 2006). In
making this study, the chapter draws on the work of Ellison (1997), who argues
that contemporary sociological perspectives on citizenship in late modernity
are problematic because they fail to properly appreciate that citizenship
can serve as a resource for negotiating social change. Ellison's own proposal
highlights the notion of citizenship as a form of the 'reflexive condition of
defensive engagement' (1997, 714). In this chapter, we consider these issues of
citizenship, reflexivity and defensive engagement, by drawing as a case study
on the successful attempt by the Singapore state to persuade Singaporeans
that recently legalized casino resorts should legitimately discriminate between
'locals' and 'foreigners'.

In Chapter 7, 'Governing the Citizen-Consumer: Citizenship, Casinos and
"Cathedrals of Consumption"', we look at the relationship between citizenship
and what Ritzer (2010) calls 'cathedrals of consumption'. While the study
of citizenship has taken into serious consideration the effects of migration
and settlement, attention to the citizen as consumer remains a relatively
neglected area of study. In this chapter we analyze the context of a more
dynamic definition of citizenship as a result of globalization, and examine
these relationships within the context of the cathedrals of consumption in
Singapore as well as the US. We focus on the issue of casinos as an example of
cathedrals of consumption and compare how they impact consumption in the
US, Macau and Singapore. Through these examples, we explore the dynamic
relationship between citizenship, consumption and the role of the state in late
modernity.

In Chapter 8, 'Regulating Consumption and the "Pink Dollar"', we move
to a different arena of consumption, that of the gay lifestyle. Aldrich (2004)
explores the historical relationship between cities and homosexuality and
maintains that homosexuals often preferred to live in cities to escape the sexual
and social limitations of suburban life. He also shows how homosexuals were
influential in both transforming the urban landscape and creating a particular
urban ethos and style. Gay culture is of course not a recent phenomenon, and
as will be shown in Chapters 8 and 9, many cities such as San Francisco, Paris
and Sydney have a long history of homosexual culture. For example, Aldrich
(2004, 1720) cites Gore Vidal's *The City and the Pillar* (1948), which described
the homosexual underworld in Hollywood and New York. In addition,
Armistead Maupin's *Tales of the City*, which was published between 1978 and
1989, 'chronicled gay life in San Francisco, from the coming out of small-town

boys come to enjoy the Bay city in an ebullient period of gay liberation to the physical and emotional trauma of AIDS'.

We set our examination in the context of a comparison between the gay communities in Singapore and a number of other cities including San Francisco, Sydney and Stockholm, as well as drawing on other cities such as Los Angeles, Rio de Janeiro and Bangkok. We show that in cities such as San Francisco there is no need for discreet consumption vis-à-vis the gay lifestyle and where it is a prominent and important part of the inclusive social fabric of San Francisco. But unlike Singapore, which is trying to inch its way toward a city that is 'gay friendly', San Francisco is struggling to maintain its reputation as a 'gay mecca'. These differences help to further bring out some of the problems facing cities as they aim to deal with issues of consumption.

The state in Singapore has shown itself to be fairly pragmatic on gay issues because it realizes the strategy to reinvent itself as a global/cosmopolitan city involves keen competition among different cities. Precisely because of this competition, in addition to legalizing casinos, the state has also been quite explicit about adopting a pragmatic attitude toward the gay community, because it appreciates that the 'pink dollar' can make a significant contribution to Singapore's economic growth. Gay tourists (and gay locals) are encouraged to enjoy themselves in Singapore so long as this is done in a discreet manner that does not make the more conservative segments of society uncomfortable. In both these cases, the state is therefore attempting to regulate consumer behavior, albeit in different ways: locals are encouraged to exercise restraint in the case of the casinos, leaving these as far as possible to foreigners; in the case of the 'pink dollar', both locals and foreigners are asked to pursue their activities with consideration for more conservative elements. We explain why it is that in the case of the gay lifestyle a call for abstention is not an option. Instead, the focus is on discretion. We then examine in detail the politics of discreet consumption.

Chapter 9, 'States as "Midwives" to Cities: Cosmopolitanism, Citizenship and Consumption in the Modern State', further broadens discussion beyond Singapore to consider the relationship between states and cities. Our discussion brings together the various themes that we have focused on in the preceding chapters, and highlights at least one important way that the state continues to function as an important 'midwife' to globalization (adapting Sassen's 2006 use of the term). Different cities need to establish distinctive identities in a competitive global environment, and in this regard, it becomes useful to ask just what roles states can or should play in facilitating this. In developing our discussion, we draw on Wright's (2009) notion of 'real utopias'. Our key argument in this concluding chapter is that it is at the city scale where social ideals can find greatest purchase.

As we will see in this book, the criteria for assessing global cities and the attitude of cities, and indeed states, toward any aspirational goal of becoming global has changed significantly due to the demands and expectations of both consumption and consumer groupings. As Stevenson (2013, 125) observes, 'Within the nexus of cities around the world, the criteria for assessing the situation occupied by any one city at any particular time now extends beyond the economic and financial to encompass lifestyle, "liveability" and the cultural/creative.' Beyond the issues of creative cities she notes that 'it is really not possible to understand any city, its culture or economy without considering its location (aspirational and material) within, outside and in relation to worldwide circuits and flows that reconfigure everyday life and urban space' (130).

Chapter 1

CONSUMPTION, REFLEXIVITY AND CITIZENSHIP IN GLOBAL CITIES

Introduction

The notion of reflexivity has emerged as an arena of intense sociological debate not least because, in the context of globalization, institutions and individuals alike are forced to negotiate a slew of rapid and unpredictable social, economic and political changes. Individuals become particularly reflexive under these conditions, it is claimed (Adams 2006), because they can no longer rely on institutional solidities or because they experience a sense of cognitive dissonance created by such changes. There is of course no uniformity in response, as the ability of individuals to respond reflectively is differentiated by complex conglomerations of gender, class, ethnicity and status, among other factors (Brooks 2008; Beck 1992; Beck and Beck-Gernsheim 1996; Skeggs 1997, 2005). Adams (2006) in fact maintains that reflexivity is now characterized by hybridity and there is no consistency in its application.

In this chapter, we illustrate the sociological significance of reflexivity with reference to three themes: cosmopolitanism, citizenship and consumption, highlighted not only because they recur prominently in ongoing scholarship, but also because they are relevant to the study of how states attempt to transform themselves or the cities within them into global cities. However, we also show that, despite its significance, sociological interventions into reflexivity have tended to focus primarily on the reflexivity of individuals, giving relatively limited attention to institutional reflexivity, such as that of the state. These observations concerning the broad thematic significance of reflexivity and the curious neglect of its manifestations in institutions within sociological research will set the stage for the theoretical framework that we present in the next chapter.

Negotiating Reflexivity in Late Modernity

Reflexivity involves self-objectification, where the social actor becomes aware of itself in relation to its various circumstances, and a reflective response is one that is informed by this awareness. In this way, a reflective response differs from an unreflective response, with the latter being more automated or routinized in nature, so that an actor's self-awareness is not a factor. Even in cases where self-awareness is a factor, however, it is useful to further distinguish between an actor who is able to reflect on the various circumstances that might impede or facilitate its pursuit of certain goals or wants, on the one hand, and an actor whose reflexivity goes a step further such that it starts asking questions about the viability or appropriateness of these goals or wants. As regards the former, the actor is primarily concerned with how it ought to be responding to external circumstances, whereas in the case of the latter, the actor is more concerned with identity-related issues such as the kind of entity that it ought or wants to be.

These two kinds of self-awareness need not of course be mutually exclusive, since it is usually the case that the former will lead to the latter, and vice versa. But the distinction is an important one, and it is one that we will return to in greater detail in the next chapter, when we discuss the difference between first- and second-order reflexivity. For now, regardless of which kind of self-awareness we are looking at, we want to suggest that in cases where the actor's reflective response involves not merely introspection but public articulation and deliberation, this constitutes a negotiated response.

The preceding statement implies that negotiated responses are a subtype of reflective responses, and it raises the question of whether there are negotiated responses that are unreflective. We think not. Negotiated responses are characterized by the justification of specific positions and the bargaining of resources (symbolic or otherwise) associated with those positions. It is not possible, we suggest, for an actor to engage in such responses without reflecting on its own position within the relevant state of affairs circumscribed by the negotiation process. However dimly unreflective particular actors may be, the very fact of negotiating with an interactional other will at the very least lead the negotiating parties to become appreciative of their own positions in relation to each other, which, in this case, involves reciprocally induced self-objectification.

Negotiated responses are particularly relevant when one of the actors involved is the state. This is because of the critical role that the public arena plays in shaping state–society relations. Regardless of whether the state in question is highly authoritarian or not, some public dissemination if not actual discussion of state-initiated policies and their rationales – aimed at garnering support from the general public, or at the very least, assuaging any sense of public unease – is to be expected. And in fact, it is the failure to seriously consider the reflexivity of the state and the potentially creative responses it might mount in the face of the concerns posed by globalization that has resulted in premature announcements concerning its 'demise' (Ohmae 1996). However, as Sassen (2006, 227) observes:

> But this perspective leaves out the fact that global systems insert themselves in national domains where they once were nonexistent. The outcome of this negotiation between standardizing global systems and the thick environments of the national can easily be packaged as national even though its actual content pertains to new global systems.

An example of a city-state that is transforming itself in late modernity is Singapore. Singapore is responding to globalization by attempting to transform itself into a global city. At the same time, the measures that the state undertakes to effect this transformation do not always sit easily with its attempts to also maintain Singapore's identity as an 'Asian nation-state'. The need to manage potential conflicts between the global city and Asian nation-state narratives thus leads to a variety of negotiations between state and society. Given our focus, negotiated responses as objects of analysis become especially relevant. As Sassen's (2006) remarks above indicate, the state is not simply going to fade away or wilt as a result of globalization. In considering Singapore, we think that it is useful to provide a comparative perspective in order to better understand the problems and constraints states face. Hence, we also discuss other states and cities, including Malaysia, Hong Kong and San Francisco.

Globalization is first and foremost about change – change resulting from the development of new technologies, from the movements of peoples and ideas, and from the apparent weakening of some institutions (such as, arguably, the state) and the strengthening of others, possibly at the subnational (such as cities) or transnational levels (such as nongovernmental organizations or free trade blocs) (see Sassen 2001, xviii). These changes, of course, do not occur in isolation from each other, and a major issue in theorizing globalization has to do with how to capture the interrelationships that exist between various types of changes. Not surprisingly, then, metaphors for talking about globalization abound, whether these be a 'space of flows' that arises from the effects of new communications technologies (Castells 1996, 1997), a 'power geometry' that treats the global as emerging from the interconnections established by multiple local relationships (Massey 1994, 1999), or a multiplicity of '-scapes', such as ethno-, media-, techno- and ideoscapes (Appadurai 1996). These different metaphors are aimed in their own ways at trying to capture the manifold processes and effects that we variously associate with the phenomenon called 'globalization'.

One way to start getting a handle on these various processes and effects is via the notion of competition, which is often highlighted in discussions of globalization, particularly in the form of economic competition and its impact on the workplace (du Gay 1996; Gee, Hull and Lankshear 1996). But there is also competition between states for highly skilled and mobile elite individuals (Ong 1999, 2006a). We will see that for the state in Singapore, the attempted transformation into a global city is precisely a response to this global competition between cities for mobile talent. And competitions constitute just the kind of circumstances under which self-objectification and hence reflexivity arises. Entities involved in competition are inevitably aware of how they stand in relation to other potential competitors, not least because the competitive gaze involves competitors constantly sizing each other up. Moreover, especially if competitions are recurrent, competitors then have to make decisions about whether it is worth competing at all, or whether withdrawal from competition is a feasible option. Such considerations amount to precisely the kind of second-order reflexivity that we mentioned above, and we argue below (Chapter 2) that the techniques of governmentality in modern life go beyond Foucault's (1977, 1980) Panopticon or even Poster's (1991) Superpanopticon in interesting ways that cannot but help induce competitive reflexivity among both individuals as well as institutions.

For now, however, we want to show that the analysis of negotiated responses involving the state can be usefully viewed through the lens of sociological themes such as cosmopolitanism, citizenship and consumption. These themes are connected to the notion of competition because as far as the state in Singapore is concerned, a successful global city (i.e., one that is more successful than other cities) is one that induces the 'right kind' of people to not only visit but to also settle down.

These themes therefore provide the rubrics by which we organize our discussion in the rest of the book. In the case of cosmopolitanism, it is common to raise questions about the ability of the state to serve as a framework for community membership when cosmopolitan intellectuals apparently can have their pick of peoples and places to experience (Clifford 1994; Robbins 1992; Rabinow 1996). For Singapore, a key impetus for wanting to be seen as a global city comes from the state's awareness that many well-educated and relatively affluent Singaporeans are choosing to work and live overseas, and may even take up foreign citizenship. These cosmopolitan individuals are attracted to other places that are deemed to provide greater opportunities for realizing their particular visions of the good life. Transforming itself into a 'global city' is therefore part of Singapore's competitive strategy to remain as attractive as possible to individuals who may have multiple options in terms of places to live, work and play.

Many citizens, however, are concerned that the state's desire to bring in 'foreign talent', seen by the state as critical to economic growth, may lead it to bestow privileges on these foreigners that undermine the locals' sense of worth. This is where a focus on citizenship becomes relevant because, as Ellison (1997, 714) points out, citizenship can and should be understood as a 'reflexive condition of defensive engagement', particularly in late modernity. This debate is fully developed in Chapter 6. The role of the state in terms of the intersection of reflexivity and citizenship is developed at this point using the example of how the state in Singapore has attempted to intervene in the lives of its citizens and the response of citizens to these interventions. It highlights the significance of reflexivity in both the citizens and the state in terms of 'defensive engagement'.

Finally, consumption is relevant because the state in Singapore has realized that, if it is to enhance its reputation as a global city, there must be sufficient 'buzz' that makes it attractive to mobile and affluent individuals. Examples of the way the state in Singapore has designed itself as a 'consumption hub' include its emphasis on the opening up of casinos, attracting high-end designer fashion labels, establishing shopping malls to give visibility to high-end consumption, celebrity restaurants, world-class architecturally designed buildings, Formula 1 racing and sports events such as the Youth Olympics in 2010. This has also led the state to reconsider its ban on casinos and its attitude toward homosexuality. But especially when consumption activities raise the specter of gambling addiction or are potentially at odds with more conservative sexual mores, reflexivity enters the picture because the state finds itself needing to explain to a concerned citizenry why it is prepared to allow these controversial activities. As mentioned above, this constitutes a case of negotiated response, and hence reflexivity, on the part of the state. Moreover, one of the ways in which the state aims to regulate consumer activity is by calling for consumer self-discipline (in the case of gambling) and consumer discretion (in the case of homosexuality). This is essentially a call for greater reflexivity and responsibility on the part of consumers. These cases are developed in the following chapters.

In the rest of this chapter, we present an overview of discussions concerning cosmopolitanism, citizenship and consumption, in order to underscore the point that attention to reflexivity – institutional as well as individual – is critical if advances in understanding these themes are to be made.

Cosmopolitanism as Elite Individual Subjectivity

Featherstone (2002, 4) tells us that 'a cosmopolitan sociology needs to investigate the "imagined presence" of distant others and distant worlds'. There is, in Featherstone's advice, an implicit acknowledgment of the role of reflexivity here, since to engage in such a cosmopolitan gaze is to at the same time situate the self in relation to these 'distant others and distant worlds'. Indeed, the study of cosmopolitanism is rich with attempts to capture the characteristics of this cosmopolitan gaze (Beck 2000; Clifford 1994, 1997; Rabinow 1996; Robbins 1992; Sassen 2006).

Three problems remain, however. One, the cosmopolitan gaze is typically attributed to specific classes of individuals, and denied to others. Two, even if this correlation between class and cosmopolitanism were to be addressed in a more nuanced manner, the role of institutionalizing forces – such as that of the state in shaping such cosmopolitan subjectivities – is still largely missing from these accounts. Three, once it is acknowledged that institutions such as the state play important roles in shaping cosmopolitan subjectivities, it then becomes pertinent to ask if these institutions themselves should be credited with some form of cosmopolitan imagining. In the remainder of this section, we elaborate on these three problems in turn.

Regarding the first problem, consider Ong's (1999, 13–15) discussion of Clifford's (1994, 1997) 'discrepant cosmopolitanisms', which focuses on the cultural subjectivities of traveling intellectuals, and Robbins's (1992) interpretation of cosmopolitan subjectivity, which looks also at the social and political consciousness of worldly intellectuals traversing the globe. Ong (1999, 13) observes that 'both Clifford and Robbins seek to link the study of cosmopolitanism with their belief in the cosmopolitan individual as a well-informed, politically progressive modern subject'. Making a similar point, Sassen (2006, 299–300) observes that there is general tendency to 'equate the globalism of the transnational professional and executive class with cosmopolitanism', despite the fact that various 'global classes', including transnational immigrants and international elites, are each 'embedded, in often unexpected ways, in thick, localized environments: financial and business centers, national governments, the localized microstructures of daily civic life and struggles, and the translocal insertions of immigrants'.

Sassen's reference to being embedded in various localized environments leads us to the second problem by reminding us that subjectivities (cosmopolitan or otherwise) are to significant extents shaped by the presence of institutional forces. In this regard, even Rabinow's notion of a 'critical cosmopolitanism' (see Ong 1999, 14), which is aimed at correcting the association between cosmopolitanism and Western elites, and which calls for greater attention to cosmopolitan intellectuals who are sensitive to 'the inescapabilities and particularities of places, characters, historical trajectories and fate' (Rabinow 1996, 56), does not go far enough in recognizing the role of institutions. Thus, Ong (1999, 14) concludes, 'What is missing from these accounts are discussions of how the disciplining structures – of family, community, work, travel, and nation – condition, shape, divert, and transform such subjects and their practices and produce the moral-political dilemmas, so eloquently captured in these studies, whose resolutions cannot be so easily determined.'

Consequently, studies of diaspora and cosmopolitanism, Ong (1999, 15) observes, fail to sufficiently 'link actual institutions of state power, capitalism, and transnational networks' to observed 'forms of cultural reproduction, inventiveness and possibilities'. Accordingly, (ibid.; emphasis added):

> This is a significant problem of method because it raises hopes that transnational mobility and its associated processes have greater liberatory potential (perhaps replacing international class struggle in orthodox Marxist thinking) for undermining all kinds of oppressive structure in the world. In a sense, the diasporan subject is now vested with the agency formerly sought in the working class and more recently in the subaltern subject. *Furthermore, there are frequent claims that diasporas and cosmopolitanisms are liberatory forces against oppressive nationalism, repressive state structures, and capitalism, or that the unruliness of transnational capital will weaken the power of the nation-state.*

This brings us to the third problem, the erasure of institutional reflexivity, such as that of the state. Even Beck's (2000) nuanced and insightful distinction between 'simple globalization' and 'reflexive cosmopolitanization', which is otherwise prepared to ask about the implications of cosmopolitanization for 'images of political community', assumes that 'the cosmopolitan project contradicts and replaces the nation-state project' and is primarily concerned with changes in 'people's cultural, political and biographical self awareness [...] if they no longer move and locate themselves in a space of exclusive nation-states but in the space of world society instead' (90). In this way, the nation-state as a disciplining force is *a priori* discounted on the assumption that the cosmopolitan society is necessarily a postnational one. More seriously, there is little credit given to the strategies of which states might avail themselves, as they try to re-establish spaces and relevancies for themselves in a globalizing world. But to even begin to give serious analytical consideration to such strategies is to credit states with some form of institutional reflexivity – not simply as an empirical fact but as a fact that merits theoretical accommodation.

By way of closing this section, we provide a brief example from Singapore of the state's influence in shaping cosmopolitan subjectivities. The state has, in recent years, introduced into its public discourse a distinction between Singaporeans who are 'heartlanders' and those who are 'cosmopolitans'. The former supposedly refers to individuals who are relatively less educated, less affluent or less well travelled, who live in public housing and speak a language other than English (e.g., Mandarin, Hokkien, Malaysian or Tamil).

But compared to their cosmopolitan counterparts, heartlanders are also supposed to be more traditional in their values and possibly more loyal to the country.

Cosmopolitans, in contrast, are better and usually highly educated, attending major global universities to gain their qualifications, more affluent and more mobile. They are supposed to be 'in demand' globally and are apparently in a better position to explore options for migrating to other countries. But because of this, they are also often stereotypically presented as likely to be more detached toward Singapore and what it means to be Singaporean. They are constructed as economic and social pragmatists, frequently having relationships with and marrying foreigners.

The state's portrayal of cosmopolitans bears some rough resemblance to the descriptions presented by those scholars critiqued by Sassen and Ong (above). But it is crucial to bear in mind that this portrayal is a political image crafted by the state to serve specific purposes, such as shaping loyalties to the nation. At the very least, we should observe that the portrayal avoids the question of whether the political leaders themselves (being well educated but presumably very loyal to Singapore) are better categorized as heartlanders or cosmopolitans, or whether, for whatever reason, these categories do not apply to them. We should also notice that this characterization of mobile Singaporeans as cosmopolitans imbues the state's own discussion of the Singaporean diaspora with very specific attributes: migrant Singaporeans who are less educated are erased from the diaspora discussion. Migrant Singaporeans who are considered significant enough by the state to be publicly discussed and perhaps constitute the targets of specific policies are the better educated ones.

We therefore need to ask just what purpose might be served by the public introduction of subject categories such as heartlanders and cosmopolitans. And here, it becomes essential to not only view the state's disciplining influence, but also its reflexivity – that is, its appreciation of its own position in relation to Singapore society and the world at large, as well as its construal of what goals or futures it envisages for the country.

Citizenship as an Ethical Regime

The concept of citizenship draws attention to the rights and responsibilities that accrue to individuals on the basis of their membership in a community, with the latter typically understood to be that of the nation-state. Models of citizenship originally emerged from political frameworks that were linked to nation-states (Marshall 1963). This traditional conception is still relevant as a politico-legal model which views the nation-state as the key distributor of citizenship entitlements, based on political membership.

In recent times, though, the concept has come under significant interrogation, with questions raised about whether it is possible to imagine citizenship beyond the confines of the state (Faulks 2000). Because the concept of citizenship is fundamentally normative in nature – that is, because it highlights the reciprocal (though by no means symmetrical) arrangement of rights and duties that grounds the relationship between an individual and the nation-state – it is useful to consider citizenship as an ethical regime. According to Ong (2006a, 22),

> An ethical regime can therefore be construed as a style of living guided by given values for constituting oneself in line with a particular ethical goal. Religions – and, I would argue, feminism, humanitarianism, and other schemes of virtue – are ethical regimes fostering particular forms of self-conduct and visions of the good life. Ethical notions of citizenship include the expression of national spirit, a style of being subjects who express the key values of a particular nation. In the formation of nation-states, national culture, humanism, and religions have interacted in shaping an 'imagined community', a shared vision of the common good.

Considered as an ethical regime, it becomes easier to see why multiple forms of citizenship can arise, since individuals concerned with different aspects of 'the good life' may connect their particular sets of values to the concept of citizenship in order that these may then gain some political purchase in society at large. Thus the potential for conflict here is significant. It is because of the possibility of such conflicting interpretations arising that citizenship needs to be understood as 'a productive and disciplinary category, which is regularly deployed within formal and informal relations of power' (Carver and Mottier 1998, 2–3). That is, interpretations of citizenship are always open to active contestation and negotiation, even under the most authoritarian of states. This means that even as the state mobilizes its resources to persuade, cajole or coerce the citizenry to accept particular representations of 'the citizen' (3), these representations will have to be mediated through the already extant sociocultural representations that are part of how the citizenry constructs itself and its relationship to the state.

A useful attempt to think about such mediations comes from Ellison's proposal that 'contemporary citizenship' needs to be understood as a 'reflexive condition of defensive engagement' (1997, 714). That is, an increasingly fragmented and complex public sphere necessarily leads to a reflexive form of citizenship, one where 'social actors, confronted with the erosion, or transformation, of established patterns of belonging, readjust existing notions of rights and membership to new conceptions of identity, solidarity and the institutional foci of redress' (711). The notion of reflexivity evoked here draws attention to how individuals attempt to negotiate their memberships in various kinds of groupings in response to ongoing social and political changes.

While we find Ellison's proposal to have considerable merit (see Chapter 6), our concern here is that reflexivity is, once again, seen primarily as the attribute of individuals to the point where institutional reflexivity is hardly given any recognition. But as we now demonstrate, institutional reflexivity cannot be easily divorced from that of individuals in studies of citizenship. We do this via a discussion of the ways in which the state in Singapore has attempted to regulate intimacy among the citizenry, and we attempt to clarify the implications of this for the notion of sexual citizenship. Sexual citizenship as an ethical regime can be seen to arise when the concept of citizenship intersects with issues of intimacy (Plummer 1999, 2003) – that is, the set of social practices and mores that pertain to the conduct of interpersonal relationships, including dating, marriage, divorce, reproduction, family dynamics and sexual orientation (2003, 5). The difference between sexual citizenship and intimate citizenship is that the latter (Lister 1997, 128; emphasis original) 'only constitutes a sphere of citizenship *practice* when its claims are made in the public sphere', and 'citizenship claims, made in the name of the intimate, are being theorized through the notion of "sexual rights"' (Lister 2002, 199). Thus, sexual citizenship, in contrast to intimate citizenship, is specifically concerned with the ways in which the state attempts to regulate intimacy practices along lines that differentiate citizens from noncitizens, as well as different categories of citizens. The latter point is worth noting because citizenship – including sexual citizenship – is not merely a 'simple on/off concept', where one either has citizenship or not; it also involves 'gradations of esteem' (Carver 1998, 13–4), where subgroups of citizens may be singled out for reward (e.g., tax rebates) or punishment (e.g., criminalization of homosexuality). Realizations of sexual citizenship are thus often refracted differently across the population.

In the case of Singapore, the relationship between the state and its citizens has been an ambiguous one characterized by a mixture of self-interest, economic and social pragmatism, and an increasingly complex and changing conception on citizenship (see Brooks 2010a, 2010b; Brooks and Wee 2008, 2010). The state in Singapore, in an attempt to encourage the establishment of intimate relationships among its citizens, set up the Social Development Unit in 1984 because it was concerned that graduate women were marrying later, and even worse, giving birth at a rate that was too low to make up for the decline in population numbers. Even though nongraduate women were apparently reproducing at a healthy rate, this was not considered an acceptable solution to the problem because, according to the Singapore's state's reasoning, it was 'graduate mothers [who] produced genetically superior offspring, [their] ability to complete a university education attesting to superior mental faculties, which would be naturally transmitted to offspring through genetic inheritance' (Heng and Devan 1995, 197). This line of reasoning clearly involved a belief in eugenics, and under this perspective, the children of nongraduate women were unlikely to possess the same intellectual qualities as the offspring of graduate women. The consequences of this 'reproductive crisis' were spelt out by the then prime minister Lee Kuan Yew in his 1983 National Day Rally speech:

> If we continue to reproduce ourselves in this lopsided way, we will be unable to maintain our present standards. Levels of competence will decline. Our economy will falter, the administration will suffer, and the society will decline. For how can we avoid lowering performance when for every two graduates (with some exaggeration to make the point), in 25 years' time there will be one graduate, and for every two uneducated workers, there will be three? (*Straits Times*, 15 Aug 1983)

To address the problem, the state introduced a number of measures that favored graduate women over their nongraduate counterparts. Graduate women were promised tax breaks and even priority in admission for their children to some of the top schools in the country. Nongraduate women, in contrast, were encouraged to refrain from having more than two children, and were also offered monetary incentives of S$10,000 if they underwent tubal ligation. These measures were clearly elitist in that they discriminated according to class – at least, as manifested in terms of educational qualifications and income. Moreover, there was also an attempt to equate childbirth with patriotism, an attempt that, not surprisingly, was met with serious resistance from many women who felt it to be an unwarranted and serious intrusion into what was essentially a private matter:

> Cabinet ministers began to exhort graduate women to marry and bear children *as a patriotic duty*. Obediently taking their cue from the government, two (nonfeminist) women's organizations accordingly proposed, in a disturbing collusion with state patriarchy, that women be *required* to bear children as a form of National Service – the equivalent, in feminine, biological terms, of the two-and-a-half-year military service compulsorily performed by men for the maintenance of national defense. (Heng and Devan 1995, 201)

Public unease with such discriminatory measures was extremely high among the citizens of Singapore, and it is therefore no accident that just one year later, in 1985, the scheme for the children of graduate mothers to be given priority in the choice of schools 'was terminated by the Ministry of Education on the ground that it did not produce the desired results' (Hill and Lian 1995, 162; citing Lee, Alvarez and Palen 1991, 67). Furthermore, public resistance to the state's articulation of this 'reproductive crisis' increased with the perception that there was also an ethnic component in the state's agenda. This was because most graduate and professional women turned out to be members of the Chinese ethnic majority, while working-class women were largely members of the Malay and Indian ethnic minorities (Heng and Devan 1995, 198).

The state in Singapore has learned quickly and adapted accordingly to the demands of its citizens. As a consequence of the lack of positive response to its attempts at encouraging marriage and procreation among graduates and nongraduates, the state has since been steadily fine-tuning its measures, all of which indicate a steady trend toward greater awareness of the need to show respect for personal autonomy and to shy away from class bias and certainly eugenics. Thus, 2004 saw a new tack being adopted by the state. In contrast to the earlier line of argument, the state now emphasized that marriage and children were important for personal fulfillment rather than for the well-being of the nation. In the words of the current prime minister Lee Hsien Loong in his 2004 National Day Rally speech:

> We want people to have babies because you want them and you love them. [...] You can have the most successful career, you can be the richest man on Earth or the most powerful man or woman on Earth, but if you don't have a family or don't have children, I think you're missing something. [...] It's fulfilling. [...] It's up to you. What we can do is we'll make it easier for families to marry and to have children. You make the decision. (PMO Singapore 2004)

As a reflection of this new approach, the measures introduced in 2004 included longer maternity leave (up from the previous 8 weeks to 12 weeks), a five-day working week in the civil service, financial support to encourage companies to develop family-friendly work practices, and tax rebates for working mothers that dispensed with any reference to the mothers' educational qualifications (Thang 2005, 91). The developments in 2004 and subsequently in 2009 are significant because the state's willingness to actively consult the citizenry and to back away from heavy-handed regulation, when taken together, indicate its growing appreciation that citizens are not 'inert blocks of wood to be moved here and there according to someone else's grand design' (Sowell 2004, 7–8), as well as its ability to reflexively modify and adapt the way in which it engages with citizens.

Regulating the Consumer

Bauman (1998, 24), writing about advanced Western democracies more generally, notes:

> Ours is a 'consumer society' in a similarly profound and fundamental sense in which the society of our predecessors […] used to deserve the name of a 'producer society'. […] The way present-day society shapes up its members is dictated first and foremost by the need to play the role of the consumer, and the norm our society holds up to its members is that of the ability and willingness to play it. […] The difference is one of emphasis, but that shift does make an enormous difference to virtually every aspect of society, culture and individual life. The differences are so deep and ubiquitous that they fully justify speaking of our society as a society of a separate and distinct kind – a consumer society.

One salient aspect of consumption in late modern societies is its importance for individuals' identity constructions, and since a consumer society is defined largely by the wide variety of goods that can serve as markers of identity, the notion of *choice* (Bauman 1998, 30; Giddens 1991, 197) becomes of the utmost importance. The consumer can be held responsible for the choices s/he makes in the kinds of objects or activities s/he consumes *regardless* of whether or not such choices are freely exercised (Warde 1994, 881). With responsibility and choice comes the need to be *reflexive*. For Beck (1992, 131) and Giddens (1991, 81), reflexivity is an important feature of late modernity since the outcomes of sociocultural (as well as scientific-technological) practices involve risks, and therefore need to be constantly monitored and fed back into the conduct of the practices themselves. Their interpretations differ. For Beck, reflexivity is less about reflection than about the inevitable confrontation with the consequence of risk brought about by scientific and technological advances. For Giddens, in contrast, reflexivity is understood more familiarly in terms of reflection about possibilities and choices. Our discussion of reflexivity is more in line with Giddens's than Beck's (see Chapter 2) since we are not focusing on the issue of risk.

Thus, actors who are more reflexively oriented can be said to have an advantage over actors who are less so. The emphasis on choice also makes it a rational strategy for the consumer to avoid being overly committed to a particular commodity or identity since this might preclude future choices. As Bauman (1998, 28) puts it: 'Identities, just like consumer goods, are to be appropriated and possessed, but only in order to be consumed, and so to disappear again. As in the case of marketed consumer goods, consumption of an identity should not – must not – extinguish the desire for other new and improved identities, nor preclude the ability to absorb them.' Bauman thus argues that the capacity for reflexivity is directly related to the capacity for choice: 'All of us are doomed to the life of choices, but not all of us have the means to be choosers' (86).

Adams (2006, 511) raises the issue of how the relationship between identity, reflexivity and choice might need to be reconfigured in the context of changing social structures (see also Cremin 2003; du Gay 1997; Sennett 1998). The establishment of this relationship has important implications for consumption and, in this regard, Elliott and Lemert (2006, 15) draw attention to the importance of individualism when they comment that 'from Singapore to Tokyo, from Seoul to Sydney, the individualist creed of the new individualism features significantly in the private and public lives of its citizens'.

One aspect of the private lives of individuals that intersects directly with consumption is the area of intimacy and sex. Changing attitudes to sex and intimacy are directly related to consumer capitalism, as Elliott and Lemert (2006, 114) show:

> Sexuality increasingly becomes a terrain on which the impact of global capital, ideas and ideologies are brought to bear. This is particularly clear in terms of the ways in which sexuality is framed and regulated today through advertising, mass media and information culture. Second, sexuality becomes a key focus of personal identity, a reflexive condition of meaning in social relationships, intimacy and eroticism.

Thus as Elliott and Lemert observe, the new individualism is characterized by an 'expansive, emotional literacy and cultural cosmopolitanism', encouraging the development of lifestyles which are tied to consumption. At the same time, it is necessary to recognize that reflexivity can be commodified and is not necessarily something that is accorded equally to each and every actor (Adkins 2002; Wee and Brooks 2010). As Adkins (2002, 123; emphasis added) points out, 'The self-reflexive subject is closely aligned to neo-liberal modes of governance, indeed is the *ideal and privileged subject* of neo-liberalism.' In this regard, the capacity for reflexivity can be seen as a resource that facilitates mobility and the establishment of 'privileged positions' in late modernity (130).

All this focus on the reflexivity of the individual consumer, however, leaves out the disciplining role that the institution as a reflexive actor might play in its attempts to regulate the consumer. A useful way to approach this issue is to start with Ong (2006a), who provides highly valuable insights into the ways in which institutions – in this case, states – attempt to manage the behavior of their populations. Ong's thesis of 'neoliberalism as exception' asserts that even in countries where neoliberalism 'is not the general characteristic of technologies of governing' (2006a, 3), there may nevertheless be 'sites of transformation' where 'market-driven calculations are being introduced in the management of populations and the administration of special spaces' (4). While such sites may refer to zones that are territorially demarcated, they can also refer to more abstract subject categories involving specific kinds of persons (e.g., 'citizen', 'foreigner', 'investor'). The establishment of such sites, where neoliberal values are actively encouraged and cultivated by the state, is a governing strategy that points to the reflexivity of the state. It indicates the state's awareness of its own accountability to its population and its own attempt to preempt and manage the potential tensions that might arise as neoliberal values come into contact with other values. The strategic significance of these sites therefore lies in their status as 'political *exceptions* that permit sovereign practices and subjectifying techniques that *deviate* from the established norms, [since] neoliberal forms articulating East Asian milieus are often in *tension* with local cultural sensibilities and national identity' (12; emphasis added).

Thus, in China, for example, the establishment of special economic zones and special administration regions serves to mark out identifiable locales where special taxation, investment schemes and a higher degree of political autonomy are allowed to hold sway (Ong 2006a, 18–19). This move is legislated by article 1 of the Regulations on Special Economic Zones, which proclaims that (quoted ibid., 105):

> The special zones shall encourage foreign citizens, overseas Chinese and compatriots from Hong Kong and Macao and their companies and enterprises (hereafter referred to as 'investors') to set up factories and establish enterprises and other undertakings, with their own investment or in joint ventures with our side, and shall, in accordance with the law, protect their assets, the profits due them and their other lawful rights and interests.

And, as we mentioned earlier, in Singapore, subject categories such as 'citizens' and 'foreign talent' constitute a significant part of the ongoing political discourse between the state and the populace (see especially Chapters 6 and 7). Consequently, a major issue of contention surrounds the kinds of rights and responsibilities that distinguish citizens from noncitizens.

Though Ong's (2006a) observations concerning the establishment of sites by states are well taken, it should be noted that her discussion has tended to focus on the state's regulation of 'producers' rather than 'consumers'. That is, both the setting up of special zones in China and the attempt to attract 'foreign talent' to Singapore are intended to bring in individuals and companies with the relevant expertise or financial capital to create new employment opportunities and drive economic growth. Ong's focus on producers raises the question of how techniques of governing might be applied by the state to regulate consumer activity.

This question is interesting because, in a globally competitive environment, a key quality that distinguishes successful individuals and institutions from their less successful counterparts is the ability to respond to fluctuating market conditions – in particular, changing consumer preferences. This is not easy, given that in a 'consumer society' (Bauman 2005, 23; du Gay 1996, 76; Rose 1990, 102) consumer preferences are actually encouraged to constantly change. That is, consumers, unlike producers, are generally encouraged to be undisciplined since their capacity for consumption depends on them being constantly unsatisfied. As Bauman (2005, 26) points out:

> To increase their capacity for consumption, consumers must never be given rest. They need to be constantly exposed to new temptations in order to be kept in a state of constantly seething, never wilting excitation and, indeed, in a state of suspicion and disaffection. The baits commanding them to shift attention need to confirm such suspicion while offering a way out of disaffection: 'You reckon you've seen it all? You ain't seen nothing yet!' [...]
>
> They [the consumers] are the judges, the critics and the choosers. They can, after all, refuse their allegiance to any one of the infinite choices on display – except the choice of choosing between them, that is. The roads to self-identity, to a place in society, to life lived in a form recognizable as that of meaningful living, all require daily visits to the market place.

Similarly, Abercrombie (1991, 173; emphasis added) points out:

> Producers, and regimes of production are associated with the forces of rationalization and order; the activities of production cannot be conducted without high levels of organization. Consumption, on the other hand, especially modern (or post-modern) consumption, is associated with undisciplined play and disorder; it does not require organization and may, indeed, actively deny it. More institutionally, any increase in the importance of consumption and consumers involves a diffusion of authority. [...] *It is a change from social organization dominated by a relatively small and well-structured group of producers to one consisting of a more diffuse and much larger assembly of consumers.*

Attention to consumer preferences and how this might impact the market therefore requires regular, if not constant, vigilance on the part of producers, as well as the capacity to quickly adapt and exploit those preferences.

All this is not to suggest that establishing special zones and identifying subject categories are not relevant as techniques of governing. But locales such as malls, museums, or theme parks are typically intended to be maximally inclusive, drawing in as many consumers as possible, rather than controlled and exclusive zones of neoliberal exception. And consumer-based categories such as 'shopper', 'diner' or 'tourist' are only temporarily inhabited by individuals in contrast with producer-based categories such as 'foreign talent', 'investor' or 'migrant worker', which are attached to specific individuals in a more sustained or durable fashion. The latter, as a consequence, can become the basis for regulatory activities that are within the control of the state, such as the allocation of tax benefits or work permits. The general point is that the state can exert greater control over the criteria for ascribing producer subject categories (e.g., who counts as a 'foreign talent' or 'investor'). In contrast, consumer subject categories are more often than not self-selected by individuals in a more ephemeral and ad hoc fashion, depending on the particularities of their tastes and the extent of their disposable income at a given point in time.

Thus, our case study of Singapore's decision to legalize casino gambling (and then facing the need to regulate access to the casinos) and its willingness to recognize the economic value of the affluent 'pink dollar' (and then facing the need to manage the various activities associated with homosexuality) represents an initial step in what is an increasingly important issue – namely, the broader question of how consumption activities in general might actually be governed. The importance of this issue derives from the fact that the neoliberal emphasis on consumer-driven markets may well lead to conflicts with other ideologies and values. For example, the consumption of cigarettes may over time lead to an increase in healthcare costs, and the uncontrolled private ownership of vehicles may have adverse effects on the environment or the flow of traffic. And of course, as this book demonstrates, participation in casino gambling or higher visibility of gay lifestyles gives rise to concerns by the more conservative segments of society about their possible impact on families and on the community in general, concerns that the state cannot afford to ignore.

The management of these concerns is particularly challenging for any society that is becoming more complex and diverse, not least because the effect of globalization is to open up societies economically, socially and culturally, leading to changes in the prevailing social order that must be grappled with. In this regard, it is critical, from a social governance perspective, to start giving greater attention to how the consumer may be regulated, especially since under the logic of neoliberalism, producer activity or in the case of this book, state policy is increasingly justified as a response to consumer demand.

Conclusion

This chapter has reviewed the significance of the concept of reflexivity in the context of late modernity. Three thematic concepts have been used to highlight the significance of reflexivity: cosmopolitanism, citizenship and consumption. These provide useful benchmarks for a theoretical analysis as well as being relevant to the study of Singapore's transformation into a global city. We highlighted each of these categories via examples of how the state in Singapore has intervened in the establishment of 'cosmopolitan identities', 'sexual citizenship' (through its intervention in the intimate lives of its citizens), and, finally, in its regulation of consumption, particularly through the introduction of casinos and attitude to the 'pink dollar' and gay lifestyles. In the following chapters, we explore these examples more fully and outline the analytical value of reflexivity in the context of social change in Singapore.

Chapter 2

ORDERS OF REFLEXIVITY

Introduction

In Chapter 1 we reviewed the significance of reflexivity within the context of contemporary social and cultural theory. We build on this in the present chapter and our goals are twofold. First, we aim to present an account of reflexivity that acknowledges its transformative potential and thus, its relationship to agency.[1] The relationship between reflexivity and agency is an important consideration because, as we show below, discussions of reflexivity are often intertwined with debates about agency, particularly in relation to the capacity for identity work. Reflexivity is usually argued to facilitate agency because an entity that is aware of the circumstances it finds itself in, it is claimed, is then better able to consider the possibility of acting upon and changing those circumstances. There are contrarian voices, however, that are far less sanguine about this characterization of the relationship between reflexivity and agency. Our account recognizes both sides of the debate and, on balance, is cautiously optimistic about reflexivity's potential for agency.

Our second aim is to extend the account we present to accommodate institutional reflexivity. While we are aware of the dangers of reifying institutions as thinking or sentient entities, we also wish to point out that institutional forces are recognized to constrain the activities of individuals and organizations (Greenwood et al. 2008; Scott 2008). Individuals and organizations acting as agents of the state, for example, are vested with responsibilities and powers that would not accrue to them otherwise.

Both these goals are developed in this chapter, drawing on theoretical and empirical discourses.

Debating Reflexivity and Agency

Adams (2006) provides a useful guide to the debates over reflexivity when he distinguishes between 'two dominant tropes'; one claiming that reflexivity

---

1 The account of reflexivity (excluding the discussion of institutional reflexivity in the latter half of this chapter) draws upon Brooks and Wee (2008), Wee and Brooks (2010) and Stroud and Wee (2012).

'increasingly constitutes self-identity in late-modern societies' (512), and the other suggesting that reflexive awareness is 'necessarily rare' (514). The main contrast between these two positions lies in (i) the extent to which social actors can actually be said to be reflexive, and (ii) whether from such reflexivity necessarily follows the possibility for actors to actively fashion their identities. In other words, the points of contention between these positions revolve around the issues of scope. How widespread is reflexive awareness and agency? Does reflexivity necessarily mean that individuals now have a greater opportunity to shape their identities?

The first position is associated prominently with the works of Beck (1992, 1994) and Giddens (1991, 1992) (see Chapter 1). The core idea here is that individuals find it increasingly difficult, if not impossible, to rely on institutional structures and traditions to help make sense of social life. Rapid institutional changes and the detraditionalization of social norms in late modern societies mean that individuals are increasingly unable to rely on existing social structures for guidance about how to live their lives, leading them to take on greater personal responsibility for the choices they make. This leads to an emphasis on self-reliance and this in turn creates a reflexive awareness of the contingent relationship that individuals bear to their surrounding material conditions. Kennedy (2001, 6; emphasis added) usefully summarizes what might be called the 'extended reflexivity thesis' (Adams 2006) in the following manner: 'Individuals are *compelled* to take greater control over the kinds of social identities they wish to assume [...] because once-powerful solidarities such as class, occupation, church, gender and family are slowly *declining in their ability to define our life experiences.*'

Because traditional sources of identity no longer 'define our life experiences', the resulting vacuum creates not just the need for actors to become reflexively aware, it also (at least according to the theorists associated with this position) leaves open a host of possibilities and opportunities for actors to take control of the kinds of identity work they wish to engage in. Hence, for proponents of this extended reflexivity thesis, the increase in the scope of reflexivity is treated as simultaneously marking a concomitant increase in agency, as seen in the claims (cited in Adams 2006, 513) that 'people have to turn to their own resources to decide what they value, to organize their priorities and to make sense of their lives' (Heelas 1996, 5) and 'the self today is for everyone a reflexive project' (Giddens 1992, 30). Note that the extended reflexivity thesis is about the reflexivity of individuals rather than that of institutions. And indeed, the former is claimed to emerge primarily because of widespread institutional failure. Conversely, under the extended reflexivity thesis, there is an implication that the reflexivity of individuals is likely to become dormant or even incapacitated if institutions regain their abilities to 'define our life experiences'.

In contrast to the extended reflexivity thesis, the second position is much more skeptical about the ubiquity of reflexivity. And even where reflexivity is acknowledged to be present, this position tends to be also more skeptical about the possibility of actors actually shaping their identities. Nevertheless, this second position too tends to be mainly concerned about the reflexivity of individuals and, like the extended reflexivity thesis, is relatively silent on the subject of institutional reflexivity. This second position has been most widely explored with respect to the issue of gender, and finds its inspiration from Bourdieu's (1977, 1990) argument that actors in a social field carry with them a habitus that predisposes them to respond in ways that tend to reproduce the existing social structure. The habitus is a set of dispositions inculcated in individuals by virtue of their socialization experiences, and so everyone inevitably has a habitus simply because everyone willy-nilly undergoes some form of socialization. What will vary, of course, is the specific nature of the habitus that is acquired, since human beings are habituated into different forms of practice by virtue of their exposure to specific experiences. The kind of habitus acquired by particular individuals or classes of individuals therefore varies, and this has significant consequences for their social trajectories (Bourdieu and Passeron 1977; Fowler 1997; Lareau 2003; Sullivan 2001).

A good example of a Bourdieu-inspired approach to reflexivity comes from McNay's (1999, 2000; see also Skeggs 1997) argument that even though ongoing social changes may have led to a mismatch between (gendered) habitus and field, such mismatches and any emergent reflexivity must always be understood in field-specific terms. For McNay, it is not possible to simply assume that reflexivity is an inherently universal capacity of subjects. Instead, reflexivity emerges instead only with the experience of dissonance, as is the case when individuals experience a sufficiently drastic mismatch between the kind of habitus they have acquired and the expectations of the field that they are encountering. Consequently, even as certain aspects of gender relations are destabilized, other aspects may yet be further entrenched (1999, 103). In this light, proclamations about the status of reflexivity as a widespread societal condition foisted upon all individuals are deemed premature, since the possibility of reflexivity is supposed to depend on the actual details of the habitus–field interaction.

While McNay's (1999) appeal to dissonance might be reminiscent of the extended reflexivity thesis' claim concerning institutional failure, there are two key differences. The first is that McNay does not necessary implicate institutions – or more specifically, institutional failure – in her account of dissonance. Individuals can experience dissonance even in conditions of relative institutional stability. For example, individuals might be highly mobile, moving from one job situation to another. As different employers provide different levels of support for women to achieve work–life balance, dissonance might arise simply through the interactions between particular individuals and particular companies. The second difference lies in the assumption concerning scope. For the extended reflexivity thesis, the phenomenon of institutional failure is supposedly general enough that extends across most if not all institutions. For McNay, in contrast, the scope is much narrower so that even if some institutions may fail to provide the requisite solidarities (resulting in uncertainty about, say, gender appropriate expectations or behaviors), others may step in (to reinforce more conservative gendered values or to create the impetus toward a re-evaluation of such values).

While these two positions differ importantly in how they approach the issue of reflexivity, the differences internal to each should be noted as well. Among theorists associated with the first position, the claim that reflexivity is widespread has led, not surprisingly, to proposals for distinguishing between different types of reflexivity. Lash (1994; see also Lash and Urry 1994), for example, has made a distinction between cognitive and aesthetic reflexivity. Cognitive reflexivity refers to agents' monitoring of conceptual symbols ('flows of information'), whereas aesthetic reflexivity refers to their monitoring of mimetic symbols ('images, sounds and narratives making up the other side of our sign economics') (135). In response to Lash, Giddens (1994, 197) has disputed this distinction, suggesting that the cognitive–aesthetic separation is not quite as clear-cut as Lash makes it out to be: 'Is there such a thing as aesthetic reflexivity? I don't really think so or at least I wouldn't put it this way. I am not at all sure that, as Lash puts it, there is "an entire other economy of signs in space" that functions separately from "cognitive symbols".'

For social theorists coming from the second position, the concern is with addressing the rather pricklier question of how the existence of a habitus can be reconciled with reflexive awareness. If habitus informs practice by being a disposition to act and react in certain ways (Thompson 1991, 12), a logical question that arises concerns the engine of practice: what drives actors in their varied practices of social life? Bourdieu's answer is that actors are habituated to accept and embrace the normative goals that constitute the field of their habituation. Different forms of capital (symbolic, cultural, linguistic, economic) and the values attached to them are, of course, specific to different fields. Depending on the details of a given field, the actors within are then motivated by the need to retain capital already acquired or the need to pursue capital deemed to be within reach. Bourdieu's notion of misrecognition is important here as it captures a fundamental postulate that social interactions, particularly those involving unequal relations of power, must always rest on some set(s) of shared understandings, beliefs or worldviews. Such understandings or worldviews are typically inculcated as part of the habitus, but the concept of misrecognition is worthy of 'recognition' in its own right because it draws our attention to the fact that such inculcation concerns not only content but also modality, where actors come to have a *shared commitment* to certain values and ideals despite their fundamentally arbitrary cultural character.

However, because the Bourdieusian habitus is presented as reflecting an 'unconscious mastery' (Bourdieu 1977, 79) of how actors are expected to respond in relation to a specific field and, as a result, 'cannot be touched by voluntary, deliberate transformation' (94), this leads to a conceptual conundrum about the relationship between the unconscious nature of the habitus and the conscious deliberation associated with reflexive awareness. That is, it is not clear how the former can (ever) give rise to the latter, or how the two can even coexist. This is a puzzle with far-reaching consequences, since unless the habitus can be reconceptualized so as to accommodate conscious deliberation or reflexive awareness, any potential for transformative agency would appear to remain muted.

One possible approach toward addressing this conundrum is to start with the general Bourdieusian picture of a fit between habitus and field, but to then argue that as actors move across fields, this degree of fit is likely to vary. As we noted above, this is the tack taken by McNay, who suggests that where the lack of fit is sufficiently strong, actors may then experience a sense of dissonance, which rudely forces them to become reflexively aware of their relations to their surrounding social structures. In this picture, the sufficiently wide disjuncture between field and habitus that might prompt the emergence of reflexive awareness is more the exception than the rule. However, McNay's proposal has been countered by the argument that such habitus–field disjunctures are in fact sufficiently common as to constitute a prevailing characteristic of actors' experiences – this is arguably the case in a highly mobile society or a society undergoing rapid social changes. But while it is conceded that this might mean that reflexive awareness is fairly widespread, any assertions concerning a rise in agency (as in the case of the extended reflexivity thesis) is mitigated by the suggestion that it is now appropriate to speak of reflexivity itself having become incorporated into the habitus (Adkins 2003; Sweetman 2003). Thus, Adkins (2003, 35) makes the intriguing point that even the presence of reflexivity may not be sufficient to warrant any discussion of agency, since it may be the case that 'reflexive practices are so habituated that they are part of the very norms, rules and expectations that govern gender in later modernity, even as they may ostensibly appear to challenge these very notions'.

At this point, it seems clear that if any kind of agency is to be recovered from the concept of a habituated reflexivity, the understanding of the habitus has to be changed in a fundamental way. Skeggs (2004, 25), in fact, makes this clear when she argues that the habitus (contra Bourdieu) is fundamentally characterized by ambivalence, since 'identities are a limited resource, a form of cultural capital that are worked and uncomfortably inhabited'. Skeggs (2004, 29) thus points out, 'Bourdieu cannot account for that ambivalence, as Adkins (2003) shows, because he places ambivalence outside of the realm of practice, he understands norms to be incorporated, […] he assumes that the field is a precondition of the habitus and the habitus will always submit to the field.'

Skeggs's suggestion that ambivalence is a critical feature of the habitus goes directly to the very heart of Bourdieu's claims about how the dispositions of actors are thoroughly informed by their socialization experiences. But while useful, it is still insufficient to address the issue of reflexivity since ambivalence and reflexivity are in principle independent properties. That is to say, it is possible for someone to be ambivalent without them being aware of being ambivalent (ambivalence without reflexivity). And conversely, one could adopt a metaperspective on one's social situation without necessarily feeling any ambivalence (reflexivity without ambivalence). It is therefore necessary to arrive at an account of the relationship between ambivalence and reflexivity, and how these are bound up with the habitus – in other words, to understand in what way the habitus is always/already characterized by *both* ambivalence and reflexivity. The work of James Bohman proves useful in this regard.

Bohman and the Transformative Potential of Critical Reflexivity

Bohman (1999, 130) acknowledges that a significant advantage afforded by Bourdieu's notion of habitus is that it provides 'a constitutive account of cultural constraint without the traditional conception of regulative rules or internalized norms'. This is because the habitus is fundamentally *formative* in nature: it is a set of dispositions and orientations that does not merely regulate the behavior of agents, but helps to define who they are. Thus, 'it is in virtue of being socialized into a common background of pre-reflective assumptions and orientations that agents have goals at all' (ibid.).

However, Bohman argues that Bourdieu's account of a 'pre-reflective habitus' is too 'one-dimensional' and makes no place for 'deliberate processes and practices' (1999, 146). Consider, for example, Bourdieu's (1990, 59; see also Bourdieu and Passeron 1979, 27) assertion that, with the habitus, 'the most improbable practices are therefore excluded, as unthinkable, by a kind of immediate submission to order that inclines agents to make a virtue of necessity, to refuse what is anyway denied and to will the inevitable'. Bourdieu's tendency to downplay the possibility of critical deliberation has the effect that his theory ends up being overly deterministic so that it is 'at its best, therefore, a theory of reproduction, and is at its weakest as a theory of transformation' (Calhoun 1993, 72; see also Adkins 2003; Collins 1993; Lash 1993).

To mitigate this determinism, Bohman (1999, 145) suggests that what is required is a conception of agency that is both reflective and transformative, one that recognizes 'the capacities of socially and culturally situated agents to reflect upon their social conditions, criticize them, and articulate new interpretations of them'. To develop such a conception, Bohman finds the work of Frankfurt (1988, 11–25) particularly instructive. Frankfurt starts with the observation that even though human beings are not unique in having desires or in making choices, they are unique in being able to form second-order desires (1988, 12; emphasis original): 'Besides wanting and choosing and being moved *to do* this or that, men may also want to have (or not to have) certain desires and motives. They are capable of wanting to be different, in their preferences and purposes, from what they are.' Frankfurt therefore suggests that autonomy comes about when there are second-order desires, or the desire to have or not have a desire. Such second-order desires, as we shall see in the following chapters, are typically called upon when agents experience the need to resolve conflicting first-order desires regarding literacy practices.

While we agree with Bohman and Frankfurt that second-order desires can lead to a transformative reflexivity, it is necessary to remember that reflexivity *per se* need not necessarily involve second-order desires. As we pointed out earlier (Chapter 1), an actor can also be reflexive to how various circumstances impede or facilitate its pursuit of certain goals or wants, and this need not involve the actor asking questions about the viability or appropriateness of these goals or wants. Consequently, it is useful to recognize different orders of reflexivity. First-order reflexivity simply concerns the actor objectifying itself in relation to various circumstances, and may thus be active or reactive without necessarily being transformative. Second-order reflexivity, in contrast, corresponds more specifically to the actor evaluating its identity and values, and is therefore more likely to open up transformative possibilities.

Bohman expands on Frankfurt's ideas by situating them in relation to Bourdieu's sociological theorizing so as to open up a less deterministic conception of the habitus. Some second-order desires, Bohman acknowledges, are apparently constrained by cultural experiences, such as the hypercorrectness of petit-bourgeois speakers in France (1999, 146). However, there are other desires that are much more deliberate in character, such as the desire to be the sort of person who has particular sorts of desires or goals, or even the desire to be critically reflective. Bohman insists that, far from being anomalous, there are in fact clear historical precedents where, in the context of particular communities or social movements, 'care for the self can open up a cultural space for greater self-interpretation and deliberate choice' (1999, 146).

Some of the examples that he gives include the various aesthetic and moral disciplines pursued by the Greeks, Buddhists and the Jesuits. In a more modern context, Bohman (147, emphasis added) points to institutionalized practices of legal review, scientific peer review and democratic debate, which are 'the institutional equivalent of practices of *character planning*, in which second-order beliefs and beliefs about the demands for justification lead people to reject certain sorts of widely accepted beliefs, such as those that depend on ignoring legitimate protests of others or that could not withstand free and open debate.'

Second-order desires highlight the fact that reflexive mechanisms can lead to the revision of beliefs, even where such mechanisms are institutionalized. In this way, the kinds of examples cited by Bohman speak directly to Adkins's concern that the habituation of reflexivity may be anathema to identity transformation or 'character planning'. For example, a scientific peer review process is not simply a process that relevant agents in the field become accustomed to as they gain experience with the process of reviewing scientific articles or applications for grants. Precisely because the process requires/encourages an attitude of critical scrutiny – albeit of certain institutionalized objects (grant proposals, manuscripts) – there is always the potential for a 'spillover' where the actors may begin to question if the institutional status quo is adequate to the goals that it is supposed to serve. In such a situation, the reflexive practice acquires a second-order status. Actors no longer work within an established system of review, but can begin to question if the system itself needs to undergo a review of its own. Also, actors might even begin to ask about the kinds of individuals who might be best suited to undertake the reviewing responsibilities – that is, what kinds of attributes should such individuals possess and perhaps whether the incumbent actors themselves qualify as appropriate reviewers. Questions of this sort point inevitably to the presence of a reflexive engagement with the review system. More importantly, such a scenario does not require that actors weaken or renounce their commitment to the process in order to begin being reflexive (as might be the case with McNay's thesis of dissonance – see above).

Moving from the narrow example of scientific review to broader societal phenomena, Bohman (1999, 147) goes on to suggest that:

> The more pluralistic a society is the less likely it is that its integration can be achieved pre-reflectively in common dispositions, even in sub-groups. [...] The issue for practical reason in such a situation is the revision of beliefs and desires in explicit ways in accordance with more public and inclusive conceptions of legitimacy and authority. Reflexive agency in such societies requires not only changing beliefs and desires, but also the social conditions under which agents reflect, deliberate and cooperate

with each other to widen their universes of discourse. By doing so, they may also change their existing relations of power.

While Bohman's concluding remarks may seem to echo that of the extended reflexivity thesis, there are actually important differences that are worth remarking upon. Recall that under the extended reflexivity thesis, individuals are apparently compelled to fall back on themselves because institutional structures are no longer reliable.[2] This leads to an account of identity transformation that tends to eschew the possibility that institutional influence can actually be facilitative of individual reflexivity. What is needed therefore is a more nuanced and relational account of the self, one that allows for the possibility of individual reflexive awareness even in the context of pervading institutional structures. Such an alternative account would have the advantage of acknowledging that it is the 'experience of the day-to-day limits of self-reliance and control, set by constraints of political economy on the one hand and family and intimate relations on the other' that creates a sense of reflexivity or 'self-awareness' (Webb 2004, 735).

It is precisely in the combination of the ideas from Frankfurt and Bohman that we find such an alternative account. As Frankfurt points out, individuals are always to some degree already reflective of their own goals as well as that of their surrounding institutions *regardless* of whether the latter are 'solid' or not. And as Bohman suggests, there are in fact institutions that even insist on reflexivity as part of their own institutional norms, so that individuals are required to be reflective not in spite of institutional failings but (contra the modernization theorists and their extended reflexivity thesis) *because of* institutional fiat.

Multiple Markets, Ambivalence and Reflexivity

But even if, as Bohman and Frankfurt suggest, individuals are always reflexive to some degree or other, it is still unclear how ambivalence can ever enter the picture, especially if there are times when individuals are in fact encouraged to be reflexive by their institutional milieu. The answer, we suggest, is this: individuals are always ambivalent about their relationship to a field or market for the simple reason that no single market ever completely exhausts the totality of any individual's social experiences. All actors are simultaneously embedded

---

2 Our remarks in the preceding paragraph acknowledge that there are clearly different kinds of institutions (academic, nonprofit, political, military, etc.), but developing a typology of institutions is not relevant to our current enterprise, since our concern really is to emphasize the need to attend to the fact of institutional reflexivity regardless of what kind of institution may be in question.

in multiple markets, and because of this, the potential for ambivalence is always present, since different markets will be characterized by different norms and values. As a consequence, individuals are always faced with the need to reconcile the potentially conflicting demands – including demands relating to identity work – which various markets may impose on them.

Bourdieu (1984, 1990) in fact tells us that social life can be construed as a series of multiple, overlapping and even hierarchically embedded fields or markets. Of course, the greater autonomy a particular market enjoys (and this autonomy is always only ever a matter of degree), the more it is able to set its own logic, governing (among other things) the kinds of capital considered relevant to the market, the convertibility of different forms of capital, and the kinds of ends that actors in the market ought to be oriented toward. For example, the more autonomous a literary or artistic market is, the more possible it becomes for the actors in this market (artists, art dealers, art critics) to mask their concerns with money or power by appearing to be only interested in the 'disinterested' world of 'aesthetic purity' (Thompson 1991, 16).

The assertion that interests in power and money are masked is intended to reflect Bourdieu's claim that multiple markets exist in relation to the more general 'field of power', where the latter is mainly characterized by the pursuit of economic capital more so than any other. This means that markets that are high in cultural capital, but low in economic capital are still often at a disadvantage in relation to, and thus open to influence from, other markets where economic capital is most valued. As Calhoun (2003, 299) puts it: 'Directly economic capital operates in a money-based market that can be indefinitely extended. Cultural capital, by contrast, operates as a matter of status, which is often recognized only within specific fields.' It also means that completely autonomous markets simply do not exist. Markets always exist in relations of power to other markets.

From this, we can go on to make a number of guiding assumptions. First, it is reasonable to treat the continuum from macro-institutions to micro-interactions (and any intermediate levels of analysis) as markets of varying sizes and influence. However, smaller markets (families, social cliques) should not automatically be treated as proper subsets of larger ones, since what counts as capital in one market is informed by the activities in other societies. For example, the literary or artistic market is not properly contained within the state, since the associated activities cut across state boundaries to operate at the international level. Thus, the relationship between markets, regardless of their size, is better conceptualized as a dynamic multidimensional network of lattices rather than as a rigidly defined strict hierarchical structure.

Second, since all actors participate in multiple markets, we have to recognize the potential for conflict as well as reinforcement between a given actor's different market-related activities. In this sense, ambivalence is more likely to be present when actors are confronted with conflicting market demands. But even in the absence of such conflict, ambivalence is still present, we reiterate, by virtue of the fact that actors are always embedded in multiple markets.

The formation of identities on markets is therefore mediated by both reflexivity and ambivalence. By complementing the work of Bohman and Frankfurt with a sociological perspective involving multiple markets, we are able to insist on the potential for reflexivity and ambivalence as ever present in any habitus.

On Institutional Reflexivity

The foregoing remarks concerning the reflexivity of individuals also apply to that of institutions since institutions achieve their goals via the actions of individuals who are acting in their capacities and identities as institutional agents. In fact, qua institutional agent, an individual may even be required to override his/her personal commitments to other goals or values, should these conflict with those of the institution.

At this point, some terminological clarification is in order. There is some awkwardness here involving the terms 'institution' and 'organization'. These terms are often used interchangeably, and in this book we do the same. This interchangeability of terms arises and is to some extent justified because of the influence of 'institutional myths' on organizational structure, which can lead to a point where organizations might even become isomorphic with their institutional environments (DiMaggio and Powell 1983; see also Lewin, Weigelt and Emery 2004, 134). This is perhaps one reason why organizations are sometimes also described as institutions. Strictly speaking, though, a distinction between the two could be made in that institutions are essentially social norms that are entrenched to varying degrees. Marriage, religion, education, family and language are all institutions. An organization is then isomorphic with its institutional environment to the extent that it represents specific institutions (a school or a religious group). However, our decision to speak of 'institution' and hence 'institutional reflexivity' rather than 'organization' and 'organizational reflexivity' in this book is also due in no small part to the fact that we are focusing on the state and the various related state apparatus. And the state is more commonly described as an institution (Fisiy 1995; Skocpol 2003) than an organization because it (qua political entity) is usually distinguished from other institutions such as civil society and the public sphere. The latter are more unambiguously institutions rather than organizations.

While institutions cannot be said to experience ambivalence in the same subjective sense that individuals can, there is little doubt that institutions are embedded in multiple markets. For example, a state may be part of a regional as well as international grouping. It will of course also have domestic obligations that, depending on the internal organization of the state itself, may be further diffracted along territorial or municipal lines. Moreover, the state may find itself needing to address religious, communal, economic and military issues, all of which necessarily lead it to being embedded in different kinds of markets. Precisely because of these involvements in multiple markets, while we would not want to claim that the institutions themselves have 'feelings', institutions undoubtedly 'experience' ambivalence in a more structural sense – that is, from having to juggle and balance the demands of multiple markets.[3]

A useful way of thinking about these involvements is in terms of ethical regimes (Ong 2006a, 22; see Chapter 1), which refers to the fact that the construction of lifestyles is increasingly guided by the need to attend to the expectations of particular value sets, such as those of environmentalism, multiculturalism or enterprise culture. Ethical regimes are not coextensive with markets, but it is clear that different markets are marked at least by the differential ordering of ethical regimes.

So, in education, the search for knowledge is supposed to be prioritized over the profit imperative, while the reverse is arguably true in the business world. Nevertheless, the public character of institutions means that they are, perhaps even more so than individuals, expected to demonstrate how their activities are consonant with various kinds of ethical regimes. This is no easy matter, since even in the case of individuals, reconciling the normative expectations of different ethical regimes can pose considerable difficulties. Thus, individuals concerned with climate change and environmental sustainability may attempt to mobilize community resources or push for formal legislation that would compel the adoption of 'green' technology or ban the use of nonrecyclable materials. But it is entirely possible that these different regimes may be in conflict with each other, since their associated priorities and values are not necessarily compatible. At the very least, disagreements may arise over how to prioritize particular goals and allocate finite resources toward the pursuit of those goals.

---

3 It is of course possible to argue that the individuals serving as institutional agents experience ambivalence subjectively. This is certainly true. But we do not wish to emphasize this too much because the distributed nature of an institution's activities often means that the individuals themselves need not necessarily experience ambivalence if they are limited to highly specific goals with limited awareness of the agendas being pursued by their institutional colleagues. Thus, regardless of how actual individuals subjectively apprehend their relationships to institutional goals, we think it is more useful to attend to the fact that the institutions themselves are structurally embedded in multiple markets.

But individuals acting in their personal capacities (that is, notwithstanding those with highly public personas, such as celebrities) often have more leeway in deciding just how to balance their commitments to different ethical regimes. Institutions, on the other, are more easily subjected to some degree of public scrutiny and evaluation, and their failure to properly live up to particular ethical expectations may have repercussions for their ability to successfully live out their institutional lives. In the case of the state, for example, simultaneous commitments to ethical regimes pertaining to political governance, ethnic diversity, economic growth, defense, tourism, education, care for the environment and public health represent just some of the many different considerations that it needs to take into account, and to be publicly seen as so doing. However, among these various ethical regimes, it is that of neoliberalism – or more specifically, enterprise culture – that is particularly significant. As we will see in the rest of this book, in Singapore (and elsewhere also), enterprise culture is a dominant ethical regime that frames the ways in which other ethical regimes are understood (du Gay 1996; Ong 2006a). Over the next few sections, then, we illustrate how the influence of enterprise culture influences the reflexivity of individuals and institutions.

Reflexivity, the 'Ranked List' and Enterprise Culture

As a political philosophy, neoliberalism asserts that individuals and institutions perform their best within the demands of the free-market economy (Harvey 2005). The development of reflexivity is inextricably embedded within the cultural frameworks around performance that are linked with neoliberalism. This is an assertion that emphasizes the development of qualities such as the ability to 'optimize choices, efficiency, and competitiveness in turbulent market conditions' (Ong 2006a, 6). Consequently, one notable offshoot of neoliberal ideology has been the emergence of enterprise culture, in which qualities such as those just mentioned are regarded as 'human virtues and promoted as such' (du Gay 1996, 56), with the result that the 'character of the entrepreneur can no longer be seen as just one among a plurality of ethical personalities, *but must rather be seen as assuming an ontological priority*' (181; emphasis original).

This elevation of the entrepreneur to the status of a character worthy of emulation has led to a broad spectrum of scholarly interest in the impact of enterprise culture on various aspects of society, including education policy, workplace communication, the construction of citizenship, and even personal relationships (Cameron 2000; du Gay 1996; Gee, Hull and Lankshear 1996; Ong 2006a; Wee 2008; Wee and Brooks 2010). A common thread in these studies concerns how the enterprising self and its associated qualities might be developed, using techniques of governmentality (Foucault 2000) to remake individuals and institutions as 'self-governing' and 'self-enterprising' (Ong 2006a, 14).

But as many scholars have observed, the recognition of specific emotions or attributes as being present is dependent on some form of social endorsement. For example, in professional performances discussed by Hochschild (1983) and Leidner (1993) of the airline, insurance and fast-food industries, workers are expected to engage in "emotional labour" (Hochschild 1983, 7), projecting specific emotions (such as sincerity, enthusiasm or warmth) in ways that are organizationally acceptable. What is deemed a professionally acceptable manifestation of a specific emotion may even be 'styled' or 'scripted' (Cameron 2000). More recently, Bucholtz and Hall (2004, 385) point out that the quality of being authentic is in fact a socially negotiated attribute that may be bestowed upon, or denied to, various individuals or groups. Similarly, Goodwin and Goodwin's (2004, 225; see also Goffman 1981) concept of participation framework focuses on how different parties 'build action together' by reflexively monitoring each other's contributions toward the construction of a situated activity. Such contributions can include the public imputation of intentionality as well as the attribution of qualities such as anger, sadness, integrity, etc.

All of this applies no less to the cultivation of enterprising qualities. This means that the techniques of governmentality aimed at developing enterprising qualities need to be examined for how they go about sanctioning what counts as enterprising. In short, the expectation to be enterprising cannot be easily divorced from the processes via which the associated qualities receive ratification.

The Ranked List

By way of illustrating our case in this chapter, we compare some of the ways in which individuals and institutions are differently constrained in terms of how they manifest their reflexivity. We do this by demonstrating how one specific technique of governmentality, the 'ranked list',[4] is being used to remake individuals and institutions as bearers of enterprising qualities. We recognize, of course, that the ranked list is not specifically confined to issues of governmentality, but the frame of reference is a useful one in addressing the individual/institutional divide.

We maintain that the ranked list, as we show below, creates a strong reflexive awareness among individuals and institutions that are being monitored for their ability to demonstrate specific attributes. This is of course a structurally imposed form of reflexivity. Moreover, the competitive

---

4 The discussion of ranked lists is largely based on Wee (2011).

nature forces these ranked individuals and institutions to respond in various ways that point to the presence of second-order desires and thus reflexivity. This discussion of the ranked list is especially useful also because, as we see in the following chapters, the state in Singapore is particularly sensitive to how aspects of Singapore are ranked in various global lists. The ranked list can of course refer to subjects as diverse as global rankings of universities, research rankings of disciplinary areas and universities around research assessment frameworks such as the Research Assessment Exercise (RAE) and Excellence in Research for Australia (ERA), as well as rankings such as quality of life and 'best cities to live in' and the *Forbes* (and others) 'rich list'. Even states themselves may be directly ranked in terms of efficiency or incorruptibility.

One example of the way the ranked list operates is shown below:

World's Top 10 Airports

2009		2008
1	Incheon International Airport	3
2	Hong Kong International Airport	1
3	Singapore Changi	2
4	Zurich	8
5	Munich	5
6	Kansai	6
7	Kuala Lumpur	4
8	Amsterdam	11
9	Centrair Nagoya	12
10	Auckland	20

(World Airport Awards 2009)

In this list of the world's top ten airports in 2009, notice that the list also indicates how the individual airports were ranked in the previous year, thus making it possible to see whether a particular airport has moved up or down the rankings from 2008 to 2009.

The ranked list is interesting for three reasons. One, just about anything that we can conceive of (people, places, experiences, etc.) can be ranked, and these rankings can in turn range from the frivolous to the serious. For example, an online men's entertainment magazine has a list of the top ten 'Modern Femme Fatales' (Barnett 2010), while the Political and Economic Risk Consultancy (PERC) generates an annual list of the least corrupt nations. Two, it is no exaggeration to say that the ranked list is ubiquitous as a means of representing information, indicating that it has become widely accepted and normalized as a particular communicative genre (Swales 1990, 58). Third, this is a genre with properties that make it particularly potent as a technique of governmentality in enterprise culture. We elaborate on these points below.

Most modern ranked lists are generated from information stored in databases because the tracking necessary to generate comparisons of rankings across different years and the use of survey information involving a large number of respondents rely on the sorting capability of an electronic database. But the surveillance logic behind the Panopticon (Foucault 1977) and the Superpanopticon (Poster 1991) also represents an organizational culture that creates interesting tensions with the qualities of innovativeness and autonomy that are emphasized in enterprise culture. In the workplace, for example, this means that employees are expected to 'deploy their "autonomy" and "creativity" *correctly from the organization's point of view*' (du Gay 1996, 62; emphasis added), with peer reviews and appraisal schemes representing just some of the organizationally 'correct' ways in which enterprise can be recognized and rewarded (du Gay 1996, 63, 69). This can, on occasion, result in employees being rewarded more for their ability to satisfy the surveillance criteria than for any genuine attempt to be creative. For example, in their study of one company's attempts to encourage greater initiative, Gee et al. (1996) observe that workers are provided training in topics such as 'effective team meetings', 'problem-solving skills', 'understanding differences', 'effective listening', 'handling problems' and 'accepting change' (1996, 87). Workers are also regularly selected to participate in competitions where work teams display their grasp of these topics and their ability to apply them to onsite problems and issues. Unfortunately, it appears that work teams are rewarded more for their polished presentational styles rather than for any actual attempts to substantively address problems, something which leads to worker cynicism and disillusionment (Gee et al. 1996, 127).

The ranked list, not surprisingly, creates similar tensions between trying to encourage and reward enterprise on the one hand and monitoring conformity to whatever set of criteria is being used to assign rankings on the other. Moreover, it has various features that are particularly interesting when it comes to the cultivation of enterprising qualities:

(i) Foucault and Poster have drawn attention to the monitoring of individuals by various institutions. But what the ranked list demonstrates is that it is not just individuals who are being monitored. Institutions are themselves monitored by other institutions as well.

(ii) The monitoring institution typically presents itself as impartial. The tracking and ranking of entities such as individuals and institutions is therefore apparently being done not for the direct benefit of a particular monitoring institution. Rather, this monitoring institution usually claims to be acting on behalf of a generalized group of interested consumers. This group of consumers could also include the very entities being ranked, since some of the ranked individuals and institutions might have an interest in how they compare with their 'peers' as well as with their 'past selves'. This encourages competition between the monitored entities.

(iii) Because individuals and institutions usually are aware that they are being ranked, the issue here is not uncertainty about whether or not they are monitored. Rather, it is the awareness of being constantly monitored, particularly in the case of 'prestigious' lists that may be generated on a regular basis, such as annual lists.

Ranked lists help define what it means to be enterprising by creating the expectation that truly enterprising individuals or institutions would be recognized by the ranked list. It is worth bearing in mind that such lists do not necessarily need to directly recognize enterprise. They can do so, of course, by ranking countries as least or most entrepreneurial, for example. Or they can focus on other attributes such as popularity, wealth, trustworthiness, etc. But importantly, in either case, enterprise is cultivated not so much by what the ranked list directly recognizes, but by the kinds of qualities and activities it encourages in individuals and institutions as they strive to improve their rankings. Enterprising individuals or institutions are expected to appear at or near the top of the list, or at least aim to do so.

This expectation imposes somewhat different constraints on the responses available to these individual and institutions. In general, it might be said that ranked individuals have somewhat greater agency in ignoring ranked lists, especially if they are being ranked in a personal rather than professional capacity. For example, *Forbes*'s 2010 list of the world's billionaires has Bill Gates ranked second (Miller and Kroll 2010). The Mexican tycoon Carlos Slim holds the first place. Whether or not Gates would wish to 'reclaim' the first place is up to him and, perhaps more accurately, up to his ego. But for other individuals, how they rank might have professional repercussions, as in the following:

In 2007, when she was not among MediaCorp's Star Awards Top 10 Most Popular Female Artists, she was upset. She had made the list every year since 2003, after her star-making turn as the innocent Mo in the drama series, Holland V. [...]
'I cried. It was sudden, after doing so well.' (Lui 2009)

The above is from an entertainment news extract, and it describes the distress of a Singaporean television actress when she did not make the list of most popular female artists. In this case, the loss of popularity could conceivably affect the actress's ability to land important acting roles as well as attract endorsement deals.

But unlike individuals, institutions do not have a 'personal' capacity. Therefore, institutional actors typically do not have the luxury of ignoring ranked lists, especially if these might negatively affect the institution's ability to pursue its goals. This means that ranked lists are typically more consequential for institutions than individuals. Thus, rankings such as the World Bank's 'World's Most Business-Friendly Countries' (Nasri 2012), which ranks 183 countries on how easy it is to conduct business in them, can influence the ability of countries to compete for the inflow of capital.

The question, of course, is not whether the ranked list is necessarily good or bad. The question, rather, is whether rankings are the right way to go about evaluating the quality of individuals and institutions. There is no easy answer to this. On the one hand, the use of rankings can have beneficial effects. Those individuals and institutions that are highly ranked benefit from having their 'excellence' being made public, which helps in attracting consumers who want 'the best' or 'the most popular'. Consumers themselves are provided with some guidance as to which particular individuals and institutions to engage. And those individuals and institutions that are not highly ranked can be induced to improve themselves. On the other hand, there is also a risk that by subjecting the ranked individuals and institutions to the same set of measures, the influence of localized and idiosyncratic factors that might be relevant to judgments of quality is obscured. Quality is reduced to a one-dimensional or monolithic attribute (Cortright and Mayer 2004, 34–5).

Conclusion

This chapter began with a discussion of debates over reflexivity and agency, and showed that one way of mediating between these different perspectives is to acknowledge (i) that the habitus is necessarily characterized by ambivalence because individuals participate in multiple markets, and (ii) that individuals are capable of second-order desires, which leads to reflexivity. We then extended this account of individual reflexivity to institutions. Finally, we closed with the question of how, in the context of enterprise culture, techniques of governmentality might be implemented and negotiated by their intended subjects. By examining one such technique, that of the ranked list, we saw how it creates a highly competitive environment that compels both individuals and institutions to accept responsibility for the possession of enterprising qualities, or lack thereof.

Chapter 3

RESCALING FOR COMPETITIVENESS

Introduction

A major impetus for state initiatives comes from the changing relationship between a modernist state and the late modern conditions of existence. That is, states need to adapt to the more uncertain and plural conditions of late modernity. In doing so, some states may find it strategically valuable to reinvent themselves. Given that we are concerned with global city aspirations, the adaptions that states need to make if such aspirations are to be fulfilled become of interest. Unlike modernist states, which tend to be focused on developing unity as a nation, cities are mainly associated with the functions of residence and business. Cities do not carry the same connotations of commitment to a national identity; instead, they are better able to conceptually accommodate a culturally plural and diverse population. The idea of a global city inherits these properties of a city, but adds to them other properties such as extensive importance and modernizing influences in the global context.

In this chapter, we approach this pursuit of a global city descriptor in terms of a 'politics of scale' (Herod and Wright 2002, 13), showing how attention to scale negotiation provides insights into the state's attempts to demonstrate its commitment to multiple scales (nation-state, global city). This discussion provides an ideal illustration of second-order institutional reflexivity. We draw on examples from Singapore to explain the state's attempts to convince Singaporeans of the strategic value of transforming Singapore into a global city. We also make comparisons with other cities within Asia, such as Kuala Lumpur and Hong Kong, as well as global cities such as Sydney and San Francisco, in order to assess different constraints and enabling factors related to the 'politics of scale'. A number of issues arising from our discussion of rescaling are then pursued in greater detail in the subsequent chapters.

Globalization and Global Cities

While there has sometimes been a tendency to think of globalization as a primarily economic phenomenon (Perrons 2004, 35–54; Wade 2001), globalization is in fact better understood as a multidimensional set of processes that include the political, technological and cultural as well as the economic (Giddens 2002, 10; Kennedy 2001, 8). The key characteristic of globalization, according to Giddens (1990, 64), is 'the intensification of worldwide social relations which link localities in such a way that local happenings are shaped by events occurring many miles away and vice versa'.

The reciprocal effects that local and distant events can have on each other means that globalization needs to be more properly understood as something that happens on a variety of scales, from the micropersonal here-and-now to the macrodistant out-there-and-beyond, and everything in between. However, Giddens's (1990, 1991) argument that identity, particularly in the era of late modernity, is a 'reflexively organized project' sustained through narratives raises the issue of whether we can detect in institutional narratives specific manifestations of the effects of globalization – in particular, negotiations of scale with indices of reflexivity.

This focus on the intersection of scale with reflexivity is especially intriguing because it bears on a prominent theme in globalization studies: the extent to which the state is in late modernity still relevant as a cultural frame (see Chapter 1; see also Bauman 1992; Wallerstein 1996, 92) for the construction of identities, the management of economies, and the protection of individual rights (Berking 2004, 51; Giddens 2002, 8–9). It has been claimed that the economic power of global corporations effectively undermines the state's ability to act autonomously, particularly where states need to make themselves attractive to foreign direct investment. Furthermore, it has been suggested that the transnational flows of highly mobile 'cosmopolitans' may have weakened their allegiance to and identification with the state, since such individuals not only have the means, but increasingly the willingness also, to transplant themselves in order to pursue the lifestyles that they desire.

At this point, it is important to note that there is sometimes a tendency to elide the differences between state and nation-state (Blommaert 2005, 217–18). However, the differences are crucial, because the nation-state is arguably far more vulnerable to the effects of globalization than the state *simpliciter*. Since the nation-state is traditionally defined in terms of a shared language, heritage, ethnic origin and geographical location (Kennedy 2001, 2), and one of the effects of transnational migration is the reproduction of a 'deterritorialized culture' (Mir, Mathew and Mir 2000, 28), coethnics may continue to feel that they share a language, heritage or origin, but this shared ethnic identity may be detached from any sense of physical territory. Because physical location is an inescapable fact of existence and the state is defined primarily in terms of territorial sovereignty (Berking 2004, 52), all individuals may accept and recognize, with varying degrees of permanence, their membership in a particular state. However, these same individuals may not be willing to go further and construe themselves as members of a nation that is bounded by the limits of the state's territory – that is, as members of a nation-state.

Therefore, while the state remains valued as an institutional arrangement that provides legal protection and economic and political security for those categories of individuals resident within its territory, it may, qua nation-state, no longer be looked upon as relevant for articulating a richer set of values and ideals, particularly those associated with specific ethnolinguistic or national identities, especially because one prominent feature of global cities is their ethnic and social diversity (Rampton 2006, 7 and references therein). The distinction is needed because some national identities are multi-ethnolinguistic, as in the case of Singapore.

But at the same time that globalization theorists debate the obsolescence of the state, and particularly the nation-state, they also acknowledge the ascension of global cities such as London, New York, Tokyo and Hong Kong (Sassen 2001a, 2001b). Originally defined (Sassen 2001a) as the command centers of multinational corporations, major banks or other financial institutions, the term has 'very positive connotations; it implies importance, modernity and being at the center of world affairs and not surprisingly many cities seek this standing, creating some fusion or confusion between the term global city as a status symbol and as an analytical concept' (Perrons 2004, 204, 231).

It is certainly important not to confuse status symbols with analytical concepts, but there are good reasons for not being unduly exercised by the porous nature of the distinction here. One, the original definition of a global city was decidedly economic in nature, but as we noted (see also Chapter 8), globalization is better understood as a multidimensional phenomenon that includes, but is not limited to, the economic. Hence, the expansion of what it means to be a global city in order to include 'softer' criteria such as perceptions of modernity is a natural outcome of embracing a richer notion of globalization. Two, as different cities compete for global city status, they inevitably seek to impose different definitions in order to play up their strengths. Thus, the blurring of the distinction is in fact an analytical necessity, one that results from adopting an emic perspective on shifting and competing ideas about what actually counts as a global city.

To address this, we focus on narratives produced by the Singapore state as it attempts to reinvent Singapore as a global city. As mentioned, Singapore is seeking this global city status. In the early years after independence in 1965, Singapore was primarily concerned with establishing itself as a nation-state. And its ethnically and linguistically diverse society meant that its articulation of a national identity required developing a sense of cohesiveness among the different ethnic groups. However, Singapore has a rather unique advantage among nation-states: its small landmass means that it also has the option of referring to itself as a city. And this other descriptor has become particularly prominent in more recent state-initiated narratives as Singapore attempts to 'scale down' and re-present itself as a global city. The notion of scale is a key feature of globalization and this deliberate attempt by Singapore at rescaling demonstrates how scalarity is fundamentally a social construct.

Our goal in this chapter is to explore how the shift toward a global city narrative is marked discursively in ways that differ from the nation-state narrative. In this way, the imperatives motivating the state's decision to transform Singapore into a global city emerge with greater clarity.

Singapore: A Brief History

The Federation of Malaysia was formed on 16 September 1963, as the result of a merger between the states of Malaya, Sabah, Sarawak and Singapore. Singapore's leaders were especially keen on the merger because they felt that, as a small island without any natural resources, Singapore could not survive as an independent state. However, the management of ethnolinguistic diversity proved to be a major bone of contention. While the central government preferred a form of affirmative action that favored ethnic Malays, Singapore preferred a policy of 'multiracialism' (Benjamin 1976), which guaranteed separate and equal treatment for the three major ethnic groups: Chinese, Malays and Indians. Consequently, Singapore's membership in the federation was short lived, and in 1965 it was removed and became an independent state.

Singapore's departure meant that its leaders were faced, quite suddenly, with the task of building a nation out of an ethnically diverse population. The narrative of Singapore's origins, then, as articulated by its first prime minister, Lee Kuan Yew, includes the following elements (Wee and Bokhorst-Heng 2005):

(i) Singapore reluctantly came into being only because it was ejected from the federation;
(ii) it has no natural resources, and thus continued success and development depends purely on the industry and intelligence of its people;
(iii) and because the people of Singapore are of different ethnic backgrounds, such sensitivities must also be respected.

In addition to providing an account of Singapore's origins, this narrative also helps to emphasize the values expected of its citizens (hard work, resourcefulness, respect for ethnic differences). Today, Singapore's population of about 3.7 million is officially 74.1 per cent Chinese, 13.4 per cent Malay and 9.2 per cent Indian. The remaining 3.3 per cent, classified by the state as 'others', consists mainly of Eurasians, Europeans, Japanese and Arabs, among others (Singapore Department of Statistics 2010).

The state's modernist orientation is manifested in its focus on the management of ethnic diversity, where each ethnic group tends to be construed in relatively stable and homogeneous terms, and also in its construction of a nation-state as a territorially bounded entity where Singaporeans are understood primarily as residing within this territory. As it moves toward grappling with late modern conditions, the state manifests greater appreciation of a Singaporean diaspora, as well as cognizance of the need to deal with social and economic diversities, in addition to ethnic diversities.

In a 2011 speech, the prime minister, Lee Hsien Loong, while using both the country and city as frames of reference, acknowledged the 'discomfort' and 'anxiety' felt by Singaporeans regarding various 'rapid changes'. At the same time, he pleaded for understanding that the state has to introduce certain changes if Singapore is to avoid becoming 'just like any other city in Asia'.

> If you look and compare today with five years ago, I think we can honestly say incomes have gone up some, people have jobs and homes, our city has been upgraded and Singapore is better. But unfortunately, it was such a powerful storm that even with a big and strong umbrella, we could not avoid getting a little bit wet. So Singaporeans felt the discomfort, the anxiety – compounded because of the rapid changes which we could not predict and which left us worrying what tomorrow would bring. […]
>
> Do we want to be still an exceptional country, one which is unique and which people look up to around the world? Or are we content for Singapore to be an ordinary country getting by but no different from so many other cities all over Asia?
>
> It is not hard to be ordinary. You can get by, but without a hinterland, it will become just like any other city in Asia, then there is no reason for people to be here to invest here, for talent to stay here or even for able Singaporeans in the next generation to want to remain, and then Singaporeans may leave for bigger and better opportunities elsewhere. (Lee 2011)

Lee Hsien Loong's references to being 'exceptional', 'unique' and avoiding being 'ordinary' highlight the issue of intercity competition and marks what we have described as second-order reflexivity. That is, he is asking Singaporeans to decide on what kind of country or city they want Singapore to be ('Do we want to be still an exceptional country […]? Or are we content for Singapore […]?'). Where the state is concerned, if Singapore is to be attractive to talented people, including the next generation of Singaporeans, then being 'ordinary' is not an option; Singapore needs to clearly stand out among the various cities. Getting the citizenry to accept that standing out is important represents one problem for the state. But an even greater problem is getting them to agree on the kind of policies that this objective might entail.

In this sense, this attempt to shift to a global city scale cannot be achieved unilaterally by the state. Instead, it requires the involvement of multiple social actors (the state, citizens and even 'foreign talent' – see below) working together to produce the relevant scale. As Herod and Wright (2002, 10) point out, 'Practices of scale jumping and negotiation, then, can be interpreted as instances of social actors producing new scales of economic and political organization for themselves in a process of "becoming".'

There was a shift in tenor in the speeches made in 2011, which shows that the state is clearly becoming much less authoritarian. This is especially clear when we compare Lee Kuan Yew's own description of his style of government (quoted in Mauzy and Milne 2002, 35): 'We wouldn't be here, would not have made the economic progress, if we had not intervened on very personal matters – who your neighbour is, how you live, the noise you make, how you spit or where you spit, or what language you use. […] It was fundamental social and cultural changes that brought us here.'

While an authoritarian style of government worked well in Singapore's early history, it is obviously much less appropriate when Singaporeans are better educated and globally mobile. Hence, Lee Hsien Loong's call for 'active citizens' to work together with the state marks a more consultative style of government, one where citizens are encouraged to actively participate in voicing their views on issues of national interest. The mechanisms by which such views can be voiced are discussed in the next chapter.

In addition, there is an emphasis on Singapore being attractive to overseas 'foreign talent'. Attention must be paid to 'softer' criteria: Singapore must be fun, vibrant and exciting. The state has even adopted a more tolerant attitude toward homosexuality and also approved the construction of casinos as part of 'integrated resorts' (Lee 2005). This attention to the culture industries and aesthetics (Lash and Urry 1994) also contrasts sharply with the earlier speeches, which had emphasized frugality, self-discipline and national achievements. These changing attitudes on sexuality and gambling suggest that the state accepts that 'the presence of a significant bohemian concentration in a region indicates an environment that is open and attractive to high human capital individuals' (Florida 2005, 128; see also Chapter 8).

Both the nation-state and global city scales still operate as 'technologies of bounding' (Herod and Wright 2002, 6), serving to construct social spaces within which the Singaporean identity can remain distinct. The global city scale, however, is also more explicitly networked, so that the city becomes construed as one (bounded) unit/node that is embedded in complex, shifting and multidimensional relationships with other units/nodes (Herod and Wright 2002, 8; see also Latour 1996, 370). Note, therefore, that the shift into a global city narrative sits rather uneasily with the narrative of Singapore as an Asian nation-state. Nevertheless, this other narrative is not easily abandoned because it provides a sense of biographical continuity. Recall that in the narrative of Singapore's origins, its departure from the federation and independence as an Asian state (rather than a Malay, Chinese or Indian state) came about because it refused to privilege any particular Asian ethnicity. And, as we have seen, subsequent attempts at fostering a sense of nationalism have relied heavily on distinguishing (Asian) Singapore from 'the West'. Thus, even as there are attempts to convince Singaporeans that the society must be more 'open', completely jettisoning the Asian connection appears to be too drastic a step to take. The contradictions between a thoroughgoing cosmopolitanism and an Asian identity are not addressed and remain unresolved at this point in time.

While we will focus primarily on the casinos and the 'pink dollar' in the rest of this book, it is useful, by way of closing this section, to briefly consider at this point how Singapore and other cities and states handle alcohol consumption. This brief comparison helps to highlight the issues of reflexivity and the relationships between cities and states that will occupy us in the later chapters.

Singapore has thus far no serious problem with alcoholism, even though there has been an increase in the prevalence of binge drinking from 1992 to 2004, with the most pronounced increase observed among women aged 18–29 and 30–49 (Lim et al. 2007). The state presently imposes a relatively high sumptuary tax on alcohol. An excise duty of S$70 per liter of alcohol is levied, making Singapore one of the more expensive places in which to consume liquor. Indeed, it might be argued that imposing a high tax is one of the measures needed to keep alcohol consumption under control (Elder et al. 2010). However, as Singapore aims to be 'fun' for tourists, it may at some point have to decide if this high tax is worth maintaining and balance this against the need to avoid a society-wide problem with alcoholism. These are fundamentally identity-related concerns; they involve a second-order reflexivity on the part of the state about what kind of society it wants to be, and what policy changes it is prepared to make in order to achieve its global city aspiration. As we will see later, the state's decision to legalize casinos – despite worries that this might lead to an increase in problem gambling – shows that it is prepared to make some rather controversial policy decisions in order not to lose out on the competition for the tourism dollar. And because

Singapore is both a city and a state, what the state decides is essentially what the city also deems to be good policy, and vice versa.

Contrast Singapore now with South Africa, which has a very clear problem with alcohol abuse. South Africa has been described as a 'hard-drinking country', and the World Health Organization 2011 report states that it has one of the highest per capita consumption rates in the world (Seggie 2012). South Africa has also been using tax as a device to deal with the problem. But because it has a regressive tax on alcohol with the highest taxes imposed on sorghum beer and malt beer, and the lowest on wines and spirits, the effectiveness of its tax policy in tackling alcoholism remains unclear (Ataguba 2012). The issue of institutional reflexivity arises because South Africa is well aware that it has a drinking problem, and the South African government has even recently imposed a ban on the advertising of alcoholic beverages (du Plessis 2013). But this also means that the policies of individual cities in South Africa are constrained by the state. For example, Cape Town has been dubbed the 'drinking capital of SA' (Maregele 2012). But any attempts by the city to move away from a regressive tax to a flat tax or one that is progressive, for instance, will have to deal with potential conflicts between the city's and the state's own policies.

Finally, consider Sweden, where the state has a monopoly on the sale of alcoholic beverages. Known as Systembolaget (literally 'the System Company'), this is a chain of state-owned retail stores throughout Sweden. Since the minimum age for purchasing drinks with more than 3.5 per cent alcoholic content is 20, the Systembolaget is seen as one effective way to ensure that only those meeting the legal age limit are allowed to buy alcoholic beverages. Despite this, Sweden is also concerned about alcohol abuse, with the Swedish National Institute of Public Health reporting that, between 2003 and 2007, the number of female alcoholics increased by 50 per cent and that of male alcoholics by 25 per cent (Sarjent 2008). Like South Africa, then, any city-level initiative regarding the regulation of alcohol consumption will have to negotiate a policy space that does not give rise to conflicts with the state. In this regard, it is therefore worth noting that Stockholm has recently been involved in a pilot project where alcohol purchases are delivered directly to homes. It is important to note, however, that this is project is run by Systembolaget in tandem with local authorities. Thus, the CEO of Systembolaget was quoted as saying (*Local*, 2012): 'The reason we have started in Stockholm is that this is where we have the capacity to carry out deliveries. We have the local authorities and other decision-makers with us in the decision to start here.'

Using the issue of alcohol consumption, what the foregoing demonstrates are a number of points that should be borne in mind in the rest of this book. One, consumption of just about anything can be seen as a problem.

To name just a few examples, the overuse of plastic bags is now considered an environmental issue, soft drinks are seen as leading to serious health problems, and there are increasing concerns that addiction to video games can result in significant social problems. Two, when these problems become sufficiently widespread, decisions about how to respond involve second-order institutional reflexivity. That is, what measure does the state or city, for example, consider to be appropriate and how would such measures cohere with the ways in which the state or city sees itself? Three, when both the state and the city are the essentially the same entity, as in the case of Singapore, policy responses are easier to implement, notwithstanding the need to negotiate the responses of the general populace. But when the state and the city are not coincident, then there are greater constraints on how each can respond. In this sense, our institutional reflexivity corresponds roughly to Archer's (2012, 13) 'communicative reflexivity', which she defines as 'internal conversations [that] need to be confirmed and completed by others before they lead to action'. We say 'roughly' because Archer's definition also includes informal discussions among individuals in their private/personal capacities, whereas we are specifically interested in more formalized arrangements where individuals are acting in their capacities as city or state representatives and where, under the conditions that we have described as negotiated responses (Chapter 1), individuals respond to such representatives in their capacities as citizens. All these points become even more interesting when we place them in the context of global city aspirations. The global city is not just a place of work. It is a place to live in and play, and thus, increasingly, a place to consume. The problems raised by the need to manage consumption while striving to be recognized as a global city is an issue of major sociological significance.

Concomitants of Rescaling: Time and Space

Places are not simply physically locatable entities, but are also socially constructed, with narratives being particularly important devices for achieving such social constructions (Anderson 1983; Johnstone 2004). In the era of late modernity, the state is particularly concerned with mitigating the effects of globalization. In the case of Singapore, we have seen that the state is intent on re-embedding the Singaporean identity, which it feels is in danger of becoming increasingly detached from the physicality of the island. So, when Singapore's second prime minister, Goh Chok Tong, speaks of Singaporean communities being located in other cities, he is effectively constructing Singaporeans, regardless of the particular ethnicity involved, as a new kind of 'global tribe', reminding them where their 'true' home is. But in a highly mobile world, the state must also face up to the possibility that these Singaporeans may never return. Singapore therefore needs to be attractive to non-Singaporeans also, drawing them to the island first as 'foreign talent' and eventually, perhaps, as new citizens.

The shift to a global city narrative is thus intended to present Singapore as a place where people of different nationalities, not just Singaporeans, can feel welcome. Consequently, the narratival scaling down from nation-state to global city is part of a strategy to construct Singapore as a place that is attractive and relevant to both Singaporeans and non-Singaporeans alike. This is a narratival shift that also involves other thematic changes that we have had occasion to observe: abandoning a strong 'us versus the world at large' dichotomy, adopting a more consultative approach to political governance, emphasizing fun and vibrancy as part of the Singaporean lifestyle, and becoming more future oriented.

We will say much more about the Singapore state's attempt to adopt a more consultative approach to governance in the next chapter. For now, we wish to highlight two specific themes, temporality and competitiveness, since these will also feed into our discussion of governance. Both temporality and competitiveness follow from the state's rescaling of Singapore from nation-state to global city.

Competitiveness follows quite clearly as an 'extrinsic' factor given that the global city narrative is intended to advantageously position Singapore in a new global landscape of cities, where cities compete to be as attractive as possible to globally mobile talent.

Temporality follows but perhaps less obviously. It is an 'intrinsic' factor in that shifts in scalarity do not occur without concomitant shifts in temporality. Thus, Blommaert (2006, 4–5) points out that scaling is not just a spatial notion; it is a semiotic phenomenon that involves both space as well as time:

> Against this separation [of space and time], Wallerstein pits the notion of TimeSpace – a 'single dimension' which locks together time and space (Wallerstein 1997, 1; also Fals Borda 2000). Every social event develops simultaneously in space and in time, often in multiply imagined spaces and time frames. So here is one critical qualification: a notion such as scale refers to phenomena that develop in TimeSpace. Scale is not just a spatial metaphor. [...] The semiotization of TimeSpace as social contexts always involves more than just images of space and time. [...] A move from one scale-level to another invokes or indexes images of society, through socially and culturally constructed (semiotized) metaphors and images of time and space.

What this means is that the shift into a global city narrative cannot merely be understood in spatial terms; it also carries temporal implications. In particular, this spatial shift in scale also means that that the state in Singapore, as well as its citizens, will need to be ever more adaptable and flexible, given the rapid changes in the global landscape. Of course, to the extent that such changes are positioned as external forces existing outside Singapore, then, regardless of whether the state adopts a nation-state or global city narrative, adaptability and flexibility are still going to be valuable attributes. But crucially, a nation-state narrative, with its modernist orientation toward homogeneity and stability, will highlight the need for long-term planning and the search for ways to maintain homogeneity. In contrast, the global city narrative, because of its orientation toward diversity and fluidity, engenders an attitude where rapid change becomes something that is both expected and even welcome as a source for opportunistic strategizing. In this way, when compared with the nation-state narrative, the global city narrative semioticizes 'TimeSpace' on both a smaller spatial scale as well as on a more accelerated temporal scale.

Given the more networked nature of cities as compared to that of nation-states (the latter – or more precisely states – are in international law usually regarded as sovereign entities, a view that can be traced as far back as the Peace of Westphalia of 1648), both competitiveness and temporality at the city scale are also more easily affected by changes that take place in other cities. The scale of the nation-state emphasizes the regulating of boundaries and political autonomy (especially in relation to other nation-states, international organizations such as Amnesty International or Human Rights Watch, and even the United Nations). There is therefore a tendency to highlight the nation-state as an entity whose domestic affairs are supposedly 'internal' and beyond the jurisdiction and interference of external bodies.

At the scale of the city, in contrast to that of the nation-state, the regulation of boundaries is less of an issue, not least because for cities within the same nation-state, movement across city limits is usually understood as something that citizens have the right to do and tourists should be encouraged to do (or at least not prevented from doing). Political autonomy, as we have seen, is far less established at the international level, and mediated by the more established autonomy of the nation-state. In fact, with cities, it is their very porosity (allowing fairly free inflows and outflows of peoples) and their malleability (the ability to mount relatively rapid responses to infrastructural needs and to implement policies as a result of highly dynamic demographic changes) that makes them such key actors in late modernity. This is all the more so when cities sometimes come together to collaborate on larger socioeconomic projects, as in the case of the Iskandar Project. Though this project, which involves the setting up of a special economic zone, was the result of an agreement between the states of Malaysia and Singapore, the realization of the project proper involves establishing various commercial, financial and residential districts around the Malaysian city of Johor and various adjacent towns. Cities can also cut across state-to-state diplomatic relations or lack thereof. A good example comes from the Northern Californian city of Berkeley, which has the Cuban city of Palma Soriano as its sister city. This is even though, at the state level, the US government has no diplomatic ties with Cuba. But Berkeley's decision to initiate a sister city relationship with Palma Soriano was precisely intended to encourage the US government to relax its travel and embargo restrictions on Cuba (Dinkelspiel 2012). Unlike nation-states, then, cities have a greater capacity to respond rapidly and flexibly to developments occurring elsewhere. It is no wonder then that, as we have seen in the preceding sections of this chapter, the state in Singapore has decided to adopt a more consultative approach to government as it shifts toward a global city narrative. This more consultative approach is a governance strategy in order to better meet the uncertainties as well as the fluid and changing realities of life in late modernity.

Global Cities: Aspirations and Concerns

Nevertheless, the problems faced by the state in making this move toward a more consultative approach are multiple (as the various chapters in this book, and the following chapter in particular, will demonstrate), and by way of contextualizing such problems, we now make comparisons with other (aspiring) global cities. Consider the city of Kuala Lumpur, the capital of Malaysia. Singapore and Malaysia share a strong history, due in no small part to the fact that Singapore was for a brief period a member of the Federation of Malaysia. But Singapore's departure from the federation was due to a large extent to political and philosophical differences over how to govern an ethnically diverse population. While Malaysia was committed to the idea of special rights for ethnic Malays, Singapore was uneasy with this elevating of one ethnic group over others. In one sense, this makes it easier for Singapore than Kuala Lumpur to attempt to become a global city. The latter is still today facing controversies arising from the notion of Malay rights, and political parties (both the ruling Barisan Nasional as well as the opposition Pakatan Rakyat) are faced with the need to delicately balance the desire to appeal to an ethnically diverse group of voters while not alienating those who would see any abandonment of ethnic Malay rights as a fundamental betrayal of the country's national values. Thus, when compared to Kuala Lumpur, Singapore's departure from the federation has given it relatively greater freedom to maneuver in its global city aspiration.

In this regard, Hong Kong provides a nice example that is the converse of Singapore. Hong Kong's return to China in 1997 represents a political trajectory that goes in the opposite direction to Singapore's departure from the Federation of Malaysia. This return has resulted in significant concern among Hong Kongers about how much of the city's distinctive identity might be lost as the mainland exerts its political influence. Thus, Ko (2012) reports on a recent survey where 'the number of respondents identifying themselves first and foremost as Hong Kong citizens was the highest in 10 years, while the number who saw themselves primarily as Chinese sank to a 12-year low'. According to Ko (2012):

> In part, Hong Kong people's negativity toward mainland Chinese reflects discontent over the Communist government's control over the supposedly autonomous region. The dominant political forces in Hong Kong are pro-China, and the Hong Kong government is viewed as regularly kowtowing to Beijing. Hong Kong is politically distinct from the mainland, most notably with its laws governing freedom of speech and freedom of protest, and any muddling of this distinction is 'frightening' to locals, says Gordon Mathews, a scholar on Hong Kong identity at the Chinese University of Hong Kong. 'The greatest fear Hong Kong people have is Hong Kong becoming just one more city in China.'

Significantly, much like the state in Singapore, Hong Kongers appear to be worried about being ordinary, where their city becomes 'just one more city in China'. But the political influence exerted by the Chinese mainland means that Hong Kong has far less political autonomy than Singapore. Thus, a city's political freedom to maneuver with minimal interference from the state is critical as it strives for global city status, and Singapore is fortunate in this regard when compared with Hong Kong. Unlike Hong Kong, the nation-state and the global city are essentially the same political entity in the case of Singapore.

However, while political freedom provides the autonomy that is needed to implement various policies, there is always still the issue of values to reckon with. In the case of Singapore, we will see that multiracialism, meritocracy and even Asian conservatism constitute key values that need to be taken into consideration if policies proposed by the state are to gain legitimacy among the citizenry. In this regard, it is worth making a brief comparison with Sydney, which, like Singapore, was ranked an 'Alpha+' city in 2010 by the Globalization and World Cities study, making Sydney a 'peer city'. Like Singapore, casinos are also legal in Sydney. Singapore, however, has two casinos while Sydney has just one, the Star. But Sydney is already planning for another precisely in order to compete with Singapore for tourism dollars (Pearlman 2012). The actual number of casinos (in Singapore or Sydney) is less interesting sociologically than the fact that, unlike Singapore, casinos in Sydney are not controversial. Singapore has been (and is still) grappling with public concerns about gambling addiction arising from the state's recent decision in 2004 to legalize casinos, and the potentially negative effects that casinos and gambling might have on the family unit. In a somewhat similar vein, neither is gay tourism controversial in Sydney, which has been hosting the annual Gay and Lesbian Mardi Gras since 1978. In contrast, while the state in Singapore acknowledges the value of the 'pink dollar', it has to still remain fairly circumspect about its support for gay tourism lest it ends up offending the more conservative segments of Singaporean society (see Chapter 8).

Conclusion

Scales are ultimately semiotic constructs. They rely significantly on the ability of actors to influence the symbolic interpretations of resources in order that the actors' activities can be read as taking place at the relevant scale. In the case of Singapore, much of the state's attempts to influence such interpretations are discursive, taking the form of public speeches to the general population, as we saw above. These attempts also involve the deployment of material resources, such as the construction of casinos. Nevertheless, it is important not to forget that attempts at 'upscaling' or 'downscaling' (Blommaert 2006, 9) are not without constraints.

A state cannot simply decide to scale down to reinvent itself as a city, given that a typical state already tends to contain within itself multiple cities. And neither can a city simply decide to scale up and represent itself as a state, given that cities are usually parts of states (although this scaling up may be a possibility if the city secedes from the state, but even so, secession is a fraught process with uncertain outcomes). It is therefore important to appreciate from our discussion of rescaling that this is not an option that is realistically always available to many states or cities. Singapore is something of an exception in this regard, which is why its global city aspirations merit special consideration.

However, even as the state in Singapore embarks on its global city initiative, it has its own set of 'enabling factors' (such as political autonomy without having to be answerable to a larger state) as well as constraints (such as the kinds of social values that need to be grappled with) that we need to pay attention to. These constraints contrast with the constraints faced by Malaysia and Kuala Lumpur on the one hand, and Hong Kong and mainland China on the other. The key point to bear in mind is that Singapore has the advantage of being a city-state. What this means is that the political leaders can address simultaneously the potential tensions associated with being a city and those associated with being a state. This gives Singapore the tremendous advantage of being in a better position than Malaysia or Hong Kong to mitigate the contradictions and conflicts between what it means to be a city and what it means to be a state.

In the case of Malaysia, the state needs to be inclusive enough to accommodate a fairly wide range of different cities, with Kuala Lumpur being just one. Some of these cities in Malaysia are arguably on the cusp of being global cities and possibly eager to be accorded that status, whereas other Malaysian cities are far less sanguine about embracing globalization and are unsure about its impact on traditional values, especially those relating to religion. Establishing a state-level narrative that comfortably allows all these different cities to each move closer toward or further away from the global city label, while still ensuring that Malaysians located across the cities all feel sufficiently unified as a nation, poses a significant problem – one that Singapore does not have to confront. It is not an option for the Malaysian state to adopt a completely hands-off approach where national identity is concerned. This is because contemporary conceptions of the state – even in late modernity – still associate it with the cultivation and promotion of national identity. A purely instrumental view of the state – as a politically autonomous institution that 'merely' provides its citizens with defense, jobs, healthcare and education, among others, within the context of a bounded territory – is not viable because the activities involved in running a country still depend on a sense of shared identity, and many citizens themselves also look to the state to help promote a national identity. There is reliance, therefore, on the strength of the national identity in motivating both ordinary citizens as well as agents of the state to perform many of the activities needed to keep the country going.

In the case of Hong Kong, the worry is to ensure that the city does not lose its 'edge' as it strives to maintain both political and economy autonomy. As a city that has, for long periods of its history, been used to functioning with high degrees of freedom, Hong Kong is clearly currently chafing under political rule from China. The same issues that we just noted in connection with Malaysia also apply to Hong Kong. At the state level, the Chinese government has to make sure that the state-level narrative is constructed in a manner that is able to accommodate not just Hong Kong but many other Chinese cities as well. The fear from Hong Kongers, while not exactly articulated in terms of city-level versus state-level narratives, is that, over time, the construction of this state-level narrative would exert pressure on Hong Kong to become more like its other Chinese city counterparts. Or conversely, the state might want to push other cities to become more like Hong Kong. In either case, the danger that Hong Kongers worry about is their city losing its distinctiveness.

The foregoing remarks about Malaysia and Hong Kong are of course not meant to suggest that Singapore's own route to being a global city is completely smooth and unproblematic. At the very least, the citizenry – which is far from being a homogeneous entity – may have mixed feelings about Singapore being a global city, or may be enthusiastic about the global city status but uncertain about some of the specific policies and measures that may be implemented as a consequence. Exactly how these factors contribute to the Singapore state's attempts to convince the citizenry that the various steps it has taken toward ensuring Singapore's global city status – legitimizing casinos, tolerating gay tourism, encouraging the in-migration of foreign talent – are in fact warranted will be discussed in the rest of this book.

But before we discuss these specific steps, it is useful to have a more general understanding of the nature of state–society negotiations in Singapore. We do this in the following chapter. This focus on state–society negotiations in Singapore will provide us with the sociopolitical background needed to better appreciate how Singapore, when contrasted with other cities and states, handles issues relating to consumption and migration. In addition, this focus on state–society negotiations also serves to highlight how the state in Singapore, despite its reputation for being highly authoritarian, is nevertheless – given the increasingly complex nature of life in late modernity – slowly but surely embarking on a more consultative style of government. And given our emphasis on second-order reflexivity, we also show that the move toward greater consultation is inextricably tied up with broader issues pertaining to the kind of society that both the state and the citizenry envision Singapore being and, relatedly, the Singaporean identity.

Chapter 4

THE DYNAMICS OF STATE–SOCIETY NEGOTIATIONS

Introduction

In this chapter, we look closely at the various mechanisms initiated by the state in Singapore as it embarks on a more consultative style of government, in order to provide a broader understanding of the dynamic nature of state–society negotiations in Singapore. We are not just interested in Singapore in this book, of course, and in the following chapters (see also the preceding chapter) we make comparisons between Singapore and other cities as well as states. But as Chua (2011) points out, Singapore is often treated by other governments as a model: its generally successful experiences in economic planning and housing development, among others, has resulted in both admiration and the desire to emulate, as well as perplexity and the characterization of Singapore's success as due to a fortuitous and exceptional set of circumstances. Be that as it may, the fact that the Singapore experience represents something of a model that at least some other governments are striving to emulate means that it is necessary to inquire further into the nature of this experience – in particular, into how the state has tried to get Singaporeans to accept its various policy initiatives in the move toward global city status.

Even in a society that is as traditionally authoritarian as Singapore, the state has increasingly found that it needs to explain and defend its policies in order to ensure that these gain traction among the general population. Here, we focus on the various ways in which public engagement is manifested, including the feedback mechanisms installed by the state, the state's initiation of 'Our Singapore Conversation' (OSC), and its organization of 'Singapore Day'. We show in these examples that the state is highly concerned with consistently spelling out the rationales behind various policy initiatives and, significantly, these rationales are usually articulated in terms of specific recurrent values, such as pragmatism, communitarianism, meritocracy and multiracialism. The highly reflexive nature of the state is thus thrown into relief. But the articulation of what kind of state and society Singapore is or ought to be also has implications, of course, for what kinds of individuals Singaporeans ought to be. The second-order reflexivity of the state, then, is in dialectical relation with that of its citizens. More significantly, the dialectics of state–society negotiations are such that citizens are not simply at the receiving end of state initiatives. Where such initiatives are not considered to be legitimate because they conflict with the values just mentioned, citizens have been known to reject them.

The State in Singapore and the Institutionalization of Reflexivity

States are by nature reflexive entities, not least because the well-established institution of sovereign statehood carries with it the implication of reciprocal recognition among an international community of nation-states, where the actual realization of such reciprocity is mediated by the fact that different nation-states possess different degrees of economic clout, political standing and military might (DiMaggio and Powell 1991, 8). That the state in Singapore is reflexive therefore comes as no big surprise. Nevertheless, because there has been scant attention paid to the notion of institutional reflexivity, what we want to provide in this chapter is a more concrete demonstration of why it is interesting and important to attend to the institutional reflexivity of the state.

Our key point is that, in the case of Singapore, the institutional reflexivity of the state has led to a process where reflexivity itself is becoming institutionalized as part of how the state and the citizenry are expected to engage each other. In making this point, we demonstrate how the state's willingness to encourage greater reflexivity among the citizenry is part of its very own survival mechanism. That is, the state is aware that its management of the citizenry and the legitimacy of its policies are both increasingly dependent on this institutionalization of reflexivity.

Our demonstration follows three different trajectories. One trajectory looks at the initiation of the Feedback Unit, a government agency set up in 1985 for the public to register their concerns, and its revamp in 2006 as REACH ('Reaching Everyone for Active Citizenry @ Home'), which is intended to facilitate a deeper level of engagement between government and citizenry. A second trajectory reviews three major attempts to get Singaporeans involved in thinking about the nature of Singapore society: the Singapore 21 project in 1997, the Remaking Singapore exercise in 2002, and most recently, the OSC exercise in 2012. The latter was initiated in August 2012 and is envisaged as a series of dialogues between the state and the citizenry on the kind of society that Singapore ought to be. The third and final trajectory focuses on how the state aims to maintain a sense of connectedness across the Singapore diaspora. The state launched in 2006 the Overseas Singaporean Portal, a website for Singaporeans living outside Singapore. And since 2007, it has also regularly organized Singapore Day, an event that is held in different cities where there are large communities of Singaporeans, with the goal of helping overseas Singaporeans stay in touch with various aspects of local culture.

In each of these trajectories, we show that the pattern of engagement is such that both the state and the citizenry are actively concerned with second-order reflexivity – in this case, the issues of what it means to be Singaporean, what kind of society Singaporeans should aim to create, and how some general consensus can be arrived at on these matters.

We noted earlier (Chapter 2) that there is some debate about whether or not institutionalized reflexivity actually leads to agency. If reflexivity becomes routinized as part of how interactions are to be conducted, then there is a question about the extent to which reflexive agents can actually challenge the very social norms that legitimize such reflexivity in the first place. There, we cited Bohman's (1999, 147) suggestion that, however institutionalized reflexivity may be, in the context of large-scale societal pluralism – with its attendant complexity and the fundamentally open-ended nature of human interaction – beliefs, desires and relations of power are unlikely to remain unchanged regardless of the degree to which reflexivity may be institutionalized. And this point certainly holds in an ethnically and socially diverse society such as Singapore. But while we draw empirical attention to this in the current chapter, our main interest is to foreground the fact that institutionalized reflexivity is as much a form of defensive engagement (Ellison 1997) for the state as it is for the citizenry.

From Feedback to REACH

In 1985, the state set up a formalized Feedback Unit, as 'a forum [for the public] to understand major policies, ask questions, make suggestions and generally participate in working out a solution'. Precisely because of the unit's status as a government agency, there was some discomfort from the public about how freely feedback, especially negative feedback, could be given and how seriously such feedback would be treated by the state. As O'Hara (2008, 12) points out:

> In most Western democracies, feedback to government is supplied by a non-compliant media, lobby groups and the real chance of the political opposition becoming the government. In Singapore, none of these institutions obtains, and instead negative feedback is modulated

through a government agency, the Feedback Unit. The Singaporean government is well-known for its love of acronyms, but a number of citizens have commented on the irony of the acronym for Feedback Unit.

Thus, there was fairly general public dissatisfaction with the level of engagement emanating from the state. This even led the then chairman of the Feedback Unit, Dr Amy Khor, to describe the Feedback Unit as 'a black hole from which no light emits' – that is, citizens who submitted their concerns via the Feedback Unit often were frustrated by the lack of response or, where a response was given, by its 'infuriatingly official and non-committal' nature (Tor 2006). The Feedback Unit, then, was seen as providing a relatively superficial level of engagement and as insufficiently dialogic. The state was perceived as using it to primarily gauge responses to various policy initiatives and then tweaking these initiatives where necessary.

Nevertheless, Singapore's third prime minister, Lee Hsien Loong, has suggested that the Feedback Unit's 'biggest achievement [...] is that it has succeeded in changing mindsets both in the civil service and the public' (Ramesh 2006). According to Lee (quoted in Ramesh 2006):

> In the Government, public consultation is now part and parcel of all major policy initiative. Feedback is systematically solicited. Exposure drafts of policy papers and legislative changes are published for comments. To facilitate face to face discussions, we have brought together focus groups involving a wide spectrum of Singaporeans, including with industry and professional associations and the unions. All this has improved policy making in Government.

Some of the specific examples of changes implemented by the state as a consequence of feedback from the unit include the use of sign language for the National Day broadcast, deferring land reclamation works at a beach after concerns were expressed by nature lovers, and the modification of Medisave (a government health insurance scheme) to allow it to be used for outpatient treatments. These examples, while noteworthy, are also highly specific and narrow in scope, and are generally more concerned with mitigating the effects of policies rather than critiquing the rationale behind the policies themselves. Put differently, they are more concerned with debating the means by which ends can be achieved rather than the viability of the ends themselves.

The state itself recognized this and, as a consequence, in 2006, launched REACH ('Reaching Everyone for Active Citizenry @ Home') 'to move beyond gathering public feedback, to become the lead agency for engaging and connecting with citizens'. According to the REACH website:

The three key roles of REACH are to:

Gather and gauge ground sentiments
We continue to feel the pulse of the ground and keep the government apprised of key issues of concern amongst Singaporeans.

Reach out and engage citizens
We work closely with community and grassroots organisations to reach out to more heartlanders, as well as voluntary welfare groups, professional groups and groups with specific needs and interests.

We have a wide variety of traditional and new media channels for citizens who are interested to engage the government, such as public forums, dialogue sessions, SMS, telephone, email, Facebook and Twitter.

Promote active citizenry through citizen participation and involvement
We will facilitate the formation of workgroups to develop ideas into concrete proposals for the Government's consideration.

Moving ahead, REACH will continue to encourage and promote public participation in shaping government policies. (REACH 2012)

There can be little doubt that REACH is an improvement on the Feedback Unit in that it is attempting to engage Singaporeans at a more substantive level about more fundamental issues. Thus, the range of issues discussed is broader, and the modes of engagement are wider: there are public consultations, snap poll findings and discussion forums hosted on the site.

Despite this, the REACH initiative has also raised concerns about the privacy of its participants (O'Hara 2008, 12):

[The website] allows a number of functions including citizen blogging, but there have been comments in the blogosphere about the privacy invasion even of the registration process, which includes ethnicity, marital status, highest educational qualification and income as mandatory fields. User names are neither assigned randomly nor chosen by the citizen – they are instead fixed as one's identity card number. A number of commentators have worried about the privacy issues involved, as well as wondering why the government hosts citizen blogs rather than simply following conversations about its functions in the blogosphere.

While REACH represents a significant step in the state's desire to actively engage the citizenry, there are still qualms about the extent to which any contribution from private citizens are subject to government monitoring. Such qualms are obviously not likely to go away anytime soon, given the state's history of authoritarian rule (see Chapter 2). Nevertheless, there is also a point at which private citizens have to exercise good faith and accept that, despite occasional stumbles, the state is by and large sincere about wanting Singaporeans to participate in a broad-based discussion about various issues and problems confronting Singapore society. As we now see, this is where the Singapore 21 project and its ilk come in.

Conversations about Singapore

In 1997, Prime Minister Goh Chok Tong launched the Singapore 21 project:

> Singapore 21 is about what the people of Singapore want to make of this country. More than a house, Singapore must be a home. The Government can provide the conditions for security and economic growth. But in the end, it is people who give feeling, the human touch, the sense of pride and achievement, the warmth. So beyond developing physical infrastructure and hardware, we need to develop our social infrastructure and software. In Sony Corporation, they call this 'heartware'. We need to go beyond economic and material needs, and reorient society to meet the intellectual, emotional, spiritual, cultural and social needs of our people. (NLB Singapore 1997)

Here, we see a theme that will continue to resonate in the later discussions about Singapore, such as Remaking Singapore and OSC: the notion of Singapore as a 'home', and hence, the kind of home that Singapore ought to be. The use of 'home' here represents a useful lexical solution that is ambiguous enough to accommodate Singapore either as 'nation' or 'city'. This is important because at the time of the Singapore 21 project, Singapore's transformation into a global city was very much in its early stages. Therefore, it would have been premature to speak about Singapore as a 'global city' in public discourses where buy-in from the citizenry could not yet be presumed. Goh's reference to 'heartware' acknowledges that buy-in from the citizenry is something that has to be cultivated, since the state had always taken pride in its ability to deliver on the economic and material needs of the people, but was aware that more could be done in addressing the public's desire for participation and engagement in civil society.

The Singapore 21 project had a fairly narrow focus, dealing with five 'dilemmas' that were proposed by the state itself, and the solutions that were proposed by subcommittees set up under the project (Lee 2002, 106). These 'dilemmas' and their proposed solutions were (adapted from Lee 2002, 106):

(i)   Dilemma: Having a less stressful life versus retaining the drive to succeed
      Solution: Every Singaporean matters
(ii) Dilemma: Looking after the needs of senior citizens versus managing the aspirations of the young
      Solution: Strong families are the foundation and represent the future
(iii) Dilemma: Attracting foreign talent versus looking after Singaporeans
      Solution: There must be opportunities for all Singaporeans
(iv) Dilemma: Aiming for internationalization/regionalization versus treating Singapore as a home
      Solution: The Singapore Heartbeat
(v)   Dilemma: Striving for consultation/consensus versus going for decisiveness and quick action
      Solution: Active citizens who can make a difference to society

The Singapore 21 project, however, has been widely criticized for being little more than a public relations exercise that did not really lead to any substantial changes. Thus, Lee (2002, 107) observes:

> Ironically, the very foundation of Singapore 21 – the five pressing dilemmas and the specially selected subject committee members – has been laid primarily in a top-down fashion. Although *Singapore 21* has been depicted, from the start, as a large-scale consultative exercise involving some 6,000 ordinary Singaporeans, it is perceived by many as yet another motherhood statement by the self-proclaimed all-knowing Singapore government. In a survey commissioned by the authorities to gauge public opinion on *Singapore 21* (in June 2000), almost one in four respondents expressed skepticism (and cynicism) at the vision statement, dismissing it as government propaganda or a political ploy. In other words, *Singapore 21* is deemed an exercise in *pseudo* participation.

There are a number of points worth noting about the Singapore 21 project. First, the agenda (in the form of 'dilemmas') was set by the state. Second, the inclusion of the fifth dilemma ('consultation/consensus' versus 'decisiveness and quick action') was seen as an attempt by the state to curtail public participation and the activities of civil groups by trying to push forward the view that the need for 'decisiveness' on the part of the state may preempt the need for it to consult the citizenry (Lee 2002, 108). Third, it is the combination of these two points that results in public cynicism about the entire project and, by extension, the state's sincerity in wanting to engage the citizenry. Fourth, the commissioning of a survey to gauge how the project was received by the public (in this case, with skepticism) means that the state cannot help but be aware of the dissatisfaction with the project. Likewise, the citizenry (either because of informal communications among individual members or via the disseminated results of the survey) will likewise be aware that there are citizens who have reservations about the success of the Singapore 21 project and who doubt the state's sincerity. This awareness – not just of the project but the meta-awareness as well of how the project was generally perceived – allows the state to calibrate its mode of engagement in subsequent attempts such as Remaking Singapore and OSC.

In this regard, it is worth considering Mouzelis's assertion about the institutionalization of reflexivity and Archer's own response to it. According to Mouzelis (2009, 135; quoted in Archer 2012, 71; emphasis original):

[It is] a reflexive disposition acquired not via crisis situations, but via a socialization focusing on the importance of 'inner life' or the necessity to 'create one's own goals'. For instance, growing up in a religious community which stresses meditation and inner contemplation can result in members of a community acquiring a type of *reflexive habitus* that is unrelated to contradictions between dispositions and positions.

Archer (2012, 71), however, objects to Mouzelis's account on the grounds that:

Although such experiences may indeed promote 'meta-reflexivity' (reflecting upon one's reflections), the mode of life that fosters 'apophatic' as opposed to 'cataphatic' reflexivity does not seem to be widespread in either Eastern or Western religious communities, much less to constitute a model for contemporary secular socialization outside them.

Contrary to Archer, however, what the Singapore 21 project and the survey that followed it demonstrates is that there is indeed 'meta-reflexivity' that can serve as 'a model for contemporary secular socialization'. In this case, it can be argued that the Singapore 21 project, together with the Feedback Unit and REACH (see above), have set a template for state–citizenry engagement. But crucially, this is a template that is not set in stone or fossilized; rather, it is one that is refined and calibrated over time, with newer iterations. This is not to say that newer iterations will necessarily arise, nor are they necessarily 'improvements' when they do arise. Such an assumption would make the mistake of treating the development of state–citizenry engagement as one that follows a form of linear progression. Instead, it is more pertinent to see newer calibrations as representing varying degrees of open-ended adjustments of earlier versions, where such adjustments represent considered responses by the state to how the earlier versions were received. In this way, the institutionalization of reflexivity certainly does not mean 'business as usual'. Transformations are not precluded since regular modifications may be introduced in order to ensure both legitimacy of content (i.e., the items discussed) as well as mode of engagement (so that the state appears sincere and does not alienate those it is trying to engage).

Aside from general skepticism about the relatively superficial nature of engagement attributed to the Singapore 21 project, Chang (2012) provides a somewhat more generous explanation as to why the project did not lead to substantive changes in Singaporean society, suggesting that the state was then focused on dealing with the Asian financial crisis:

> As for the Singapore 21 exercise, the nation's virginal foray into mass engagement, its report swiftly faded from view as the country turned its attention to a deep economic recession brought about by the Asian financial crisis.
>
> As Ang Mo Kio GRC MP Inderjit Singh, who sat on both Singapore 21 and the ERC, sums up: 'The Prime Minister didn't even bother responding to the Singapore 21 report in Parliament.'

Regardless of whether the Asian financial crisis provides a good reason for why the Singapore 21 project made little societal impact, there can be little doubt that Singaporeans also greeted with skepticism the next attempt by the state to engage them in a broad-based national conversation.

This next attempt took place in 2002, when the Remaking Singapore Committee (RSC) was constituted by Prime Minister Goh Chok Tong. The RSC was chaired by the then minister of state Vivian Balakrishnan, and members included other ministers of state, members of parliament, members of the public from the private sector, voluntary organizations and tertiary institutions (National Library Singapore 2012). A total of about 10,000 Singaporeans were consulted as a result.

Given that 'remaking Singapore' presents an extremely broad concept, the committee decided to make their task more tractable by focusing on four specific themes (RSC 2003, 13):

(i) A home for all Singaporeans: where Singaporeans, regardless of their diverse ethnic and cultural backgrounds, can 'pursue a collective search for happiness, prosperity and progress'.
(ii) A home owned: where there is 'greater choice and flexibility, more avenues for expression, and opportunities to participate meaningfully in

national and community life. […] The government will have to play a less prescriptive, more facilitative role.'

(iii) A home for all seasons: where citizens 'can count on help if life has dealt them a harsh blow'. The goal is to achieve a more gracious and compassionate society.

(iv) A home to cherish: where there is regular emphasis on social and cultural improvements, since 'what created value, fulfilment and rootedness in the past may not do so now. We need to examine which aspects of our quality of life can be advanced.' As examples, the committee noted that the patriarchal model of family has to change to recognize the contributions of women to the economy, and the 'stresses of urban life in a globalized world will need to find their relief, whether through family, friends or recreation'.

There are three points worth noting about these themes. First, the notion of a 'home' is again present in the Remaking Singapore exercise. This perhaps can be seen as lending credit to the continued influence of the Singapore 21 project. More substantively, it indicates that regardless of whether Singapore is prominently re-presented in public discourses as a nation or a global city, the fundamental concern for the state is that Singaporeans view the country as a place worth living in, one that they can commit to. This concern is particularly significant given that at the time of the Remaking Singapore exercise, the momentum toward the transformation into a global city was building up. This is clear from the fact that the RSC (perhaps unsurprisingly) endorsed the recommendation of the independent Economic Review Committee, which called for the transformation of Singapore into 'a leading global city, a hub of talent, enterprise and innovation. Singapore will become the most open and cosmopolitan city in Asia, and one of the best places to live and work' (RSC 2003, 18).

In this regard, while the RSC's recommendations were clearly aimed at facilitating this transformation, it had to be cognizant of the fact that the transformation itself was very much a work in progress and one possibly fraught with contentions from the citizenry. Hence, the continued appeal to the term 'home' was strategic in that it satisfied both a national as well as city-level scale of conceptualization without having to be explicitly committed to either.

Second, consistent with our discussion in the preceding chapter, the second theme ('A home owned') recognizes that the transformation into a global city will have to be accompanied by significant changes in how the state and citizenry engage each other. The former will have to be less 'prescriptive', while the latter will have to exercise the greater choice and autonomy it enjoys 'meaningfully' (i.e., responsibly) (RSC 2003, 11).

Third, the fourth theme ('A home to cherish') highlights very clearly the role of reflexivity and hence its institutionalization into the ways in which state and citizenry engage each other. The committee suggests that a shift in the nature of state–citizenry engagement will require that Singaporeans themselves become less 'expectation-oriented' and more 'aspiration-oriented' (RSC 2003, 12). The former are described in the committee's report as 'passive and dependent on the system'; in contrast, the latter will 'increase the dynamism of Singapore society' but are 'less likely to look to the government to improve their well-being' (12–13). The increased presence of the latter will mean that 'the relationship between the government and people will necessarily be reshaped' (13). The call for a concerted and critical examination of various aspects of Singapore society – discarding outmoded values, embracing changes and adapting to a globalized world – recalls what we have termed second-order reflexivity, since such discussions revolve around the question of what kind of society Singapore ought to be. Note also that such discussions may tend toward a notion of utopianization, where different and perhaps competing conceptions of the good life will have to be reconciled. We will say more about this notion of utopianization in our concluding chapter.

As with the Singapore 21 project, the Remaking Singapore exercise too has been criticized for not producing any real or concrete changes. Such criticism is perhaps to be expected given what we have described as utopianization, since such a notion, by its nature, tends to create idealistic, if not unrealistic, expectations. The criticism also seems rather unfair, given that some of the committee's recommendations – whether directly or not – have arguably contributed to bringing about various changes that are part of Singapore's global city transformation. These include 'instituting a five-day work week, establishing a school for the arts, and the ceasing of prior vetting of performance scripts' (Chang 2012). These are attempts by the state to enhance the quality of life in Singapore, with the latter two in particular aiming to liven the local arts scene. In addition to these changes, the RSC's report has also helped to put a greater emphasis in public discourse on 'softer' considerations such as social justice, compassion and graciousness. As we now see, the emphasis on these qualities continues to inform public discourse in the third and most recent initiative, OSC.

OSC was launched in August 2012, when Prime Minister Lee Hsien Loong announced during his National Day Rally speech that he wanted to have a 'national conversation' about the direction that Singapore should take. The prime minister's rationale for initiating this 'conversation' highlighted the themes by now familiar to many Singaporeans: the uncertainties and concerns arising from globalization, and the need to reflexively consider what kinds of values are important to them and, by extension, what kind of society they want Singapore to be.

> 'Our future ... depends on ourselves', he said. 'We have to set a clear direction, we cannot just be blown off-course or drift with the tides onto the rocks.'
>   'In a rapidly changing world, Singapore must keep on improving, because if we stand still, we are going to fall behind. You may think you may be happy as you are, but when you see how the world has moved and what the human spirit is capable of elsewhere, we will not be happy. And even if we are, our children will not be happy', he said. 'So we have to keep on moving.' (Teo 2012)

OSC is led by a committee helmed by the education minister, Heng Swee Keat. The committee itself consists of 26 members. In addition to political office holders, the members included a taxi driver, a polytechnic student, an artist and a television host. The actual conversation itself is envisaged to consist of about thirty public dialogues with various segments of Singapore society, carried out over a period of six months. It is hoped that in the course of such dialogues, some general consensus about what Singapore society ought to be like and how it ought to go about tacking various issues would emerge.

Before we say more about the initiative, it is worth noting that this comes in the aftermath of the 2011 general election, where the ruling party suffered some significant setbacks despite winning enough votes to stay in power. One key setback was the loss of a group representation constituency (GRC) to the opposition for the first time in Singapore's electoral history. In a GRC, candidates from the same party stand as a group, ranging in size from three to six individuals. And at least one of the candidates must come from an ethnic minority community (e.g., Malay or Indian). The group is voted into parliament as a unit. The GRC was introduced by the ruling party, the People's Action Party (PAP), as a means of ensuring minority representation in parliament. The popular belief was that the ruling party would never lose a GRC. This was proven wrong in 2011. Moreover, one member of this lost GRC was a well-respected and popular minister, George Yeo. The result of losing both a GRC as well as a highly respected minister led the ruling party to seriously rethink its way of engaging the citizenry.

Even in the run-up to the election itself, the ruling party was already concerned that the opposition was gaining too much ground due to dissatisfaction among voters with various state policies. Speaking at a lunchtime rally, Prime Minister Lee Hsien Loong publicly acknowledged that there had been mistakes and that things could have been better managed. He acknowledged that there was broad unhappiness with 'higher housing prices and over-crowding on trains and buses caused, critics say, by lax immigration policies and an influx of foreigners' (Gopalakrishnan and Lim 2011). According to Reuters (ibid.):

> 'If we didn't quite get it right, I am sorry but we will try and do better the next time', Lee told a rally on Tuesday in the city-state's central business district, newspapers said.
>
> Later he repeated: 'Well, we're sorry we didn't get it exactly right, but I hope you'll understand and bear with us because we're trying our best to fix the problems.'
>
> Chua Mui Hoong, a deputy editor at the pro-government *Straits Times* newspaper, said the speech was like no other from a PAP minister in recent years.
>
> 'Mr Lee's speech was remarkable for its public mea culpa. And it was remarkable for its – there is no other word for it – humility', she wrote in a commentary.

Thus, the way in which the OSC initiative is being conducted has to also be seen in light of the fact that it comes on the heels of a bruising general election as well as earlier iterations (Singapore 21, Remaking Singapore) that had already been greeted with skepticism. Given this, we can see that the state is at pains to be seen as being especially sincere in wanting to understand the concerns of Singaporeans and genuinely interested in having them play an active role in shaping Singapore's future. Thus, OSC qua an engagement exercise does present some fairly significant changes when compared to the Singapore 21 project as well as the Remaking Singapore exercise. As Chang (2012) points out:

> There are many aspects of the shape and scale of the exercise – officially termed Our Singapore Conversation (OSC) – that are indeed unprecedented.
>
> It will be larger than ever before: almost 5,000 Singaporeans will be invited to focus group sessions, with thousands more engaged through new media. And that will just be in Phase 1, as citizens are asked, in small groups across 30 sessions, to ponder three questions in an open-ended, creative manner:

- What matters most to us?
- What are the values we hold in common?
- How can we work together to meet the challenges of the future?

It will also be unstructured, and strenuously 'ground-up'. Mr Heng wants to form sub-committees only in Phase 2, and these will be based on the themes that emerge from Phase 1.

Unlike the earlier attempts, the OSC initiative thus aims to be assure Singaporeans that the agenda is a 'bottom-up' one that emerges from dialogues with Singaporeans themselves rather than being established 'top-down'. Also, while the state seems unable to conceptualize any way of getting work done without establishing committees, the committees themselves here will come about only after the themes have been clarified via the dialogue sessions. The mode of engagement is also a lot more open and less structured, in the hopes that this will facilitate a freer and more spontaneous exchange of ideas. Finally, in what could be considered a particularly significant move, the state has lifted a gag order so that civil servants may be allowed to participate in these dialogues. According to Toh (2012):

> The Public Service Division (PSD) explained that the gag order was lifted 'in the spirit of the OSC', so that civil servants can 'engage in meaningful discussions on most government policies and share their feedback on how some policies can be improved'. [...]
>
> Although the gag order was lifted, civil servants have been reminded not to 'make controversial comments' or 'publicly lobby for a different policy position', as these would hurt the credibility of the civil service. 'Public officers are collectively responsible for government policies', the circular said.

The outcome of the OSC initiative remains to be seen. Whether it leads to any substantive changes in the nature of Singapore society, and whether it is ultimately viewed as a more sincere attempt by the state to involve the citizenry in processes of policy formulation and in the more fundamental discussion about what kind of society Singapore ought to be will only become clearer in the months or years following the completion of the OSC initiative.

But what is pertinent given the focus of this book is that the OSC initiative, the Remaking Singapore exercise and the Singapore 21 project all represent increasingly critical modes of engagement between state and citizenry. Later versions are of course conducted with some historical memory of earlier attempts. In the same way that the ranked list constitutes a record for competitive self-improvement (Chapter 2), this historical memory contributes greatly to increased reflexive awareness on the part of both state and citizenry: it shapes the expectations that these parties have about the processes and their outcomes. Note that both reflexive concerns – about the ways in which state and citizenry engagement one another, and about the kind of society that Singapore ought to be – are not necessarily independent. This is because, increasingly, as Singaporeans become better educated, globally mobile and experience first-hand other societies and cultures, a prominent aspect of the kind of society that Singapore ought to be includes the ways in which state and citizenry are expected to engage one another. That is, the normative vision of Singapore grows to include the fact that many citizens want to be, and should be encouraged/allowed to be, more actively and more regularly involved in activities that were in the not-so-recent past seen as the exclusive province of the state. This includes having a say in the formulation of macro-level policy decisions.

As we have seen, the state on its part is also acutely aware of the need to be more open to, and appreciative of, the desire of citizens to be involved (or to at least be seen as being open and appreciative). The state is only too aware that some of its recent policy decisions have not gone down well with the citizenry or at least raised concerns that need to be addressed. Some of these involve immigration and the legalization of casinos, and we discuss them in the later chapters.

For now, we move on to discuss the third and final trajectory, how the state aims to engage Singaporeans located overseas.

The Singaporean Diaspora

The most important point to bear in mind when considering the Singaporean diaspora is that, because these are individuals located overseas, they are less subject to any regulatory policies that the state may introduce. For example, the state has been discouraging Singaporeans from using Singlish, a colloquial variety of English, because it fears that this may compromise Singaporeans' ability to speak Standard English and subsequently jeopardize their ability to compete economically in the global market (Wee 2007). But while it may be better able to limit the use of Singlish domestically, it is hardly in a position to change Singaporeans' language practices when they are located overseas (cf. Kong 1999).

The state recognizes this, implicitly or otherwise, and hence, in addressing the Singaporean diaspora, its focus is less on engagement with substantive issues (on which these Singaporeans are in any case able to convey their views via the mechanisms already discussed above). Rather, the strategy here involves encouraging overseas Singaporeans to maintain an emotional connection with their homeland. In this regard, we discuss two initiatives recently introduced by the state, the Overseas Singaporean Portal and Singapore Day.

The Overseas Singaporean Portal was launched in 2006, and its main goals are to cater to their 'informational', 'transactional' and 'community-building needs' (Wong 2006), by providing overseas Singaporeans with information about events back home, making easily available various government administrative services, and helping them to make contact with fellow Singaporeans. In his speech marking the event at the Regent Hotel in Shanghai, the deputy prime minister and minister for home affairs, Wong Kan Seng, made the following comments (ibid.):

> There are now more than 140,000 Singaporeans spread across the world. The Overseas Singaporean diaspora is rich in its diversity of experiences, knowledge and networks. You add to the rich fabric of our nation. It is important for us to remain engaged with one other.
>
> In an increasingly globalised world, many Singaporeans will follow in your footsteps to go overseas to study or work. Among you are some of our best and brightest talent. We want you to stay connected with Singapore, to know what is happening back home. At the same time, you can also share with fellow Singaporeans in other countries and Singapore what you are doing. Together, we can build a strong and interconnected Singaporean community that is not constrained by geographical limits or by Singapore's small size. […]
>
> We will do well to harness this to our advantage – to use this tool to bring us closer together, to stay together as one people, overcoming the constraints of physical distance. It enables us to be united as one by the Singapore spirit, even though we may be physically apart. Let us celebrate our new found proximity and connection.

As we noted in Chapter 1, studies of cosmopolitanism have tended to underestimate the role that institutions such as the state play in positioning/constructing cosmopolitan individuals. In Wong's speech, we see that even as the state acknowledges that cosmopolitan individuals have many possibilities open to them, it emphasizes their relationship to Singapore ('*our* best and brightest talent'), presents their very cosmopolitanism as something that Singapore can benefit from ('We will do well to harness this to our advantage'), and reminds them that they have a contribution to make to Singapore's success ('Together, we can build a strong and interconnected Singaporean community').

This insistent reminder of the cosmopolitan individuals' connection to their homeland was recently reinforced by Grace Fu, second minister for the environment and water resources, at the Singapore National Day Reception in Seoul. According to Fu (2012), overseas Singaporeans are 'ambassadors' of the 'Singapore brand':

On a more serious note, Singaporeans and Singaporean companies are often known for reliability, competence, trust-worthiness, and a high standard for quality and safety. We deliver what we promise and are trusted. This Singapore branding is invaluable and has helped many Singaporeans and Singapore companies land job and business deals in many parts of the world. As our community in Korea, I urge each and every one of you to be the ambassadors of Singapore and help uphold the Singapore brand here.

With globalisation, the branding of Singapore is becoming ever important. Our karma is to live with our lack of resources including water and land. Our strategy is to keep a strategy of openness to investment and trade and be a liveable and vibrant city of choice in Asia. We are a hub, a shining red-dot, connected to the rest of the world. You are part of our connection to the rest of the world. There are now more than 190,000 Singaporeans, who are like you, spread across the world. The Overseas Singaporean diaspora is rich in its diversity of experiences, knowledge and networks. You add to the rich fabric of our nation and contribute much to our Singapore brand. It is important for us to remain engaged with one another. We want you to stay connected with one another and with Singapore, to know what is happening back home. A vibrant and connected Overseas Singaporean community around the world, with strong linkages to the family and friends in Singapore, will be an asset to the country.

Fu therefore makes clear that, where the state is concerned, overseas Singaporeans have undoubtedly benefited from the 'Singapore brand', with its associated characteristics of reliability and competence. This branding has 'helped many Singaporeans and Singapore companies land job and business deals in many parts of the world'. Overseas Singaporeans therefore have an obligation to 'uphold' the brand, wherever they may be, because they 'contribute much to our Singapore brand'.

In this way, the cosmopolitan gaze that we have criticized as being attributed to specific classes and denied to others (Chapter 1) is being directed by the state toward the same focal point as that of its noncosmopolitan counterparts. That is, all Singaporeans – cosmopolitan or otherwise, located in Singapore or outside, highly talented or not – are enjoined by the state to see themselves as 'united', as still having significant contributions to make. Whether ultimately successful or not, the state's goal here is clearly to influence the second-order reflexivity of Singaporeans located overseas, so that they see themselves not only as successful individuals but, more specifically, as successful individuals who can and should continue to play a part in contributing to Singapore's development.

And in order to further strengthen this sense of connection (and, indeed, obligation) to Singapore, the state has more recently introduced Singapore Day, a largely annual event organized by the Overseas Singaporean Unit (OSU), which comes under the Prime Minister's Office. The first Singapore Day was held in 2007 in New York City, the second in 2008 in Melbourne and the third in 2009 in London. There was no Singapore Day in 2010, possibly because the country was organizing the Youth Olympic Games that year, and having a Singapore Day would stretch the budgetary and other resources. In 2011 and 2012, the Singapore Day was held in Shanghai and Brooklyn, respectively.

According to the Singapore Day website, the goal is to bring 'a slice of home' to Singaporeans around the world (OSU, n.d.):

> Every year, Singapore Day travels to major cities around the world to bring to OS communities familiar sights, sounds and tastes. It's a mega get together!
>
> Singapore Day is OSU's signature event where we organise a carnival in cities with a big concentration of overseas Singaporeans. We bring up the sights, tastes and sounds of Singapore, to give you a slice of home.

In contrast to the exhortations by Wong and Fu to overseas Singaporeans to be mindful of their responsibilities to the country back home, Singapore Day focuses primarily on more light-hearted connections. It is an opportunity for the state to remind overseas Singaporeans that Singapore can be fun and enjoyable. Thus, the website describes the three 'key components' of Singapore Day:

- authentic hawker fare served by Singapore's celebrity hawkers,
- a concert by home-grown artistes, and
- a colourful experiential showcase that showcased the latest developments in Singapore.

These reminders to overseas Singaporeans of things that they might have missed are part of the state's larger attempt to portray Singapore not only as a global city where things are efficiently run, but also as a place where people can have fun. Lee Kuan Yew, Singapore's first prime minster, recognized that mere efficiency would not be enough to attract cosmopolitan individuals (Mukherjee 2005):

> Lee Kuan Yew, the founder of modern Singapore, described his island nation in parliament this week as 'a neat and tidy place with no chewing

gum, no smoking in air-conditioned places, no this, no that – not a fun place'. [...]

With China and India chipping away at Singapore's manufacturing and service businesses, the city-state can't remain a top draw in Asia for money and talent simply because it's 'a healthy and wholesome society, safe and secure for everyone', as the 81-year-old leader put it.

While it remains to be seen if the state can actually succeed in manufacturing 'urban buzz' (Mukherjee 2005), there is little doubt that it is determined to try. Events like the various Singapore Days target overseas Singaporeans by attempting to convey to them some of the excitement and energy of life back home. But for this to succeed, there must be excitement and energy to actually convey, and of course, this imperative to create a 'buzz' cannot only rely on nostalgic desires for food or concerts by homegrown artistes. The state is well aware that if Singapore is to draw both overseas Singaporeans as well as globally mobile non-Singaporeans, more contemporary and 'world-class' events and activities will also need to be made available. Some of these, such as the legalizing of casinos, have proven controversial. Other concerns that need to be addressed involve a less regulatory approach to issues surrounding the Singaporean identity (which we discuss in the next chapter).

Conclusion

As Singapore moves toward its goal of becoming a global city, the state has recognized the need for greater engagement with the citizenry, encouraging them to actively contribute toward this goal by articulating their own ideas about how it can be achieved. In the not-so-recent past, the state would have performed these tasks of defining (for the citizenry) what it means to be a Singaporean and what it envisions Singapore society to be.

But as the various mechanisms discussed in this chapter demonstrate, these tasks now are 'to be shouldered reflexively by the subjects themselves' (Archer 2012, 107), as citizens are enjoined by the state to provide their own varying perspectives on these matters. At the heart of these mechanisms (the Feedback Unit, REACH, Singapore 21 Project, Remaking Singapore, Our Singapore Conversation, the Overseas Singaporean Portal, Singapore Day) is the attempt by the state to get Singaporeans to *care* about Singapore. And caring entails reflexivity (Archer 2012, 105; quoting Frankfurt 2004, 17–18; emphasis original):

By its very nature, caring manifests and depends upon our distinctive [human] capacity to have thoughts, desires and attitudes that are *about*

our own attitudes, desires and thoughts. In other words, it depends upon
the fact that the human mind is *reflexive*. [...] Creatures like ourselves are
not limited to desires that move them to act. In addition they have the
reflexive capacity to form desires regarding their own desires – that is,
regarding both what they want to want, and what they want not to want.

These mechanisms institutionalize second-order reflexivity, where the latter
also includes the shaping of expectations about how state and citizenry ought
to engage one another. What this means is that as the state and citizenry
deliberate about the nature of Singapore society, part of that deliberation also
includes, as we have seen, the nature of the state–citizenry relationship (see
also Chapters 6 and 7).

Chapter 5

(DE-)REGULATING ASIAN IDENTITIES: COMPARING ASIAN CITIES AND STATES

Introduction

This chapter takes up the issue of the dialectics between city and state by comparing three cities in Asia with differing positions in their relationship with states and with differing aspirations as regards becoming a global city. These cities are Singapore, Hong Kong and Kuala Lumpur, in Malaysia. Unlike Singapore, which is both a city and a state, Malaysia represents a state that is unable to plausibly descale into a city (which then leads us to briefly consider Kuala Lumpur, Malaysia's capital city). In contrast to both Singapore and Malaysia, Hong Kong represents a city that has (since the handover in 1997 to China) been co-opted back into a state. By placing our discussion in a comparative perspective, a more nuanced appreciation of the relationship between cities and states emerges, as well as the issues that need to be faced when striving for global city status.

We are not assuming that the cities and states discussed here are all necessarily interested in acquiring global city status. Rather, our goal is simply to bring out some of the identity-related issues that each might have to deal with, were they indeed so interested. Of course, each of the examples discussed here necessarily differs in the particular details. Nevertheless, it is important not to slip into a discussion of particularities, important though such details may be. Instead, we advance the argument that there are interesting generalities to be observed, which we discuss in the concluding section of this chapter.

In this introductory section, however, before embarking on the specifics of comparisons, we want to address a more general issue, which has to do with our decision to focus on Asia. As we pointed out in Chapter 1, the notion of global city as construed in this book is not the same as Sassen's (2001a) interpretation, which analytically bestows global city status on those cities that are important financial hubs. Instead, we take as our starting point Perrons's (2004) observation that many cities are striving, and thus competing against each other, in order to be seen as global cities. Under these circumstances, the notion of what counts as a global city is broadened; being a financial hub becomes just one among many other factors, and may even not constitute a necessary condition. This is because competition leads the competitors to consider and develop their own interpretations of what it means to be a global city, so that increasingly, offering world-class cultural attractions is now something that many cities are aiming to offer.

These two notions of what it means to be a global city – Sassen's more etic and analytically oriented notion, and the more emic and aspirational interpretation that emerges from the competing cities themselves – are certainly not unrelated. This is especially in the light of what Giddens (1987) calls the 'double hermeneutic' – that is, the notion that there is a two-way relationship between lay/everyday concepts and social-scientific ones. Unlike the natural sciences, where scientists study objects and phenomena (e.g., chemical processes) that lack awareness, the objects and phenomena studied by social scientists (i.e., people, society) can come (via education, the mass media, sociopolitical debates, etc.) to not only appreciate social-scientific concepts such as 'citizen' and 'sovereignty' (Giddens 1987, 20), and more recently 'diaspora' or 'inflation', but to even use them themselves. As Giddens (1987, 18–19) puts it:

> The subjects of study in the social sciences and the humanities are concept-using beings, whose concepts of their actions enter in a constitutive manner into what those actions are. Social life cannot be accurately described by a sociological observer, let alone causally elucidated, if that observer does not master the array of concepts employed (discursively or non-discursively) by those involved. [...]
>
> Unlike in the natural science, in the social sciences, there is no way of keeping the conceptual apparatus of the observer – whether in sociology, political science or economic – free from appropriation by lay actors.

In the case of the 'global city', as relevant authorities become aware of the concept, it has become something that has been appropriated by them and (increasingly) even lay members of the public. At this point, the concept begins to exemplify Giddens's description of the double hermeneutic. Second-order reflexivity is especially relevant here, as we noted in Chapter 2, because as the concept circulates in public discourses between authorities and the public, it inevitably develops beyond a purely academic understanding to ones that are more nebulous, especially as governing authorities and members of the public engage each other in negotiated responses, thus offering somewhat different understandings of the concept.

This brings us to the reason why we are focusing primarily on Asian cities in this chapter. Singapore (among other cities) is aggressively and actively trying to be seen as a successful global city. To this end, the state in Singapore has consulted well-known theorists of the city, including Saskia Sassen herself. For example, in 2006, the Monetary Authority of Singapore invited her to speak about how Singapore could be 'a major, well-rounded city' (Cheong 2013). In her most recent visit in 2013, Sassen was quoted (ibid.) as suggesting that Singapore might want to be careful to avoid overplanning, and to also ensure that it does not become

> only an economic engine for fat cats to make big money, but also a wide window in which all folk 'can execute their life projects' by innovating constantly and exchanging ideas and opportunities with everyone from everywhere else. […] For example, immigrants in a city learn to set up various enterprises to survive. Gay people feel freer in a city, as they are often persecuted in smaller communities.

Thus, the state in Singapore is well aware that it will probably have to regulate less and allow for more ad hoc and bottom-up initiatives, and maybe even embrace some version of Florida's (2005) 'creative class' thesis, which emphasizes 'Technology, Talent and Tolerance' as key to the economic growth of cities and communities. Indeed, in that very same interview, Sassen (Cheong 2013) explicitly makes the point that:

> The challenge for Singapore now, ironically, is to resist the urge to continue planning its city too comprehensively, she says.
> 'For a city to be dynamic and exciting,' she stresses, 'it has to remain complex and incomplete; it cannot be fully planned.'

This raises difficult second-order reflexivity questions for a state that has historically been more comfortable with an authoritarian style of government (see Chapter 2), and one that also has taken pride in its ability to plan comprehensively. Learning to 'let go' and allowing for the unplanned and the unregulated is not something that comes easily to a state known for its technocratic attention to detail. And Sassen's reference to the gay community is particularly pertinent. As we will see later (Chapter 8), the state faces a difficult balancing act because it wants to appear 'gay friendly' while, at the same, it needs to be seen as remaining faithful to conservative 'Asian' values.

This, then, is why a focus on Asia is useful. 'Asian-ness', however and whatever it might mean to different people, creates interesting considerations for global city aspirations, especially when states and cities in Asia have strong religious or other cultural commitments that might conflict with issues of sexual, ethnic and cultural diversity. Thus, while both Singapore and Malaysia face concerns arising from their ethnically diverse populations, the latter, being an Islamic state, needs to balance any attempt at opening up with its commitment to pro-Malay policies as well as curbing religious extremism. The issues of religion and ethnic diversity are less salient in the case of Hong Kong. Hong Kong, however, is under Chinese rule, and the issue of identity and the rights of individuals in that context is still in the process of negotiation, especially regarding the relationship between Hong Kongers and Chinese mainlanders.

Another reason why Asian cities are of particular interest comes from the fact that the push toward global city status carries with it an unmistakable neoliberal ethos. Neoliberalism is viewed (correctly) as an economic and political doctrine with historically Western roots (Harvey 2005), and managing the penetration of neoliberal manifestations and initiatives in Asian society presents a significant concern for governance, especially given that in the 'global popular imagination, American neoliberalism is viewed as a radicalized capitalist imperialism that is increasingly tied to lawlessness and military action' (Ong 2006a, 1). Thus, the neoliberal emphasis on individually based free-market enterprise may be seen as undermining state authority. This is why, in many Asian states, the 'exceptional' status of neoliberalism needs to be marked off, often via the introduction of 'special spaces' within which neoliberal activities can be tolerated (3–4). In the case of Singapore, such special spaces or zones are used to mark off the presence of casinos, whose legalization has proven politically controversial as they are potentially damaging to local communities (see Chapters 6 and 7).

We organize our discussion in this chapter as follows. We first summarize some of the key issues faced by Singapore in deregulating what it means to be Asian, drawing attention to the problems it faces as well as the advantages that it possesses. This will set the stage for a more comparative discussion, as we then introduce Malaysia (and Kuala Lumpur) and Hong Kong, before concluding with a more general review.

Deregulation of Identity: The Enigma of Singapore

Singapore became independent in 1965 when it was ejected from the Federation of Malaysia, due to political differences between the Singapore government and the central government. A key political difference concerned the management of ethnic diversity and, specifically, the issue of whether ethnic Malays ought to be granted special rights. Singapore's position was that the granting of special rights would do little to improve the status of the

Malays and would, in fact, create more problems for ethnic relations. It was this debate over special Malay rights that would be a key factor leading to Singapore's eventual departure from the federation.

Singapore's subsequent departure meant that its leaders were faced, quite suddenly, with the task of building a nation out of an ethnolinguistically diverse population, and with developing the nation's economy without access to any natural resources. This emphasis on economic development motivated Singapore's strong emphasis on learning English. But because of the country's ethnic and linguistic diversity, the promotion of English must take into account the presence of Singapore's other languages as well as the feelings of the speakers of those languages. In order to do this, the government encouraged Singaporeans to be bilingual in English and a mother tongue that is officially assigned to them on the basis of their ethnic identity. Given Singapore's ethnically diverse society, three official mother tongues are recognized for each of the major ethnic groups: Mandarin for the Chinese, Malay for the Malays, and Tamil for the Indians. Perhaps the best way to see how Singapore's attempts to become a global city may require a deregulation of identity is to begin with an appreciation of its language policy (see Wee 2012), which from the outset has positioned English as a language to be acquired only for its pragmatic value.

Although the government recognizes English as an official language, it does not wish to accord it the status of an official mother tongue for a number of reasons. One, English is to serve as an interethnic lingua franca. Two, as the major language of socioeconomic mobility, maintaining an ethnically neutral status for English helps ensure that the distribution of economic advantages is not seen as being unduly associated with a specific ethnic group, which would otherwise raise the danger of interethnic tension. And three, English is treated as a language that is essentially Western and thus unsuitable to be a mother tongue for an Asian society such as Singapore.

Thus, while English is embraced for its association with economic development and access to scientific and technological know-how, there is also a fear that exposure to English can lead Singaporeans to become increasingly 'Westernized' or 'decadent' or 'morally corrupt'. Thus, as far as the state is concerned, knowledge of English must be balanced by knowledge of one's mother tongue, as indicated by the following statement made by the first prime minister, Lee Kuan Yew (1984; cited in Bokhorst-Heng 1998, 252): 'One abiding reason why we have to persist in bilingualism is that English will not be emotionally acceptable as our mother tongue. [...] To have no emotionally acceptable language as our mother tongue is to be emotionally crippled.'

Knowledge of one's mother tongue, it is claimed, will provide Singaporeans with a link to their traditional cultures and values, and will thus serve to counter any undesirable effects of Westernization. This belief that English and the mother tongue play different roles, such that the former serves a purely pragmatic function while the latter has a cultural-symbolic value, has been described as 'English-knowing bilingualism' (Pakir 1992). However, there are reasons why this particular positioning of English as an 'emotionally unacceptable mother tongue' is problematic.

This is because, for many Singaporeans today, the language of the home is English rather than one of the official mother tongues (Pakir 2000, 262; Li Wei, Saravanan and Ng 1997; Saravanan 1998). In the case of the Malay community, for example, English use among residents aged 5 and above has increased from 7.9 per cent in 2000 to 17 per cent in 2010. In the same time period, the use of Malay has dropped from 91.6 per cent to 82.7 per cent (Singapore Department of Statistics 2010). Similarly, for the Indian community, English has increased from 35.6 per cent in 2000 to 41.6 per cent in 2010, while Tamil has declined from 42.9 per cent in 2000 to 36.7 per cent in 2010. For both these communities, the general explanation for this shift offered by community leaders has been the appreciation among Malays and Indians of the economic value of English as well as a rise in interracial marriages (Hussain 2011).

Mandarin is the only language among the official mother tongues that appears to have maintained a strong presence in its particular ethnic community. But even here, 'while the growth in the share of English-speaking households has accelerated in the last decade, the growth of Mandarin-speaking households has slowed' (Cai 2011). More interestingly, the resilience of Mandarin is aided by the inflow of Mandarin speakers from Malaysia and China. It is not unlikely, therefore, that as these new permanent residents settle into Singapore society, subsequent generations might also demonstrate a shift toward English.

Another reason why the state may need to reconsider the status of English has to do with its desire to attract foreign talent, which may result in changes to Singapore's Asian character. Goh Chok Tong, Singapore's second prime minister, has acknowledged that a consequence of bringing in foreign talent is that Singapore 'will be less Asian': 'When Singapore becomes a first-world economy, it will become more international and more cosmopolitan. This has a cost for our society. It will be less Asian. There will be many more people of different nationalities, races and lifestyles in Singapore. This place will feel and look like any other cosmopolitan city in the world' (1999; National Day Rally speech).

Finally, Singapore's already diverse population looks set to become even more increasingly varied, making it even more difficult to organize Singaporean multilingualism along the lines of ethnically determined local identities. One indicator of this is the increase in the 'Others' category, which in 2000 constituted 1.4 per cent of the population and in 2010 rose to 3.3 per cent. Another indicator comes from recent statistics concerning marriage trends. Singaporeans with foreign spouses rose from 4,445 in 1996 to 6,359 in 2006. From 2004 to 2006, the most common male foreign spouses were from Australia, Bangladesh and Canada, while the most common female spouses were from Australia, Brunei and Cambodia.

As a consequence of the trend toward interethnic marriages, the state has very recently also had to accept that there are Singaporeans who, as a result of having mixed parentage, wish to claim double-barreled or hyphenated ethnic identities. Consequently, with effect from 1 January 2011, the government introduced the possibility for Singaporeans to officially opt for hyphenated ethnic identities. However, there are also reasons to think that this move may not be quite as radical as it appears. The implementation still allows the government to cling to its more traditional view of the relationship between ethnic identity and language because the two terms in the hyphenated identity are not of equal value or importance. 'Hybrid' Singaporeans are required to reflect their 'dominant' identity in the first member of the pair. Thus, a 'Chinese-Malay' is someone who feels mainly or primarily Chinese and to a lesser extent Malay. Consequently, for this person, his/her official mother tongue will be Mandarin, following from the government's assignation of Mandarin as the official mother tongue of the Chinese community. Conversely, a 'Malay-Chinese' is someone who feels mainly or primarily Malay and to a lesser extent Chinese. For this person, his/her official mother tongue will be Malay, again, in accordance with the assignation of Malay as the official mother tongue of the Malay community.

Given the rise of English as a home language, the drive toward attracting foreign talent and the increase in interethnic marriages, the mandatory assignation of a specific mother tongue onto Singapore's ethnic and linguistic diversity, and the denial of mother tongue status to English, are simply unrealistic. Whether the state likes it or not, deregulation of identity has to be seriously considered. That is, there may be little choice but to allow for greater individual autonomy in language policy.

Malaysia: The Bumiputra Policy and Islam

A key reason for Singapore's departure from the Federation of Malaysia had to do with disagreements over whether there ought to be a policy that privileged Malay rights. Singapore's unease with such a policy has, in a sense, made it easier to aim for global city status, at least where the management of diverse ethnicities is concerned. This is notwithstanding the fact, noted in the preceding section, that the state in Singapore would still need to allow for greater autonomy in decisions over what counts as a mother tongue. But not being expected to privilege a specific ethnicity or particular religion affords Singapore greater leeway in accommodating and even absorbing diverse cultural influences.

Conversely, Malaysia's decision to institute a policy that privileges Malay rights, also known as the *bumiputra* policy – now long entrenched as part of the sociopolitical scene – raises difficult considerations for issues of national identity, because any move toward deregulation would likely be seen as undermining such rights. The problem facing Malaysia, then, is not necessarily one of deregulation. Rather, it is one of continuing to regulate the expectations and privileges that accrue to someone classified as ethnically Malay, while moderating these expectations and also managing any unhappiness that might emanate from members of the other ethnic groups. This is because the bumiputra policy provides special recognition of the rights of the ethnic Malays on the basis that, as the 'original or indigenous people of Malaya', they are entitled to specific consideration and privileges vis-à-vis other ethnic groups (Mahathir Mohamad, Malaysia's longest serving prime minister, 1970, 33; emphasis original):

> We are now in the process of building a new nation which is to be an amalgam of different racial groups. The form of this new nation and this new citizenship must be such as to satisfy all the constituent races. An understanding of the relative rights and claims of each race is important if we are to avoid the differences which selfish racial prejudices will engender [...] *I contend that the Malays are the original or indigenous people of Malaya.*

Even though the importance of Malay rights was codified in the Malaysian constitution in 1957, a refinement was implemented in 1970 in the form of the New Economic Policy (NEP). Under the NEP, 'Malays were not only given special rights in administration and education but also in terms of language and culture' (Rappa and Wee 2006, 33).

The bumiputra policy has continued to prove contentious over the years, such that in 2001, the opposition political party, the Democratic Action Party, issued the following statement during a press conference (Penang, 28 May 2001; see Rappa and Wee 2006, 44) expressing their concerns about:

> ... a narrow attitude that bumiputra students must be helped at all cost, even at the expense of other citizens who are high achievers in public examinations ... It does not make sense for Education Minister Tan Sri Musa Mohamed to propose that the much disputed quota system

be extended to the private sector which would further curb the limited opportunities available to non-bumiputra.

And even as recently as 2008, the Malaysian government has had to assert that key elements of the NEP would not be removed because bumiputras have yet to achieve the 30 per cent equity target since their share of the economy was still estimated at only 19 per cent 'and there was no increase since 1990' (*Nation*, 31 October 2008; quoted in Rappa and Wee 2006, 44). Thus, the bumiputra policy regulates identity by according special status to ethnic Malays and, by implication, making it clear that not all ethnic groups are of equal status. And this regulation of identity goes beyond the symbolic, because it carries economic and educational implications for Malaysians, depending on whether they are considered bumiputra or not.

Malaysia also has to grapple with the status of Islam as the state religion. Constitutionally, all ethnic Malays are considered Muslim. But there continue to be problems relating to whether Islamic law ought to also apply to non-Muslims. Those taking more extreme positions, such as calling for the imposition of *hudud* – where theft, for example, is punishable by amputation – have unsurprisingly created unease among the more moderate Muslims as well as among non-Muslims. There is also the dimension of gender, with better-educated Muslim women challenging the traditional restrictions imposed on them as a result of their female identity. Thus, consider Ong's (2006a, 42–3) observation that in Malaysia, feminists like the Sisters of Islam, who aim to oppose the monopoly that *ulamas* (traditionally male Islamic scholars and officials) have over Islamic ethics,

> must first legitimize their claims as rational and therefore equal moral partners (sisters) in the interpretation of Islamic texts. The first of feminists' struggles with ulamas is over women's intellectual and moral capacity to interpret Islam for themselves, instead of relying solely on ulamas' interpretations. This assertion of women's intellectual role in Islam is part of Muslim feminists' worldwide strategy to increase higher education for girls. [...]
> By arguing that ulamas' claims are not divine revelations but man-made interpretations (however authoritative), feminists have opened a space for women's voices in debates about religious truths.

As an indication of their ongoing struggles, a book recently published by the Sisters of Islam, *Muslim Women and the Challenge of Islamic Extremism* (2006), was banned by the state on the grounds that it gave a 'misleading view of the religion' ('Activists Slam Ban on Books', *Straits Times*, 16 August 2008).

These are complex problems that the state needs to grapple with as it continues to come to terms with the conditions of late modernity. For example, Mahathir's successor, Abdullah Badawi, introduced the notion of *Islam Hadhari*, in an attempt to address the intersection of tradition and modernity. By claiming that it is possible to strive for a more moderate version of Islam – one that is compatible with the demands of modernity while not compromising on traditional Islamic values – Badawi hoped to preempt accusations from the more fundamentalist sectors of Malaysian society that he was disrespectful of the religion or undermining the central position that Malays ought to occupy in Malaysian society. Despite this, Badawi's tenure as prime minister was short lived, owing to a relatively dismal showing in the 2008 general election.

Badawi's successor, Najib Razak, too, continues to grapple with this issue. Despite his One Malaysia campaign, which emphasizes religious moderation, ethnic harmony and national unity, Najib's own showing in the 2013 general elections – despite being returned to power – was even poorer than that of Badawi's. The results were attributed to voting that went along racial lines as well as following a rural–urban divide (*Malaysian Insider*, 7 May 2013), leading to calls from external observers such as Bloomberg not to give in to racial politics:

> Datuk Seri Najib Razak's Barisan Nasional (BN) must continue economic reforms and dismantle racial preferences or risk losing the next elections, international business news wire Bloomberg said in an editorial published today.
>
> In the editorial, Bloomberg said that 'if Najib begins to institute reforms, including providing a timetable for dismantling racial preferences, he can still lead Malaysia to better days.'
>
> 'If he doesn't, he is almost certain to lose next time,' said the editorial.

Thus, identity issues in Malaysia are arguably far more complicated than in Singapore. Racial preferences, long institutionalized via the bumiputra policy, will prove extremely difficult to moderate, as will any push for interpretations of Islam that are more in line with gender equality and the expectations of a better-educated and urbanized social class.

The fact that there was a rural–urban divide in the voting might suggest that some of the push for moderation might be more easily implemented in the cities, such as in Kuala Lumpur, the capital of Malaysia. And it is true that Kuala Lumpur is certainly far more liberal than many other Malaysian cities. Nevertheless, unlike Singapore, Kuala Lumpur is not a city-state but a city within a state. As such, there are real limits about the extent to which

Kuala Lumpur (and other cities in Malaysia) can be allowed to liberalize without risking the possibility of a serious political backlash at the national level. This is a risk that any ruling political party has to carefully consider. Consequently, even though the advice from Bloomberg may be well taken, Najib (or his successor) will have to carefully and very strategically decide just how far the moderation and modernization of identity expectations can go without incurring the ultimate political price of being voted out of office.

Hong Kong: Competing with Mainlanders

The reference to Kuala Lumpur and the constraints it faces from being part of a state come into greater relief when we consider Hong Kong. Unlike Singapore and Malaysia, the issue that Hong Kong faces when it comes to identity and global city status has little to do with religion or ethnic diversity. Rather, as we now see, it concerns the relationship between Hong Kongers and Chinese citizens from mainland.

Hong Kong enjoyed a relatively high degree of autonomy before its return to China, successfully attaining a global reputation as a leading financial center, a place where entrepreneurialism flourished, and where a booming movie, television and music industry could be found. The handover in 1997 was intended to assure Hong Kongers that they would continue to enjoy some reasonable degree of autonomy – hence, the city's status as a special administrative region (SAR; the other being Macau) under the 'One Country, Two Systems' principle. But because Hong Kong has never been an independent country, its residents are not technically citizens. Rather, legal residents of Hong Kong hold permanent resident status, and a Hong Kong passport is given to permanent residents who also happen to be Chinese citizens (*Wikipedia*, 2013a).

Hong Kong's Basic Law, however, provides a constitutional guarantee of political autonomy in all matters aside from defense and foreign affairs. Taken together, the Basic Law and the SAR status serve to constitute Hong Kong as a special zone, but one of political rather than economic exception – the latter being exemplified by special economic zones (SEZ) such as Shenzhen, Xiamen and Hainan Island. As Ong (2006a, 110) points out:

> SARs are fundamentally in a state of political exception. These administrative zones possess their own mini-constitutions, independent political institutions, and judiciaries. Furthermore, a spectrum of democratic rights allows for free elections and freedom of expression, at least for the immediate future. In brief, then, SEZs represent particular orders of economic and administrative autonomy within centrally

planned socialist China. SARs, in contrast, are unique orders of political autonomy within a flexible arrangement of one country, two systems.

Because the exceptionality that Hong Kong enjoys is political rather than economic, this means that, in matters of consumption, Hong Kong is freely accessible to consumers from the mainland and is also (under certain conditions) able to access the mainland as an export market. And while there continue to be suspicions among local politicians as to whether there is in fact political interference from the mainland (see below), the greater tensions – at least where identity-related issues are concerned – have to do with the influx of mainlanders and how to regulate it, if at all. In short, Hong Kong's proximity to the mainland brings with it some advantages as well as disadvantages.

   The advantage is that there is a huge market that Hong Kong can easily tap into by exporting its products to it; indeed, in 2003, the Chinese state used this as a carrot in return from certain political concessions from the Hong Kong authorities, triggering protests from prodemocracy groups (Ong 2006a, 111):

> The city and the mainland signed the Closer Economic Partnership Arrangement as a step toward even greater economic integration. The agreement gives Hong Kong–based banks and companies market access to the mainland. Tariffs on hundreds of Hong Kong products have been removed, giving the city's economy an immediate boost following the outbreak of severe acute respiratory syndrome (SARS). The trade agreement is an economic gift to sweeten the simultaneous imposition of a new national security law to curb sedition and other crimes against the Chinese state. This state intervention into the SAR political environment triggered a demonstration on July 1 by a half million Hong Kong residents who wanted to uphold the policy of one country, two systems. To prodemocracy groups such as the Human Rights Monitor, the free trade pact is a kind of payback for business leaders in the Hong Kong government who have gone along with the steady erosion of civil rights, especially in journalism and the media.

The disadvantage is that the consumption activities from mainlanders who enter Hong Kong often lead to intense competition with the locals, which can result in shortages of goods, price increases and even discrimination from Hong Kong–based merchants who favor the mainlanders because of their perceived superior purchasing power.

   These examples highlight the difficulties that a city faces in identity regulation if it is not itself an independent state. Even though Hong Kong enjoys greater political autonomy vis-à-vis China (because of its SAR status) than Kuala Lumpur does vis-à-vis the Malaysian central government, any attempts at identity (de-)regulation – especially when these rely on some distinction between those who are the city's 'proper' residents and those who are not – still raise questions about just how legitimate such measures might be, given that the city is still part of a larger state. In this regard, Singapore stands out as both exceptional and fortunate in being able to impose measures that link consumption to citizenship, as we will see in Chapters 6 and 7.

Conclusion

The conclusion in this chapter takes the form of a concluding discussion, where we make three points relating to rescaling, reflexivity and the articulation of a vision for the city and/or state.

Singapore is able to rescale from nation-state to global city because, as a city-state, it is not part of a larger state and is as a consequence politically autonomous. We shall not dwell any further on the issue of scale vis-à-vis Singapore since this has already been discussed at length in the preceding chapters. Instead, we simply want to point out that in the case of Malaysia and Hong Kong, as we have had occasion to observe in the present chapter, any similar attempt at scaling is much more problematic. Malaysia is a much larger country than Singapore, with multiple cities displaying a wide spectrum of cultural, political and economic liberalization. Some Malaysian cities are relatively modern and open, such as Kuala Lumpur and Penang. Others are seats of Islamic fundamentalism with concomitant restrictions of gender interaction and entertainment options. For example, cities in the Malaysian state of Kelantan come under a strict interpretation of Islamic law, with the state having been under the rule of the Pan-Malaysian Islamic Party (PAS) since 1990: there are single-sex queues in the supermarkets, separate public beaches for the different genders, even restrictions on public performances by women. What this means is that Malaysia cannot simply scale down to a city, given the highly heterogeneous mix of cities that it already contains. But there are also limits on what each city can do because each has to still be seen as presenting a city identity that is broadly consistent with what it means at the national level to be Malaysian.

The constraints faced by a city when it is part of a larger state emerged with particular clarity in the case of Hong Kong, which despite its SAR status still has to grapple with tensions between permanent residents and Chinese citizens from the mainland. Thus, while Hong Kongers have derided their mainland counterparts as 'locusts' (Liu 2012), some mainlanders, including Kong Qingdong, an academic from Peking University, have in turn accused

Hong Kongers of being 'dogs' for the British colonialists. Kong has been quoted as saying (*Wikipedia*, 2013b):

> 'You Hongkongers are Chinese, right? But as I know, many Hongkongers don't think they are Chinese. They claim that we are Hongkongers, you are Chinese. They are bastards. Those kinds of people used to be running dogs for the British colonialists. And until now, you Hongkongers are still dogs. You aren't human.' Kong then claimed that Hong Kong citizens had failed to accept their responsibility to speak the 'real Chinese language (Mandarin Chinese)' because of the 'residues of colonialism'. He then threatened, 'If Hongkongers keep discriminating against mainlanders (Mainland Chinese) in that way, then we won't provide the territory with water, vegetables, fruit and rice.' And asked, 'Can Hongkongers still survive? Go to seek help from your British daddy.'

The issues involved in scaling clearly require a consideration of reflexivity. As we have already pointed out in the preceding chapters, and as the discussion in this chapter illustrates, scaling from state to city requires deliberations that involve second-order reflexivity: What kind of city/state/people are we? What kind of city/state/people do we want to be? Are we comfortable with some of the possible measures that might be needed should we aspire to be more global or open? Are we prepared to accept the implications or consequences if we decide against opening up?

This brings us to the final point, that of articulating a strategy. We have already noted that Singapore is fortunate in that, as a city-state, it can scale down from nation to global city with relative ease. But because scaling involves reflexivity, this means that it cannot be a move unilaterally decided by the state. The general populace, too, has to be convinced that the global city aspiration and any concomitant measures are both useful and necessary – which brings us to the notion of strategy.

Kornberger (2012, 84–5) points out that 'cities represent the arenas in which struggles for environmental sustainability, economic growth, social inclusion and cultural diversity will be won – or lost. […] Strategy offers a theoretical framework and managerial practices that claim to be capable of addressing these concerns.' What is meant by strategy, in this context, is 'a body of knowledge concerned with the production of truth, while simultaneously being a political mechanism to mobilize people. […] It is not about the future, but a shared belief in the future' (91). Where the governance of cities is concerned, strategy involves reinventing the public via 'public gatherings, stakeholder meetings, focus groups, exhibitions, briefings and a whole array of other events to make people respond to questions they would not have asked otherwise' (98).

Kornberger's remarks about strategy and the reinvention of the public via various publicly conducted consultation events are exactly the kinds of activities that the state in Singapore has been engaged in (see Chapters 3 and 4). As Kornberger (2012, 99) explains:

> The strategy process is a mechanism to make people talk about their fears and desires, and brainstorm and collect their ideas. The political and the non-political, the private and the public, are deliberately blurred as strategy invites conversations about facts and values. Strategy spins a grand narrative where the personal idiosyncrasies of an individual captured on a sticky note are placed next to global issues. In the vision of the future, the social division of the 'I' and the 'we' appear to be overcome.

As we have already indicated, it is not the case that Malaysia and Hong Kong are unable to articulate a similar vision. For these two, the difficulty lies in articulating such a vision while reconciling the tensions between scales: that of the city and the state. Singapore, we have already noted, as an autonomous city-state faces less of a problem in this regard. We return to this issue of the relationship between cities and states in Chapter 9.

Chapter 6

CITIZENSHIP, REFLEXIVITY AND THE STATE: INVESTIGATING 'DEFENSIVE ENGAGEMENT' IN A CITY-STATE

Introduction

A key issue in theorizing about citizenship concerns the relationship between a modernist state and the late modern conditions of existence. In this regard, it is important to consider the steps taken by the state as it attempts to reinvent itself in varying contexts of rapid transformation, and how such attempts are received by the populace (Ong 1999, 2006a; Sassen 2006). According to Ellison (1997), contemporary sociological perspectives on citizenship in late modernity are problematic because they fail to properly consider citizenship as a resource for negotiating social change. This is rather ironic since a key characteristic of life in late modernity is precisely the need for individuals to negotiate a slew of political, social and cultural changes, and there is no obvious reason why citizenship cannot be strategically adduced to aid in such negotiations. Clearly the capacity of individuals to respond to these changes will be differentiated by gender, class and ethnicity, among other factors (Skeggs 1997, 2005; Beck and Beck-Gernsheim 1996). Ellison provides a useful conceptual framework for understanding the steps taken by modern states to address change as they reinvent themselves in varying contexts of rapid transformation and how such attempts are received by the populace. Ellison's work is also useful in understanding how sociological accounts of citizenship connect in an interesting way with notions of reflexivity and what he calls 'defensive engagement'.

This chapter considers Ellison's critique of contemporary citizenship and investigates what it means for citizenship to be construed as 'reflexive' and 'defensive' in the context of a particular city-state – in this case, Singapore. We employ Ellison's conceptual framework to analyze the Singapore state's attempt to negotiate social change within its populace. The case study of Singapore provides an opportunity to explore the dynamic relationship between citizenship, reflexivity and the notion of defensive engagement.

Ellison's own proposal is that citizenship needs to be understood as a 'reflexive condition of defensive engagement' (1997, 714; see below). This proposal is promising because it manages to retain the strengths of prevailing sociological accounts of citizenship, while also connecting in an interesting way the notions of reflexivity, defensive engagement and citizenship to each other. However, because Ellison is primarily concerned with critiquing prevailing accounts of citizenship before presenting his own proposal, his examples of reflexivity and defensive engagement are only discussed in a cursory manner. A more detailed discussion, it seems to us, is required to better flesh out just what it means for citizenship to be construed as reflexive and defensive. By way of contrast, we consider the concept of citizenship as developed by Turner (2011) in the context of a broader analysis of American citizenship. Turner draws on the work of Shklar (1998a, 1998b) and frames debates around civil liberties and rights in the context of arbitrary state interference within American political culture.

This chapter is organized as follows. The first section investigates Ellison's critique of contemporary accounts of citizenship as well as his own proposal as it essentially develops the relationship between citizenship, reflexivity and defensive engagement. The chapter then moves on to consider the specifics of Singapore as a case study in exploring the relationship between citizenship, reflexivity and the state. In particular, we consider the successful, albeit controversial, attempt by the Singapore state to persuade Singaporeans that the recently legalized casino resorts should legitimately discriminate between 'locals' and 'foreigners'. We then develop the implications of the case study for the notion of citizenship as defensive engagement.

Citizenship, Reflexivity and the State

Ellison identifies three major accounts of citizenship – state-centered, pluralist and poststructuralist – all of which, he argues, are problematic for various reasons. State-centered accounts, including those sometimes described as 'civic liberal' and 'civic republican' (Ellison 1997, 697), typically aim for universal inclusion on the basis of social rights (Marshall 1992) or rights and responsibilities that are incumbent upon gaining political membership in nation-states (Miller 1989). But these state-centered accounts are inadequate in the face of globalization, which has weakened or at the very least problematized the capacity of the state to serve as a framework for social cohesion and protection against the increasing complexity of social, economic and political risks (Ellison 1997, 697).

Pluralist accounts (Sassoon 1991; Young 1989), with their insistent attention on power and the identity politics of 'difference' and 'recognition', find it difficult to provide a satisfactory understanding of the nature of social inclusion. This is because pluralist accounts tend to assume that any attempt to foreground a notion of 'universal' good immediately 'raises the prospect of discrimination and exclusion within supposedly integrated communities' (Ellison 1997, 705). And while Ellison himself thinks that it may be possible to reconcile a universal notion of citizenship with an attention to difference, he is concerned with what he sees as an essentialist stance in pluralist accounts, which seem to assume that 'social actors cannot belong to, or make demands on behalf of, more than one defined identity' (707).

This desire to avoid slipping into essentialism is what leads Ellison to comment favorably on poststructuralist accounts (McClure 1992; Mouffe 1993) and acknowledge the value of their insights into the fragmented and open-ended nature of identity. The social actor is now understood as 'an ensemble of "subject positions" that can never be totally fixed' (Mouffe 1993, 77; cited in Ellison 1997, 709). However, the poststructuralist perspective is still problematic because of its 'tendency, introduced through the privilege of the decentred subject, to reduce the significance of "solidarity" as a constituent element of any processes involving intersubjective understanding' (Ellison 1997, 710). For Ellison (ibid.), this is a serious problem in developing a sociological account of citizenship:

> This line of criticism is particularly significant if we want to refashion a theory of citizenship in such a way that the original sense of the idea is not lost entirely. It is important to recognize that rights and membership claims must continue to depend on shared understandings of what is being demanded, and a shared perception of the likely sources and avenues of 'redress', but acceptance of this apparently 'traditional' view need not imply that identities need be entirely ascribed or eternally fixed.

Ellison (1997, 711) suggests that 'it is more accurate to characterize [social actors] as "centred" or integrated social agents confronted by the need to pursue a range of different claims in an increasingly dis-integrated and complex public sphere'. The notion of reflexivity evoked here draws attention to how individuals attempt to negotiate their memberships in various kinds of groupings in response to ongoing social and political changes. Such negotiations can involve the reinforcement of existing alliances or the creation of new forms of solidarity – all of which can range from the ephemeral to the durable. Consequently, it is important to appreciate that (713):

> citizenship stands as a capacity for collective resistance, but a capacity the power of which can itself be diffused amongst a variety of public spaces.

Claims for recognition and inclusion continue to be advanced, and in this way we continue to try to shape our world, but now in fragmented fashion because the 'solidarities' forged and the claims themselves are transitory. Social actors may become aware of the contingent nature of solidarity and community [...] but their 'reflexivity' involves the appreciation of the transformation of traditional concepts of belonging and the need to pursue alternatives in circumstances of constrained choice.

Ellison's proposal is valuable because it remains agnostic as to the role of the state. It is able to accommodate the activities of social actors qua citizens in arenas of resistance that may or may not involve the state. And in the case of the latter, it allows that social actors qua citizens may mobilize with – as well as against – the state, depending on the particular nature of the 'thing' that needs to be resisted. In short, the proposal has the merit of not being state centered, but neither does it dismiss the potential relevance of the state, even given the effects of globalization. This agnosticism toward the state is important because, as Sassen observes (2006, 227; see also Chapter 1), states, particularly strong states, are still influential actors in mediating the effects of globalization:

> In this regard I find Cox's thesis that strong states act as midwives, not victims of internationalization, compelling (1987, 204). Failure to differentiate state capacities, both across countries and inside a given national state, easily can keep globalization scholars from considering, let alone examining, how states may at times facilitate globalization.

In fact, Sassen (2006, 288) points out that even arguments for cultural pluralism and attempts to deconstruct the notion of citizenship (which are often brought up as clear evidence that globalization is weakening the reach and power of the nation-state) actually 'continue to use the nation-state as the normative frame and to understand the social groups involved as parts of national civil society'.

Ellison's proposal is also useful because while it acknowledges that solidarities can be formed around many different factors, it does not ignore the fact that new solidarities are often forged on the basis of extant relationships or existing shared values. New solidarities emerge by extending, modifying or rejecting prevailing relationships and/or values; they are not created randomly or *ex nihilo*.

Finally, Ellison's emphasis on the social rather than individual nature of reflexivity resonates nicely with observations elsewhere concerning the transformative potential of reflexivity (Brooks and Wee 2008). In particular, his argument that reflexivity is part of a defensive engagement coheres with a conception of agency that is both reflective and transformative, one that recognizes 'the capacities of socially and culturally situated agents to reflect upon their social conditions, criticize them, and articulate new interpretations of them' (Bohman 1999, 145).

However, despite the merits of Ellison's proposal, the examples he provides give little indication as to how reflexivity and defense/resistance are actually related. Ellison (1997, 712) cites as examples of the 'defensive quality' of citizenship the emergence of credit unions in Britain as a response to high levels of poverty and unemployment, various local initiatives in the Swedish city of Orebro to increase support for and participation in community life, and the Lega community in Italy, where the criteria for community membership now emphasize the commitment to certain ideals as opposed to the possession of ethnic attributes. While these examples illustrate the fact that various collectivities can and do come about as a way of dealing with perceived problems, they do not say much about the processes of inclusion and exclusion by which collectivities are formed and solidarities are reflexively established. These are crucial omissions for an approach to citizenship that takes as its central notion that of 'defensive engagement'.

But Ellison is not unique in this respect. There appears to be a general tendency in studies of citizenship to downplay the dynamics of engagement (an important exception is Turner 1993, discussed below). Thus Faulks (2000, 7–11; see also Clarke 1996) suggests that citizenship can be investigated in terms of at least three dimensions: its extent (i.e., the criteria that distinguish citizens from noncitizens), content (i.e., the rights and obligations that are concomitants of citizenship) and depth (i.e., the dominance that one's identity as a citizen might be expected to exercise over other possible identities and their concomitant rights and obligations). And in a similar vein, Joppke (2010, vii; emphasis original) distinguishes between 'the *status*, *rights*, and *identity* dimensions of citizenship'. These respectively refer to formal state membership, the rights that accrue to such formal status, and the various 'collective identities on the part of the citizenry' (ibid.). Notwithstanding the fact that Joppke's approach appears to fall under what Ellison might call 'state-centered accounts', both Faulks and Joppke outline various dimensions of citizenship that present citizenship in a static manner. This is not to suggest that these scholars are unappreciative of the dynamic nature of citizenship – far from it. But this dynamic nature is omitted from the theorizing itself. Consequently, attention to the dynamics of citizenship is not only of specific relevance to Ellison's proposal, it is a much-needed remedy to the way in which citizenship studies are generally approached.

This is where a detailed discussion of a specific case study from Singapore becomes useful. Singapore provides a particularly clear example of institutional reflexivity on the part of the state, firstly because of its long tradition of explicit government scrutiny of all sectors of public and private life (Chua 1995; Mauzy and Milne 2002). Secondly, even as the state aims to be more consultative (see Chapter 4), the hands-on management approach that it has for so long adopted has meant that, in recent years, categories such as 'citizens' and 'foreigners' have constituted a significant part of the ongoing Singaporean political discourse between the state and the populace, with a major issue of contention surrounding the kinds of rights and responsibilities that the state (given its power) sees as distinguishing citizens from noncitizens (Ong 2006a, 193). Thirdly, by considering a specific instance in which the state has attempted to regulate the behavior of citizens – quite successfully – we are able to draw out in greater relief the dynamic relationships between citizenship, reflexivity and defensive engagement.

Citizenship and Defensive Engagement in Singapore

Ong (1999, 208) observes that 'the structure of accountability in Singapore is predicated on the population's trusting in the expertise and cultural authority of the political leadership and the state's ability to deliver in terms of social stability and economic performance'. In more specific terms, what this means is that state policies in Singapore are usually legitimized by appealing to such values as communitarianism, meritocracy, multiracialism and pragmatism (Chua 1995; Hill and Lian 1995; Mauzy and Milne 2002).

Communitarianism emphasizes the prioritizing of collective interests (the family, the community or the country) over those of the individual; meritocracy refers to the belief that individuals should be rewarded because of their own efforts rather than any inherited features such as ethnic identity; multiracialism refers to the position that in order to maintain harmony among Singapore's ethnically diverse population, there must be respect and equal treatment accorded to each ethnic group; and pragmatism stresses that policy choices must be rationalized by how they can contribute to strengthening the country's economic competitiveness.

Among these values, pragmatism also acts as an operational 'metavalue' in the sense that it rationalizes the other values and specific policy options as being conducive to economic growth. For example, while ethnic harmony can be considered a good in and of itself, the state has also emphasized its role in attracting foreign investment. Thus, values such as communitarianism, meritocracy and multiracialism are, ultimately, themselves rationalized on pragmatic grounds: prioritizing the community over the self, distributing rewards according to talent (rather than, say, class or ethnic identity) and maintaining ethnic harmony are all essential because they facilitate the country's continued economic well-being.

The influential nature of these values can be seen in the 1990s when the state attempted to formally articulate a set of 'shared values' ('nation before community and society above self', 'family as the basic unit of society', 'community support and respect for the individual', 'consensus, not conflict', 'racial and religious harmony'; 1991) that are supposed to be representative of Singaporean society. While these 'shared values' have no legal status, they do have 'institutional and ideological significance' (Chua 1995, 33).

In what follows, we will focus on a case study where the values of meritocracy and communitarianism play key roles in the mobilization of citizenship as defensive engagement. We go on now to discuss an example where citizenship constitutes a form of defensive engagement that is mobilized by and with the state.

Mobilization of Citizenship as Defensive Engagement

Up until 2004, when the state announced that it was considering legalizing the operation of casinos in Singapore, and 2006, when the Casino Control Act was enacted, casinos were illegal in Singapore. Although other 'smaller' forms of gambling such as lotteries and sports betting were tolerated, these were tightly controlled by the state. For example, the Singapore Turf Club has specialized in horse racing since it was first set up in 1842 (as the Singapore Sporting Club). In 1988, the state created the Singapore Totalisator Board to take over racing and 4D operations from the Singapore Turf Club. In addition to the Turf Club, there is Singapore Pools, a lottery operator which covers a wider range of gambling activities, including betting on soccer and motor racing. Singapore Pools was incorporated by the state in 1968 in order to curb illegal gambling. In 2004, it became a subsidiary of the Totalisator Board.

The state has long been concerned about the association between gambling and social problems, such as gambling addiction, loansharking and bankruptcy. These problems, according to the state, can jeopardize the stability of a gambler's family unit, as well as have repercussions for the community in general. These are obviously communitarian concerns, and casinos are seen as particularly problematic because they encourage gambling on a much larger scale. Groups of gamblers come together for a period of time that is in principle open ended (since the casinos are open 24 hours a day). And because casinos are in the business of making money, they are designed to help the gambler forget about the 'world outside'. The décor and availability of alcohol are geared toward heightening the sense of excitement. Finally, casinos also bring with them the increased risk of money laundering and illegal money lending.

Bearing in mind the foregoing, the state's recent decision to legalize casinos has been described as nothing less than a 'cultural sea-change' (Smale 2004). The state decided to legalize casinos because it considers them a necessity if Singapore is to sustain its economic competitiveness and enhance its reputation as a cosmopolitan city that is attractive to the global community. Thus, 'cities all round the world are reinventing themselves', according to Singapore's third prime minister, Lee Hsien Loong (2005).

> New York City has been undergoing a renewal. [...] Paris is also getting a shake-up, even though it attracts 25 million tourists a year, 3 times as many as Singapore. [...] Hong Kong is talking about building a casino on Lantau, to compete with Macau. [...] By acting now, we seize a window of opportunity to get ahead of our competitors. If we say no, the best proposals for the IR ['integrated resorts', also known as 'casino resorts'], together with the investments and the jobs, will most likely go somewhere else in the region. Then we will be forced to play catch up, and be in a much weaker position.

The casinos are therefore intended to cater primarily to foreigners, including tourists, rather than locals. According to the prime minister, 'If gambling is one of the things [tourists] want to do, then maybe we should allow them to do that, find some way to do that, and as a result of that over 10 years double the [tourist] traffic volume. I think we should think about it' (quoted in Smale 2004). Thus, even as the state takes responsibility for licensing the operation of casinos and credit for any resulting economic growth, it also has to avoid being accused of contributing to any rise in gambling-related problems. In other words, it is clear that once the state has decided to legalize casinos, it needs to avoid charges that it has abandoned its commitment to the values just mentioned, particularly communitarianism. This was acknowledged as much by the prime minister when he admitted that the state has to 'explain how we propose to limit the negative impact of the casinos' (Lee 2005).

One of the ways in which the state attempts to do this is by arguing that the casinos are 'zones of exception' (Ong 2006a), requiring special measures to ensure that while foreigners are free and encouraged to enter, locals are not. There are basically three types of measures introduced by the state. The first involves charging Singaporeans and permanent residents an entrance fee of S$100 per day or S$2,000 per year simply to enter the casinos. This fee does not apply to foreigners. And even if individuals are willing to foot the daily or annual entrance fee, they can still be denied entry if they have been served with an exclusion order. This is the second type of measure. There are different types of exclusion orders: voluntary self-exclusion, family exclusion (where a family member can apply for the order to be served to a relative) and third-party exclusion (which applies automatically to bankrupts and those receiving public assistance). The third type of measure involves the possibility of extending credit to gamblers. Unlike foreigners, locals will not be extended credit by the casinos. All these measures help to reinforce the point that the casinos are mainly targeted toward the market of foreigners/tourists rather than locals.

There has been little widespread resentment about the introduction of these measures. In short, despite their clearly discriminatory nature, these measures have not roused much resistance from locals. There are two reasons for this. One, the economic success of the casinos has been undeniable in attracting tourists and creating more jobs for Singaporeans. The casinos are part of larger 'integrated resorts' (IRs), where shopping, concerts and theme parks constitute attractions in addition to gambling, and they are expected to provide employment for about 20,000 people as well as 'create countless further business opportunities'. Also,

> Booming tourist numbers have provided the scoreboard to keep track of Singapore's IR win. Visitors are up 30% for May to a record 946,000 arrivals (not counting land arrivals across the causeway from Malaysia) according to figures released on Monday, the sixth consecutive all-time arrivals record for a month. (Cohen 2010)

Two, the state has also been quite successful in increasing public awareness of 'problem gambling'. Following the announcement that the casinos would be legalized, and even while construction of the casinos was still in progress, the state embarked on a highly aggressive and visible series of public service announcements, warning Singaporeans about the dangers of gambling addiction and of its potential impact on the gambler's family stability. Also, the National Council on Problem Gambling (NCPG) was set up in 2005 specifically to raise public appreciation of the dangers of gambling, educate the public on how to identify the signs that point to gambling addiction, and oversee the issuance of exclusion orders. Together with the National Addictions Management and the National Problem Gambling Hotline, the public has been consistently reminded that counseling is available for gamblers themselves or their affected family members. All this is further aided by featured articles in the press and local programs that provide detailed portrayals of individuals who, through their gambling, have created misery and misfortune for themselves and their families. The distinction between foreigners and locals is invoked in a manner that suggests that the latter can be free to 'ruin' themselves gambling if they wish to do so, as long as the latter are protected.

The success of all this emphasis on problem gambling can be seen from the fact that since the opening of the casinos, the number of people applying for self-exclusion orders has increased (Musfirah 2010):

> NCPG said there have been 264 applications for self-exclusion orders since it started receiving the applications in November last year. [...] There have also been 12 family exclusion orders issued in February, bringing the total number to 31. Most of them were wives applying for their husbands to be barred from entering the casino.

In short, the state has managed to frame the casinos as zones that are economically important, but also as zones that necessarily discriminate between locals and foreigners *because* they contain dangers that, if left unregulated, could well lead to a variety of social problems. It has therefore been able to demonstrate the pragmatic benefits of legalizing casinos while showing that it is making reasonable efforts to minimize any negative social impact arising from their presence. This has not always been uncontroversial. For example, in September 2010, the Casino Regulatory Authority ordered the casinos to stop providing free bus services from residential neighborhoods to the integrated resorts, even though some Singaporeans complained that they were not necessarily intent on specifically visiting the casinos. But Vivian Balakrishnan, minister of community development, youth and sports, explained that (Portmann 2010):

> When the government decided to allow casinos [...] we made it clear that the casinos were primarily to attract additional tourists from abroad. [...] Our aim was to minimise the impact on locals,' he said. [...] The casino operators 'have been reminded that they must comply strictly with our rules', Balakrishnan said. 'Where parts of the rules need to be tightened, we will tighten', stressed the minister, noting that it was up to the regulatory authority to contemplate any penalties for the recent breach of rules.

Given the state's unambiguous and uncompromising position that the casinos are intended mainly for foreigners, the more stringent measures that apply to locals are seen, understood and even accepted by many Singaporeans as measures that are essential for the protection of the larger community. As one writer to the local newspaper opined (*Straits Times*, 17 November

2010), the state is justified in imposing entrance fees against Singaporeans and permanent residents because

> the law is helping the Government in its aim to deter citizens from excessive gambling, [and this] shows that the Government takes responsibility for Singaporeans and PRs, while foreigners are allow to access the casino freely [since any] decision to discriminate against foreign workers [...] by banning them from casinos or curbing their entry is contradictory to our treatment of other foreigners.

However, because low-wage foreign workers have been able to enter the casinos freely, they have been known to lose the money that they are supposed to remit back to their homelands. In this regard, an indication of the state's success in presenting the casinos (rather than gambling per se) as zones of danger, some foreign workers have even asked for the self-exclusion order to be made more easily available to them. At present, foreigners can only apply for a self-exclusion order in the presence of witnesses who must be Singaporeans or permanent residents, and the order itself takes a month or more to take effect (Teh and Kok 2010). This development could slowly reduce the differences in the ways the state regulates the casino participation of locals and foreigners, although it still seems unlikely that the entrance fee and lack of access to credit extension will be imposed on foreigners (or conversely, lifted from locals).

More recently, the state has decided to introduce limits, which apply only to Singaporeans and permanent residents, on the number of visits a gambler can make to a casino each month, following similar visit restrictions in Amsterdam, Austria and Melbourne. According to a news report (Tai and Lim 2013), 'The number of times a gambler will be allowed in the Marina Bay Sands or Resorts World Sentosa casinos each month will be determined by factors such as the frequency and pattern of their visits, their credit record, their work situation and information provided by family members.'

The main focus of concern is the high-frequency gamblers – that is, those who visit the casinos more than six times per month (Tai and Lim 2013):

> Data on problem gamblers will be provided by the casinos to the council [i.e., the National Council on Problem Gambling], which will then send those individuals letters requesting them to furnish information on their financial situation.
>
> A Committee of Assessors (COA) – made up of about 70 members from the council and grassroots and social service organizations – will

then decide the extent of the visit limit to impose on the gambler and, depending on the situation, may even slap an exclusion order on him.

As with the exclusion orders, there are different types of visit limits. One is voluntary, where the individual takes it upon himself or herself to apply for a self-imposed visit limit. The other is the family visit limit, where immediate family members apply for limits to be imposed on a relative's entry into the casinos. And the third is a third-party visit limit, where a committee of assessors may serve limits on those found to have poor credit records.

The measures restricting locals' ability to participate in casino gambling are thus seen as affirming (rather than undermining) the state's commitment to communitarianism, since many Singaporeans understand and accept that trade-offs are necessary (which is of course pragmatism at work). This discussion of the casinos shows that citizens and the state are acting together to harness the economic benefits that the casinos bring to the country while trying to contain the social dangers associated with casino gambling. The notion of citizenship as defensive engagement is clearly relevant here, but it is a defense that involves citizens working in concert with the state rather than in opposition to it. Moreover, it is a defense that arises reflexively out of a public state–society discourse about the pros and cons of legalizing casinos. This is a discourse that acknowledges the social risks and economic benefits involved, and one that is ongoing, as it continues to explore ways of taking advantage of the presence of the casinos while curtailing their negative effects.

Citizenship and the Politics of Inclusion in the USA

We now briefly contrast an approach to citizenship in terms of defensive engagement with one that highlights the role of practices, before returning in the following section to show that the two approaches are by no means mutually exclusive or contradictory. Turner (1993, 2) suggests that it may be useful to think of citizenship as 'that set of practices (juridical, political, economic and cultural) which define a person as a competent member of society, and which as a consequence shape the flow of resources to persons and social groups'. Thinking in terms of practices helps to identify citizenship as a 'genuinely sociological as distinct from a legal or political notion', and can help us to 'understand the dynamic social construction of citizenship which changes historically as a consequence of political struggles' (2). This means that a sociological approach to citizenship will have to give due attention to the 'social forces that produce such practices' (3).

More recently, Turner (2011) has analyzed citizenship rights in the context of American political culture and values. He claims that American social scientists operate within a framework of individual liberties rather than the social rights of citizens. Drawing on Judith Shklar's work, Turner shows that Shklar (1998a, 147) identifies the protection of minorities as being fundamental to American democracy. She claims that civil liberties occupy 'the very heart of American political values'. In other words Shklar claims that 'what comes first in American political culture is the protection of the individual from arbitrary state interference' (Turner 2011, 933).

Turner shows that debates on citizenship within the social sciences in the US have shifted to an emphasis on cultural identity rather than class position (which had been the basis of the Marshall model of citizenship). As Turner (2011, 935) comments:

> Of course new migrants are economically poor and exploited, but the membership – or rather quasi-membership – of minority communities within the host society is typically perceived as the key issue. New theories of citizenship have stressed the issue of ethno-cultural marginality in such notions as 'flexible citizenship', 'post-national citizenship' or 'semi-citizenship' in order to capture this grey world of minorities. The modern state continues to operate as a territorial sovereign power, but the global labour market assumes porous political and legal boundaries. The social inclusion or otherwise of the Latina immigrant community of California is a typical issue of American citizenship research (Coll 2010).

In the context of American political culture opposition to government has frequently taken a populist expression, as shown in the growth of the Tea Party (Amery and Kibbe 2010), which has influenced the selection of candidates and largely undermined traditional GOP politics in the US. In his book *The Civil Sphere* (2006), Jeffrey Alexander shows how 'social movements [in the context of American politics] can bring about civil repair through social integration' (Turner 2011, 937). However, in order for these movements to facilitate civil repair they have to move beyond localized to a broader set of representative interests. As Turner (ibid) comments:

> These particular interests of localized movements must be translated into wider social interests and values if they are to mobilise society for civil repair. His examples include the transformation of the women's movements into feminism with its notions of gender universalism after which the issues of gender found a wider and more powerful public, and second how the civil rights movement for racial equality for black Americans 'played an enormous role in the civil repair of racism that crystallised in the Civil Rights movement of the 1950s and 1960s.

It supplied economic and organizational power and an ideology of solidarity in the struggle against white oppression' (Alexander 2006, 286).

Turner argues that while American society still confronts significant socioeconomic and political issues, perhaps being made more visible under the presidency of Barack Obama, 'the USA has been relatively successful as an inclusive society'. The reason for such inclusivity includes 'a liberal political system, social mobility and legislation to protect minorities and their basic rights have provided an open and inclusive social framework – albeit divided by significant economic and other forms of inequality' (2011, 937).

By comparison with the US, Turner shows that in the UK 'the post-war experiment with citizenship concentrates on the failures of social inclusion' (Turner 2011, 937). Turner cites the divisive politics of the Thatcher years (having strong parallels with the extreme right-wing fringes of the current GOP in the US), the rise of new liberalism and the persistent erosion of the welfare state. Additionally, the racist tendencies of parts of the British community, which has always resisted the full integration of large waves of migration to the UK, has made the UK a divided society by class, ethnicity, nationality and region. As Turner (ibid.) notes,

> These developments in Britain have been seen as the erosion of citizenship. Britain is often seen in terms in terms of a collection of 'parallel communities' that is isolated minority groups who are concentrated into specific urban spaces with little social interaction with the host community, rather than an integrated national community.

Reflexivity and Defensive Engagement

But while Turner is undoubtedly right to draw attention to the role that practices play in informing citizenship, it is also the case that all practices are necessarily viewed or interpreted through the lens of particular social values. In this way, the social forces that produce such practices include the kinds of 'shared understandings' that membership in social groups is seen to entail (Ellison 1997, 710; see above). At this point, we can see why the notions of reflexivity and defensive engagement are particularly relevant to a sociological understanding of citizenship. Deliberations over membership categories – including deliberations about the criteria for membership and the resources that might accrue to members – are necessarily reflexive in nature, as these require individuals to consider their relationships to existing social categories and to adopt specific stances toward them. Such deliberations can be about values such as meritocracy and communitarianism, but they can in a particularly reflexive manner be about the category of 'citizen' as well. And these deliberations are defensive in nature because what is often at stake are particular resources such as special taxation benefits, privileges for members' offspring, access (or lack thereof) to casinos, or a sense of satisfaction that particular values that are being upheld.

However, reflexivity involves self-objectification (Chapter 1), where the social actor becomes aware of itself in relation to its various circumstances, and a reflective response is one that is informed by this awareness. Because different social actors occupy rather different relations to various circumstances, it is not necessarily the case that defensive engagement involves actors acting in a unified manner. Returning to the casino example, there are undoubtedly many Singaporeans with rather different attitudes toward the restrictions imposed upon them. Possibly, there are some individuals who welcome the measures as separating the 'serious' gambler from the dilettante.

There are also others for whom the measures represent inconveniences rather than strict deterrents, and these individuals are willing to pay the levy in order to access the casinos. For yet others, these restrictions are sufficient warnings as to the dangers of problem gambling and these individuals may even go on to voluntarily sign up for an exclusion order. The result on a broad level is the general population's acceptance and support of the state's decision to legalize the casinos as well as to impose measures that treat foreigners and locals differently. This can be described as a 'temporary alliance' (Ellison 1997, 712). However, Ellison overplays the homogeneity of citizenship when he stresses that it is motivated by the 'need to establish new solidarities'. Ellison is correct that citizenship can be seen as 'a defence against social changes' (714). But what this example demonstrates is that Singaporeans may have different attitudes toward the casinos and the state-imposed restrictions, and these different manifestations do not point to anything like a group solidarity or social movement. There was no unified grassroots activity where citizens voiced their support for the state. Nevertheless, the absence of any such manifested or organized display of solidarity does not undermine the fact that at the national level there has been widespread support (so far) for how the state has gone about handling the presence of the casinos.

Another point to consider is that the notions of citizenship, reflexivity and defensive engagement should not only be treated as attributes of individuals (Ellison 1997, 713). To do this would be to ignore the fact that institutions, such as the state, are also reflexive. Thus, one of the reasons why the state was able to successfully marshal general support for the legalization of casinos was because it highlighted Singapore as being involved in a global competition with other cities for the tourist dollar.

Transforming itself into a 'global city' is part of the state's competitive strategy to make Singapore as attractive as possible, in order to ensure the country's continued economic growth. And the state has long been involved in publicly articulating what it sees as the different problems the country faces and the kinds of responses it considers feasible. In particular, the state has been highly concerned with consistently spelling out the rationales behind various policy initiatives, and significantly, these rationales are usually articulated in terms of how they are consistent with values such as pragmatism and communitarianism. In doing so, the state was therefore being reflexive about the kind of future it was attempting to create for ordinary Singaporeans.

This leads to the issue that we have been emphasizing at some length. This is the tendency to underplay the reflexivity and agency of institutions. Granted, institutional reflexivity and agency is ultimately enacted by individuals. But when individuals, such as the prime minister, do so in their capacities as institutional agents, they are faced with rather different kinds of constraints arising from the fact that institutions qua highly public entities are entrusted to pursue specific programs or causes. In the absence of sufficient attention to institutional reflexivity, our understanding of the dynamics of citizenship as reflexive engagement remains incomplete since the active responses by institutional structures such as the state are not taken into proper consideration.

Conclusion

The concept of citizenship typically draws attention to the rights and responsibilities that accrue to individuals on the basis of their membership in a community, with the latter usually understood to be that of the nation-state. In recent times, though, the concept has come under significant interrogation, with questions raised about whether it is possible to imagine citizenship beyond the confines of the state (Faulks 2000). Despite the multiplicity of issues surrounding discussions of citizenship, citizenship has not usually been considered in terms of reflexivity and defensive engagement. With this in mind, this chapter has focused on the ways in which a particular nation-state in Asia has attempted to regulate access to casinos among the citizenry. Our discussion has demonstrated that despite the merits of Ellison's (1997) proposal, more attention needs to be paid to the dynamic nature of reflexivity and engagement and, as well, to the fact that the state, too, can be reflexive. Only by bearing this in mind can we hope to better understand how the concept of citizenship becomes meaningful to particular individuals and institutions, in the context of varying sociopolitical conditions.

By way of contrast we also included a different view of citizenship from a US perspective captured in the work of Turner (2011) and others. There, we suggested that because not all practices are equally valued, an appreciation of which practices come to be seen as relevant or useful in specific issues concerning citizenship will still need to draw on the notions of reflexivity and defensive engagement. In this regard, the state's attempts to discourage citizens from patronizing the casinos raises a question of more general interest – that is, how citizenship and consumption intersect such that the state needs to confront its citizens not just qua citizens *simpliciter* but in their capacity as citizen-consumers. We pursue this question in the following chapter.

Chapter 7

GOVERNING THE CITIZEN-CONSUMER: CITIZENSHIP, CASINOS AND 'CATHEDRALS OF CONSUMPTION'

Introduction

Citizenship and its links to the rights of individuals have become increasingly complex. The impact of globalization has fundamentally transformed the conceptualization of citizenship, the rights and responsibilities accruing to individuals, and the obligations of states that oversee increasingly diverse populations. The movement of peoples through migration and settlement has changed previously clearly defined homogenous populations into increasingly heterogeneous groupings made up of individuals with different racial and cultural backgrounds and forming different categories of citizenship (Glenn 2002, 2011; Nash 2010; Turner 2011). Citizenship is in fact being increasingly defined by 'gradations of esteem' (Carver and Mottier 1998), which recognize that different kinds of rights and responsibilities accrue to different categories and subcategories of citizens based on considerations of 'relative productivity'. What has been left out of these discussions is any attention to the citizen as consumer. The interface between citizen status and consumer activity is important because of the neoliberal assertion that individuals and institutions perform at their best within a free-market economy and because of the state's expectations regarding citizens' rights and responsibilities as consumers, not just as producers. Our goal in this chapter is to analyze the context of a more dynamic definition of citizenship as a result of globalization and examine these relationships within the context of a particular case study. This involves an exploration of how the state in Singapore aims to regulate the patronage of casinos, which have been recently introduced into Singapore.

Citizenship: Rights, Responsibilities and Consumption

The notion of citizenship has typically focused on the rights and responsibilities that accrue to individuals on the basis of their membership in a community, usually understood to be that of the nation-state. Depending on the specifics of the relationship between citizens and the state in question, the actual set of rights and responsibilities, including the relative emphasis of one over the other, will vary. Examples of rights may include social rights, such as having access to state-funded education or healthcare, and civil rights, such as freedom of speech or the right to vote (Faulks 2000, 63). Questions have also been raised, for example, as to whether it is possible to imagine citizenship beyond the confines of the state (Hardt and Negri 2000) as well as about the kinds of cultural protections citizens might expect if they happen to belong to a minority ethnic group (Kymlicka 1995). This way of conceptualizing citizenship also leads to analytical attention being given to the converse: individuals who are denied rights and responsibilities by virtue of their statelessness.

Ong (2006b, 499) refers to the above as the 'citizenship-versus-statelessness' model and argues that 'mutations in citizenship' are occurring that challenge the utility of this model. In Ong's (ibid., 499–500) view:

Binary oppositions between citizenship and statelessness, and between national territoriality and its absence, are not useful for thinking about emergent spaces and novel combinations of globalizing and situated variables. For instance, market-driven state practices fragment the national terrain into zones of hyper-growth. These spaces are plugged into transnational networks of markets, technology, and expertise.

Meanwhile, strict distinctions between the citizens and foreigners are dropped in favor of the pursuit of human capital. Such modes of governing engender a checkerboard patterning of the national terrain, thus producing an effect of graduated or variegated sovereignty (Ong 2000). Some sites and zones are invested with more political resources than others. Meanwhile, rights and entitlements once associated with all citizens are becoming linked to neoliberal criteria, so that entrepreneurial expatriates come to share in the rights and benefits once exclusively claimed by citizens.

For Ong, then, neoliberalism is a key driving force in framing contemporary workings of citizenship. Neoliberalism takes the position that 'human well-being could best be advanced by liberating individual, entrepreneurial freedoms within an institutional framework of private property rights, free markets and free trade' (Harvey 2005, 2). Consequently, how the state accords 'sovereignty' to the citizenry is increasingly informed by considerations of relative productivity, with the consequence that different kinds of privilege accrue to different subcategories of citizens. Productive and skilled foreigners may share in some of the same kinds of sovereignty as highly valued citizens, giving them greater commonality with their skilled citizen counterparts. This extension of neoliberalism to the point where even the notion of what counts as a 'good' citizen is influenced by transactional considerations is perhaps unsurprising since '[neoliberalism] holds that the social good will be maximized by maximizing the reach and frequency of market transactions, and it seeks to bring all human action into the domain of the market' (ibid., 3).

Because neoliberalism is just one ethical guide among many others concerning the conduct of social life (Harvey 2005, 3), its insertion into different sociocultural milieus will have to be negotiated in relation to the presence of other ethical regimes (Ong 2006b, 22), such as religious beliefs, commitments to gender equality or environmental sustainability. Consequently, various kinds of citizenship configurations are possible, leading Ong (2006a, 2006b) to explore the specific ways in which citizenship may be configured in the European Union, the US and Asia.

Ong's remarks about Asia are of particular interest, given her thesis of 'neoliberalism as exception' (2006a), which asserts that even in countries where neoliberalism 'is not the general characteristic of technologies of governing', there may nevertheless be 'sites of transformation' where 'market-driven calculations are being introduced in the management of populations and the administration of special spaces' (3–4). While such sites may refer to zones that are territorially demarcated, they can also refer to more abstract subject categories involving specific kinds of persons (e.g., 'citizen', 'foreigner' and 'investor'). The establishment of such sites, where neoliberal values are actively encouraged and cultivated by the state, is a governing strategy for managing the potential tensions that might arise as neoliberal values come into contact with other values. In drawing on data from China, Malaysia and Singapore, she suggests that the strategic significance of these sites lies in their status as 'political exceptions that permit sovereign practices and subjectifying techniques that deviate from the established norms [since] neoliberal forms articulating East Asian milieus are often in tension with local cultural sensibilities and national identity' (12; emphasis added). According to Ong, 'administrative strategies are informed by [...] "explicit calculations" about human life in terms of its growth and productivity' and, especially in 'Asian tiger states' (such as Singapore, Malaysia and Thailand), 'low-skilled workers enjoy fewer civil rights and less welfare protection than higher-skilled workers in science parks and high-tech centers' (78–9).

In this chapter, we explore further the configuration of citizenship in Asia, giving specific attention to Singapore. We complicate Ong's observations by shifting the analytical focus from productivity to consumption. This is because missing from the current focus on the productivity of the citizen is attention to the citizen as consumer. For example, as we noted in Chapter 1, the establishment of special economic zones and special administration regions in China serves to mark out identifiable locales where special taxation, investment schemes and a higher degree of political autonomy are allowed to hold sway (Ong 2006a, 18–19). The purpose of these 'special zones' is to encourage 'foreign citizens, overseas Chinese and compatriots from Hong Kong and Macao and their companies and enterprises (hereafter referred to as "investors") [to] set up factories and establish enterprises and other undertakings' (excerpted from article 1 of the Regulations on Special Economic Zones; quoted in Ong 2006a, 105). Ong's discussion of these technologies of governing, however, focuses mainly on the state's regulation of 'producers' rather than 'consumers'. For example, the setting up of special zones in China is intended to bring in individuals and companies with the financial capital needed to drive economic growth. This focus on producers raises the question of how techniques of governing might be applied by the state to regulate consumer activity instead. This question is interesting because consumers, unlike producers, are generally encouraged to be undisciplined so that the very nature of consumption thus tends to be antithetical to organization and authority (Abercrombie 1991, 173; see Chapter 1).

As we pointed out earlier (Chapter 1), consumer subject categories are more often than not self-selected by individuals in a more ephemeral and ad hoc fashion, making it more difficult to target these categories as technologies of governing. In contrast, producer-based categories are attached to individuals in a more durable manner, and because of this, are more likely to be within the control of the state, which can decide on who counts or qualifies as a 'investor' or 'migrant worker', as we saw in the China example above. The state's assignation of producer-based categories can then become the basis for specific regulatory activities such as taxation schemes or length of stay in the country. As pointed out in Chapter 1, the relationship between citizenship and consumption is significant given the influence of the neoliberal assumption that individuals and institutions perform their best within the demands of the free-market economy and points to the presence of 'sovereign consumers', who can be expected to exert 'a high degree of control over what is produced' (Keat 1991, 6–7). And if neoliberalism has indeed penetrated state–citizen relations, positioning and differentially valuing citizens (and foreigners) according to their productivity – and we agree that it has – it then becomes relevant to also ask whether and to what extent the state may be expected to encounter its own citizens in their roles as consumers.

The general research question that concerns us in this chapter, then, is this: what is the relationship between a state's neoliberal focus on productivity and its politico-ethico stress on the consumption of a non-morally problematic activity? In particular, if the success of said activity depends on its uptake by potential consumers, how does the state encourage this activity among one group of consumers (i.e., foreigners) while discouraging or regulating its consumption among another (i.e., its own citizens)? The reference to a 'non-morally problematic activity' is relevant because, where the activity is generally considered immoral or dangerous (such as drug trafficking), the issue of regulating consumption is relatively straightforward: the activity can be declared illegal and consumption criminalized regardless of whether foreigners or citizens are involved. The more interesting situation arises when the state itself is keen to encourage the activity or at least unwilling to ban it, but would like the activity to be consumed under specific conditions. Where such conditions intersect with the notion of citizenship, a particular configuration involving the 'citizen-consumer' arises. Consequently, it seems to us that any examination of the effects of neoliberalism on citizenship configurations is incomplete if insufficient attention is paid to the social positioning of the citizen-consumer.

The empirical basis for our discussion involves an investigation of Singapore's decision to legalize casinos. As we noted in the preceding chapter, because gambling is a consumer-oriented activity, this means that in addition to tourists, locals can too be expected to patronize the casinos. However, gambling is associated with a number of social problems, such as gambling addiction and bankruptcy. Indeed, the state has presented these problems as strong reasons why it was (until recently) deeply *against* the legalization of casinos. The state therefore needs make sure that it is not seen as contributing to any rise in gambling-related problems. That is, even as the state willingly takes responsibility for licensing the operation of casinos and credit for any resulting economic growth, rise in employment or the number of tourists, it also has to avoid being accused of encouraging Singaporeans to gamble. The Singapore situation therefore raises the question of how gambling can be regulated in such a manner as to encourage it among foreigners but not locals.

We suggest that the Singapore situation presents us with a different kind of consumerism. Whereas most forms of political consumerism are concerned with boycotts or even 'buycotts' (Micheletti et al. 2004, xi), the kind of regulation associated with casino gambling in Singapore is concerned with abstention. In particular, Singapore presents its citizens with an argument that prioritizes national productivity over the citizen's desire to consume, modulating the latter with a call for self-discipline and the imposition of external regulatory mechanisms. We close this chapter by suggesting in broader terms the kind of economic condition that might lead other states to adopt strategies similar to Singapore, bringing in as a possibility the issue of rice consumption in Indonesia.

Political Consumerism, Reflexivity and Citizenship

Micheletti et al. (2004, xiv) usefully define political consumerism as 'consumer choice of producers and products with the goal of changing objectionable institutional or market practices'. In political consumerism, then, individuals and groups use the market to communicate their support for or disapproval of particular policies, corporations or countries. Through boycotts – or their opposite, buycotts – consumers signal their interests and desires, and hope through the collective power of their consumption activity to persuade, cajole and coerce businesses and governments to formulate policies or take actions that are in accordance with these interests and desires (ibid.). Whereas a boycott calls for the avoidance of a particular company's products, a buycott is an attempt to actively patronize a particular company or goods from a specific producer (e.g., 'Buy American'[1]).

Political consumerism has a relatively well-established history, particularly in the West. Vogel (2004, 83), for example, argues that contemporary political consumerism in America is traceable to the 1960s and 1970s, when citizens engaged in 'consumer boycotts, shareholder resolutions, demonstrations, and selective investments and disinvestment' to express, among other things, their opposition to the Vietnam War and their support for civil rights. And Jordan et al. (2004, 161) discuss the use of eco-labeling schemes as guides to consumers who are concerned about the environment, suggesting that 'the first national eco-label was set up in Germany in 1978, and by the early 1990s more than a dozen national and multinational eco-label schemes were established around the globe'. In these examples of political consumerism, businesses are forced to react to the political values of consumers as manifested in the latter's consumption activities.

More recently, however, some businesses have attempted to preempt the effects of political consumerism by co-opting the consumer into the conduct of the business itself. An example of this is the BRANDAID Project, which describes itself as a 'new global initiative committed to closing the market divide. [...] In the belief that enlightened capitalism creates prosperity, BRANDAID Project practices market-driven business development toward

---

1 How Americans Can Buy American. Online: http://www.howtobuyamerican.com/ index.php (accessed 23 March 2011).

achieving an economically balanced world.'[2] In BRANDAID, consumers are directly addressed by a collection of businesses, and asked to provide support for these businesses in the knowledge that they are committed toward improving the revenue, living standards and working conditions of artisan communities. BRANDAID has been criticized on the grounds that its appeal to 'compassionate consumption' ends up benefiting businesses more than the communities they ostensibly are aimed at helping (Richey and Ponte 2011).

Regardless of whether consumers are co-opted by businesses or not, the very nature of political consumerism is such that it relies on the reflexivity of consumers. Specifically, it calls on their ability to see themselves as political actors who have specific interests, to appraise how existing institutional practices may or may not respect these interests, and finally, where necessary, to take market-oriented action (such as boycotts) in order to ensure that institutional practices fall in line with these interests.

The reflexive and interested nature of political consumerism fits well with Ellison's (1997) observation that contemporary sociological perspectives on citizenship in late modernity need to more seriously consider citizenship as a resource for negotiating social change. This is because a key characteristic of life in late modernity is precisely the need to negotiate a slew of political, social and cultural changes, and there is no obvious reason why citizenship cannot be strategically adduced to aid in such negotiations. As we have seen, Ellison's own proposal is that citizenship needs to be understood as a 'reflexive condition of defensive engagement' (714).

The extension of political consumerism involving boycotts and buycotts to Ellison's discussion of reflexivity and citizenship is relatively straightforward because we are still dealing with a situation where citizens mobilize themselves to bring about sociopolitical changes vis-à-vis the state or some other institution. But as we highlighted in the introduction to this chapter, there is also the intriguing question of how citizens qua consumers may be regulated by the state. In this regard, we now pursue our discussion of the legalization of casinos in Singapore. We focus here on a case study of the introduction of casinos to investigate the relationship between the 'citizen-consumer' and the state in Singapore.

Legalizing Casinos in Singapore

As we indicated earlier, the legalization of casinos in Singapore is a controversial matter. Thus, the prime minister, Lee Hsien Loong (2005), acknowledged in

2 BRANDAID Project. Online: http://www.brandaidproject.com (accessed 6 March 2012).

a major speech that this decision to legalize casinos did represent a significant policy change, but rationalized this as a necessary step if Singapore is to remain competitive in the drive to attract tourists and keep the tourism industry healthy. The casino is contained within the broader concept of the 'integrated resort' (IR).

The term 'integrated resort' serves to signal that the state has no intention of legalizing standalone casinos. Rather, the casinos are a part of IRs, where there are 'hotels, restaurants, shopping, convention space, even theatres, museums and theme parks. […] The great majority will not be there to gamble'. However, the state acknowledges that 'within this large development and slew of activities, there is one small but essential part which offers gaming and which helps make the entire project financially viable' (Lee 2005).

Importantly, while the other parts of the IR – the restaurants, shops and theatres, etc. – are open to all and sundry, the casinos are specifically intended for tourists. Thus, according to Lee Hsien Loong, 'If gambling is one of the things [tourists] want to do, then maybe we should allow them to do that, find some way to do that, and as a result of that over 10 years double the [tourist] traffic volume. I think we should think about it' (Smale 2004).

The fact that locals are not supposed to be the intended target of the casinos was made explicit by the minister for community development, youth and sports, Dr Vivian Balakrishnan, who has been quoted as saying, 'They [the casino operators] are not supposed to go after the low-hanging fruit which the local market represents but instead to focus their efforts on bringing additional tourists from abroad' (Ramesh 2010). Exactly how the state attempts to ensure that such 'low-hanging fruit' are not (too) attracted to the casinos is the focus of the next two sections.

Casinos and 'Integrated Resorts': Zones within Zones

Since early 2010, two IRs have been opened for business. One is Resorts World Sentosa (RWS) and the other is Marina Bay Sands (MBS). RWS is located on Sentosa, a holiday island resort just off the mainland. In addition to restaurants, shops and hotels, a major attraction at RWS is the Universal Studios theme park, which is very much family oriented. Although MBS too contains restaurants and shops, it contrasts with RWS by catering more to the convention and corporate sector. MBS is supposedly the second most expensive casino in the world and its casino caters more to high rollers, so the minimum gambling stakes are apparently higher than those at RWS.

The state's strategy of having casinos as part of IRs is obviously intended to treat the casinos as special zones that are located within larger zones. These larger zones are unexceptional, at least as far as 'mainstream' Singaporean values go. They are zones that are family friendly, catering to restaurant diners, shoppers, museum-goers and convention visitors. They are thus 'suitable' for locals as well as foreigners. Within these larger zones, however, are the casinos. These casinos are the 'zones within zones' and require careful monitoring to ensure that consumer access is regulated. Ironically, as we now see, one problem for the state in regulating access arises precisely because the casinos are located as part of the IRs.

In September 2010, both RWS and MBS provided bus shuttle services from parts of Singapore to the IRs. The shuttle service by MBS was not free, but the fares were redeemable at various food and beverage outlets, some of which were located in the casino itself. The shuttle service by RWS was free, and a number of its pick-up points were in the 'heartlands' of Singapore. This meant that the residents of the heartlands, some who were unemployed and others retirees, were among those who tended to take advantage of the free shuttle rides to RWS (Lee 2010). However, once the state became aware of these shuttle services, it immediately ordered that they be stopped.

This decision to put a stop to the shuttle services was taken despite the fact that not all Singaporeans who used the services were going to the IRs to gamble. Some were visiting the shops and enjoying the various leisure facilities, though there were a number who of course used the shuttles to visit the casinos specifically (Lee 2010).

By locating casinos within IRs, the state had hoped to reduce their salience. At the same time, this has had the consequence of making it difficult, if not downright impossible, for the state to be sure if passengers were indeed going to the IRs to gamble or not, since to get to the casinos, visitors must first also go to the IRs. It is also not easy for the state to decide if the IR operators were trying to entice locals to visit the casinos specifically, or just the IRs in general.

The state's decision to stop the shuttle services provided by the IR operators is a move that attempts to regulate the producer. This move regulates the citizen-consumer only indirectly by making sure that the shuttle services are no longer available. This goes back to our earlier point that proper enforcement of the producer–consumer nexus has to come from outside this dyad – in this case, the state. It also suggests that, where possible, the state would prefer to avoid having to directly regulate the citizen-consumer because regulation is politically sensitive and difficult to achieve. But as we see in the next section, this avoidance is not always possible, and because of this the state also has to consider measures that directly target the citizen-consumer.

Differentiating Consumers

The state in Singapore is well aware that it is simply not possible to completely ban locals from the casinos. According to Balakrishnan (2010), 'Our aim was to minimize the impact of the casinos on locals, to protect vulnerable groups like young persons and dependents, and to prevent the casinos from targeting the locals as their principal market.' In concrete terms, what the state has done is to put in place measures that control the access of locals to the casinos. As the above quote indicates, the state has been careful to rationalize these measures as being needed 'to protect vulnerable groups like young persons and dependents'. These measures come into play at the point of entry into the casinos themselves. There are basically three types of measures, as noted in Chapter 6, that make clear that the casinos are not intended for local patronage: charging local patrons an entrance fee, enforcing an exclusion order and prohibiting credit extension to local gamblers. This raises the question of why these measures are by and large not perceived as discriminatory by locals. This is because the state has managed to successfully heighten public awareness of gambling not just as an activity but as a potential addiction, and, moreover, one that could affect not just the gambler him/herself but the family unit as well. Once re-presented as a potentially addictive activity, the casinos are not just framed as zones of consumption but also danger zones, where exposure to the activities therein could well lead to problem gambling. The casinos are zones that necessarily discriminate between locals and foreigners *because* they contain dangers that, if left unregulated, could well lead to a variety of social problems for Singapore society.

Consequently, the more stringent measures that apply to locals are not so much seen as discriminatory as protective. They are technologies of subjection, necessarily constraining the activities of locals because the very nature of gambling addiction means that the gamblers, once addicted, cannot be counted on to discipline themselves. There is a lack of general resentment among locals toward the above measures, and this is actually quite remarkable given that the state has made it clear that it considers 'foreign talent' critical to Singapore's economic growth because it is seen as having the knowledge and expertise necessary for developing the financial and biomedical industries, among others. Many citizens, however, are concerned the state's desire to bring in 'foreign talent' may lead it to bestow privileges on these foreigners that undermine the locals' sense of worth. Consequently, a major issue of contention has surrounded the kinds of rights and responsibilities that distinguish citizens from noncitizens (Ong 2006a, 193):

> The dependence on foreign actors has split homeland and dwelling. [...] Locals have begun to reflect on what it means to be a citizen, because expatriates seem to have citizenship status, to be cajoled into becoming citizens even when reluctant to do so. Expatriates are now referred to as 'citizens without local roots', while those who are technically citizens are beginning to feel unrooted.

Given this context, the state's introduction of stringent casino-related measures that apply to locals but not foreigners could well have led to a backlash where locals felt even more discriminated against. However, by arguing that the casinos are important to national productivity, provided the gambling itself is restricted to foreigners, the state is able to justify the regulation of casino gambling among locals on the grounds that it is needed to protect them from the dangers of gambling addiction and possible financial ruin.[3]

Casinos and Consumption: A Brief History

The growth of casinos for the mass market was pioneered in 1930s by the state of Nevada in the US and provided a less class-based model of gambling compared to the exclusivity of gaming in Europe. The 1970s to the 1990s saw the expansion of the hotel resort casinos 'with 24-hour access to games, alcohol and credit. The casino became a space of desire and licence epitomizing new forms of experiential consumption' (West and Austrin 2011, 121).

Las Vegas: Casinos and the revenue-raising model

Las Vegas epitomizes the growth of casino resorts. Nevada took the decision in 1931 to legalize gambling because it was an impoverished state interested in raising revenue. It has a checkered history, having been influenced by politicians and organized crime ('the mob'). As West and Austrin (2011, 122) note, casinos were family-owned, racially discriminatory (blacks were barred as customers and from working as dealers and as bartenders) and anti-union (workers depended heavily on tips and privileges – 'juice'). The development of 'casino tourism' is not new, and links between entertainment and casinos have developed since Holiday Inn bought into the Nevada-based Harrah's casino in the late 1990s.

The Nevada pattern of using casinos to generate revenue was copied by other states, as outlined by West and Austrin (2011, 123):

The volume and concentration of casinos in Las Vegas are untypical in the US and elsewhere, with only Mississippi in the US adopting the

3 Because low-wage foreign workers have been able to enter the casinos freely, they have been known to lose the money that they are supposed to remit back to their homelands. In this regard, another indication of the state's success in presenting the casinos as zones of danger comes from the fact that some foreign workers have even asked for the self-exclusion order to be made more easily available to them. At present, foreigners can only apply for a self-exclusion order in the presence of witnesses who must be Singaporeans or permanent residents, and the order itself takes a month or more to take effect (Teh and Kok 2010).

Nevada model directly. But the number of casinos outside of Nevada increased from 53 to 300 between 1989 and 1995, as other states and cities such as Detroit and Atlantic City adopted gambling tourism, albeit that tighter controls were imposed through zoning on numbers and location. And the use of gambling to promote economic (re)generation through labour-intensive employment in the service sector has also underpinned developments in US Native American reservations.

In fact the ubiquity of legal gambling in North America is the result of the kind of expansion that has taken place since the 1960s as shown above. It has also facilitated a growing economic opportunity for Native Americans, with the expansion of native-run casinos in the US and Canada. In fact this includes the 'largest casino in the world, the Foxwoods Resort Casino, [which] is run by the wealthiest Indian tribe in the world, the Mashantucket Pequots and is located in […] Connecticut' (Cosgrave 2006, 10).

One of the key characteristics of Las Vegas casinos that has become a feature of casinos globally is the way time (or the lack of it) is used to support a gambling culture. Casinos eliminate any external sign of time of day or night. They operate on a 24-hour basis and cut out signs of sunshine and darkness. Clocks are not allowed in casinos or malls. The growth of casino tourism in Asia and elsewhere is explored below.

'Las Vegasification' of casinos

Macau, like Las Vegas, has a history of gambling, going back to the 1850s. Ritzer (2010) claims that it has been moving toward a 'Las Vegasification' in its development of the Cotai Strip, which according to Ritzer aims to rival the Las Vegas Strip. In fact, the Macau Venetian is built to resemble Old Venice. As with all Vegas-style casino hotels, Ritzer (2010) notes, it emphasizes size: at 10.5 million square feet it is the largest building in Asia; it has 3,000 suites, more than thirty restaurants and 1.2 million square feet for conventions. 'It also claims to have the world's largest casino with 3,000 slot machines and 750 gambling tables' (174). An interesting development is the fact that China has become concerned about gambling problems and 'has restricted travel to Macau for Chinese citizens through more restrictive visas that limit visitors to one trip of no longer than 7 days in a 3-month period' (176).

Loi and Kim (2010, 268) argue that Macau is the only location in China where legalized gambling is allowed and has been variously described as the '"Las Vegas of the East", "Monte Carlo of the Orient", "Las Vegas of the Orient" and "Las Vegas in Asia" (McCartney 2005; Pessahha 2008; Vong 2004)'. They point out that gambling revenue from Macau exceeded that of Las Vegas in 2006.

Despite the parallels with Las Vegas, the patterns of gambling in Macau differ markedly. As Loi and Kim (2010, 274) show, 'Approximately 96 percent of casino revenue in Macau in 2007 comes from gaming activities, whereas the figure is 42 percent in Las Vegas. Thus, unlike Macau, Las Vegas earns substantial revenue from nongaming enterprises, such as conventions, shows and shopping (Gu and Gao 2006).' Another key difference between Macau and Las Vegas is also the type of gambling that takes place. The Macau gaming industry, with its roots in Chinese gambling, relies heavily on 'high-stakes' gambling, whereas Las Vegas draws on a broader range of gamblers, not just high rollers, and most are small-stakes gamblers, many of whom are tourists with more diversified gambling through slot machines and nongaming segments. Loi and Kim show that approximately 27 per cent of table games in Macau are directed at VIP baccarat, while only 2 per cent of tables in Las Vegas cater for premium players. Also, the target gamers in Macau are of course the mainland Chinese and those from Hong Kong and Taiwan, whereas Las Vegas arguably has a broader appeal.

In Manila, Melco Crown – a company jointly owned by Macau tycoon Lawrence Ho and Australian billionaire James Packer – has recently been given government approval to add more gaming tables. As Sayson and Chan (2013) observe, 'The Philippines is among a list of Asian nations including Sri Lanka and Vietnam seeking to emulate the success of Singapore and Macau.' Melco is building yet another casino in Manila, called City of Dreams, named after Melco's flagship Macau resort (Rivera 2013). To ensure a sustained demand for the new casino, Melco is also financing junkets for high rollers from Macau and Australia. According to Lawrence Ho, co-chairman and CEO of Melco Crown (Rivera 2013):

> Naturally we have a strong client and customer base originating from China, Hong Kong, Macau and the region. […] Given the experience we have with our junket partners in Macau, we're very encouraged that between them and our own customer base, there will be no lack of demand. […] We're going to do additional things to wow them, like bring them in private jets… helicopters.

Finally, Japan represents a particularly interesting case. Like Singapore (at least until Singapore legalized casinos), gambling is banned in Japan, though horse racing, lotteries and football pools are allowed. However, casinos are controversial due to their association with the Yakuza. Despite this, there continue to be explorations concerning the building of casinos. Thus, Mitsui Fudosan Co., Japan's biggest property developer, has recently joined with Fuji Media Holdings and Kajima Corp to propose setting up a casino and resort complex in Tokyo

(Fujita and Layne 2013). This of course depends on changes being made to legislation that would legalize casinos, and in this regard there appears to be cause for optimism (at least for those keen to see casinos being set up in Japan). As Fujita and Layne note, 'After more than a decade of lobbying by lawmakers, a bill to legalize casino gambling is seen as having a decent chance of passing next year with the business-friendly Liberal Democratic Party in power and after Tokyo won the bid to host the Summer Olympics in 2020.' Until that happens, Japan is widely seen as 'one of the last great untapped markets due to its wealthy population and proximity to China' (ibid.).

If the Singapore experience is anything to go by, then Japan will find it hard to resist legalizing casinos even if this does not happen next year. The competitive pressure from other cities in the region will increase, especially if the revenues from casino gambling continue to grow and if spillover economic benefits are enjoyed by adjacent tourism industries such as hotels, shopping and heritage tourism. There is thus almost an inexorable pull: as other cities and states jump on the casino bandwagon, Japan will be hard pressed to opt out. The introduction of casinos in Tokyo would then be just the beginning; we can expect other Japanese cities to introduce casinos as well.

Casino tourism: Gambling for the masses

The shift to casino tourism, pioneered by the Nevada model, represented gambling for the mass market. Austrin and West (2005, 311) note that

> truck-drivers and guys who work in factories [were] targeted in place of the elite high-rollers, and this transformation in clientele was achieved in several ways: by big reductions in hotel room charges, a cheap buffet, […] above all by expansion in the number of slot machines which paid out bigger jackpots. […] (Earley 2001). Over 70 percent of floor space was dedicated to machines (over double that in conventional casinos), under the direction of a slots department, separate from tables management.

It does not appear as though the development of casinos in Singapore is really targeting a mass market. In fact, the hotels and restaurants within the MBS complex are expensive even by Singapore standards. The RWS is more family friendly than MBS, although the RWS galleria is still characterized by high-end shops including the first Victoria Secret boutique in Asia. However, it also has a water park and marine-life park and a Universal Studios Singapore theme park. The MBS complex is more dedicated to elite gambling and high rollers, with high-end designer shops dominating the shopping mall surrounding the casino. The Las Vegas Sands Corporation is behind the MBS in Singapore and was apparently having financial problems in building the casino hotel. Ritzer (2010, 176) claims that the Singapore government regarded the project as 'too big to fail' and discussion had taken place on whether the Singapore Tourism Board would take over much of the MBS's debt in order to complete the project.

'Cathedrals of Consumption'

In theorizing consumption within late modernity, Ritzer (2010) shows how 2008–2009 in the US was a period of 'hyperconsumption', accompanied by the growth of what he calls 'cathedrals of consumption'. Within what he identifies as the cathedrals of consumption are: shopping malls, chain stores, fast-food restaurants, superstores, cruise ships, airports, online shopping and casino hotels. Ritzer credits these 'cathedrals of consumption' as having an appeal for consumers which gives them an 'enchanted', sometimes even sacred, religious character' (2010, 7), and in order to keep attracting customers they have to keep offering something magical. Ritzer also shows how they increasingly blend into one another and overlap in their services. Changi Airport in Singapore, among other global airports, is typical of this.

An example of this process of blending can be seen in the intersection of gambling and shopping. He shows how neither gambling in centers like Las Vegas nor the idea of shopping malls is new. Ritzer notes that the Las Vegas casinos were preceded by great casinos like the one in Monte Carlo and that shopping malls have their precursors in 'the markets of ancient Greece and Rome, the souks of ancient Arab and Muslim worlds, and the arcades of 19th-century France' (Ritzer 2010, 6). He maintains that the erosion of the relationship between gambling and shopping can be seen in the fact that shopping is now an integral part of the Las Vegas experience, and gives the example of 'the Venetian, which in addition to a huge casino, 6,000 suites, and a convention center, includes a shopping mall' (122). It is also worth noting that, on a global basis, commercial gambling has gone though a normalization process. In fact, as West and Austrin (2011, 119) show: 'The normalization of a once pariah sector has moved it from the periphery to a much more central position within a number of societies across Europe, North America, Asia and Australia.' Gambling has been renamed 'gaming' and had become part of the entertainment industry, including online gambling. But it had also been recognized by states as part of the mainstream economy.

In this regard, Singapore's attempt to frame the casinos as parts of IRs is not especially new or radical. It is simply another instance of the blending process. Taken together with the normalization of gambling into 'gaming', there is probably some justification in being somewhat skeptical that the state's strategy of having zones within zones will be especially successful in discouraging Singaporeans from patronizing the casinos. Instead, it is more likely that a group or family outing to the IRs might mean that mom and dad will go to the casinos (for perhaps part of the time) while the children (most likely with domestic helper in tow) indulge in the other activities offered by the IRs.

Casino Resorts: Aspirational Category or Addiction?

As we have seen, many cities and states have introduced casinos to try and establish a competitive advantage with other cities and states as a tourist economy, to raise revenues to fund an ageing population and to offer a range of lifestyle choices. But what was surprising and sociologically interesting about the introduction of casino resorts or IRs in Singapore was the about-face on the part of the state toward bringing gaming as an industry so fully into the city-state.

'Remaking' Singapore: The shift from 'renaissance' to revenue

The state in Singapore has a history of establishing itself as highly competitive, 'relevant' and in fact as ahead of the field in a globalized world. The state in Singapore has gone through a number of 'makeovers' or 'remakes' in the last ten years. Singaporeans have witnessed a series of 'transformative experiences' as they move through a 'knowledge-based economy', a 'Renaissance city of Asia', the 'Monaco of the East', a 'biomedical hub' and a number of other state-led initiatives to maintain the city-state in the forefront of global change and development. While these transformations have broadened the city's identity to its citizens and the world there is barely time to digest one new identity before one experiences the next, and the state is now so layered with 'makeovers' that there is a sense of fatigue among the citizenry.

As shown in the preceding chapter, the Singapore government announced in 2005 that it planned to introduce casino gambling. As has been shown, this generated a great deal of surprise because the Singapore state in the form of the ruling party, the People's Action Party, had resisted the introduction of such casinos. This had been an entrenched policy over forty years, so the decision shocked a lot of people. Perhaps most surprising was the problem it posed to the Singapore 'brand' internationally, which was unapologetically staid, secure, clean, green and somewhat bland. Regardless of the impression held about Singapore, no one could doubt its success in economic, education and business terms, with a lack of natural resources, but a huge abundance of human resources. In an Asia riven by division, terrorism and corruption, Singapore was efficient, secure and incorruptible; so does the introduction of casinos change that?

Singapore has always been keen to attract wealth, and the liberalization of its policies with regard to foreign talent (opportunities to become PRs, buy property and invest in the city-state) raised the issue of how to move Singapore toward the 'aspirational' category of global city, which required attracting wealth and talent and staying ahead of the competition (cities such as Hong Kong and Manila in the Philippines) for tourist dollars in the region.

Singapore had already attracted a lot of new wealth from countries in the region, and by the late 1990s Singapore started attracting vast swathes of wealth, particularly from the immediate region. This was particularly the case with the flight of thousands of wealthy ethnic Chinese from Indonesia to escape the political turmoil after the collapse of the Suharto regime in 1998. It was estimated that 110,000 Chinese families fled to Singapore, Hong Kong, Canada and Australia. These individuals 'expatriated' an estimated US$80 billion in capital, and US$50 billion to Singapore alone (Nonini 2004).

Singapore reinforced the confidence in its safe-haven status by implementing policies specifically related to high-net-worth individuals, including the introduction of legislation in early 2000 to exempt foreign-earned income from taxation, and also modified its trust laws, guaranteeing the right of trust holders to determine who inherits their estate (Arnold 2007). Thus Singapore had already established itself as a safe haven to keep money.

However, the Singapore state also started crafting an identity as a 'Renaissance City of Asia' – a phrase that began to be used by Singapore officialdom in the late 1990s to encapsulate the desire for a vibrant, dynamic metropolis excelling in all fields of endeavor, not least in the arts and culture (Sanyal 2005; Da Cunha 2010, 19). However, by 2004 the phrase 'Renaissance City of Asia' started to disappear from official usage and in the same year the government in Singapore announced that it was considering introducing a casino as part of the development of the southern island of Sentosa. As the minister for trade and industry, George Yeo (2004) stated:

> Of course, if we decide to have a casino, we will need to put in place control measures to limit its access by Singaporeans and to make sure that there is no organized crime. [...] We will engage international consultants to help us map out the possibilities. An illustration of what is possible can be found at Atlantis on Paradise Island in the Bahamas. This is only an illustration, and what we create eventually will probably not look anything at all like Paradise Island. It will be, and it will have to be, uniquely Singapore.

The new slogan for Singapore was now 'Monaco of the East', as coined by the first prime minister of Singapore, Lee Kuan Yew. The state had already been trying to attract tourists and maintain itself in the forefront of developments in the region through the building of the new cruise terminal and the introduction of the Formula One Grand Prix in the downtown Marina Bay area in 2008.

Integrated Resorts in Singapore: Benefits and disadvantages

There is little doubt that the primary motivation of the state in introducing IRs into Singapore was to attract rich tourists and foreigners who were interested in bringing their wealth to the city. It was clear that the state wanted to reverse its steadily eroding share of the regional tourism market. As Da Cunha (2010, 44) shows: 'Casinos, as part of elaborate and upscale integrated resorts, seemed to have been viewed by the Singapore Government as one way to capture a part of that wealth. Singapore also appeared to be under pressure to reverse its steadily eroding share in the regional tourism market.'

Singapore has limited resources to fall back on as it has no UNESCO World Heritage sites and apart from shopping has little of interest to attract tourists. The expensive nature of the lifestyle – including hotels, rented apartments, restaurants and hugely expensive designer-oriented shopping – mean that it is indeed a place for high-end tourism. Hence, the introduction of IRs as opposed to cultural ventures is about economics. Examples such as the opening of the Las Vegas Sands Corporation casino in Macau made the introduction of the IRs an obvious outcome. Da Cunha (2010, 45) notes that:

> Macau [...] had opened its casino market in 2002 with the first American-style casino. The Sands – commencing operations in 2004 – could be used as a benchmark for comparison. [...] The Las Vegas Sands Corporation was to recoup its initial US $265 million investment in The Sands casino in under 12 months. [...] The Sands was to boost visitor traffic to Macau, largely from the Chinese mainland and Hong Kong. If once sleepy Macau could achieve such spectacular results with just one standalone casino, i.e., not even part of an integrated resort, it must have dawned on Singapore policy-makers that having two elaborate IRs with casino components to them could achieve even more spectacular results for the island-state.

The second economic factor that was identified by the state as important in the introduction of the IRs was job creation. By 2009 the expected number of jobs to be created was revised to 20,000 and for the more indirectly created jobs it was 30–40,000 (Lim 2009). Jobs included those directly related to casinos in hotels, restaurants, high-end shops and other related attractions: there was an expectation that the resorts would help ease structural unemployment, as they would 'employ both blue-collar workers as well as older white-collar workers who may have been made redundant' (Da Cunha 2010, 46).

Local resentment and fear around employment has been a long-standing issue for the population of Singapore because of the decision to allow skilled, semiskilled and unskilled workers to work there. Despite reassurances from Prime Minister Lee Hsien Loong regarding the allocation of jobs to citizens and PRs there is still more than a little concern.

There was a flutter in early 2009 as regards employment of foreigners in the new casinos, when the Philippine press quoted President Gloria Arroyo as saying that the Philippines had secured 5,000 jobs for Filipinos at the RWS. In fact, the Universal Studios theme park wanted to hire Filipino entertainers and performers. In Macau, where there are standalone casinos, the government states that all casino openings for dealers, croupiers and other casino workers must be filled by locals. However, more managerial and supervisory positions can be filled by expatriates.

The third economic factor was the expectation that the Singapore economy would receive a direct boost. The increase was expected to be in the region of 1 per cent to GDP initially and in the long term would be around 1.8 percent assuming an increase of 10 per cent in visitor arrivals to Singapore and a 1 per cent rise in government spending related to IRs (Da Cunha 2010, 49). The long-term outcome on this remains to be seen.

A Cosmopolitan City or Asian Nation-State?

There has long been a debate in Singapore between those who have aspirations for the city-state to become a 'global city' and those who wish to retain its identity as an Asian nation-state. The focus of cities that have achieved the status of global cities, including London, San Francisco and Sydney, has been their cosmopolitan populations. Prime Minister Lee Hsien Loong (2005) was emphasizing diversity even in 2005:

> I always use this example. If you walk along a New York Street, you will see the most diverse sampling of humankind anywhere in the world. [...] And that's what makes New York so special, vibrant. [...] If you want to eat any food, you can get it in New York. And if you want to have anybody with a new thought to start off something, it happens in New York. [...] We want to be something like that, a cosmopolitan city. But if the whole of America were like New York, I'm not sure that it would be one country. So we have to keep a balance, creating cohesion and this diversity.

The issue around the management of change is the essence of what is happening in Singapore and the issue of the casinos is located in that broader debate about change and what voice the citizenry of Singapore have in the future development of the country. The citizenry does become vocal on some issues.

Some of the more contentious issues concern the issue of population growth in Singapore and the issuance of the White Paper (2013) on population, as the government announced its objective of increasing the population to 6.5 million by 2050 or thereabout. Clearly the emphasis on growth from immigration has created significant anxiety among Singaporeans. Initially the growth in population from the 1970s to the first half of the 1990s consisted of foreign nationals who were either working in the high-end job market – managers or professionals – as 'foreign talent' or at the low end of the job market – domestic 'helpers' (maids) or construction workers – as 'foreign workers'. However, there was a significant change in the mid-1990s, with foreign nationals occupying service jobs as a result of the diversity of hubs that emerged in Singapore. This resulted in a shift in the attitude toward population growth. As Da Cunha (2010, 163) notes:

> In June 2008 it was revealed that Singapore's overall population had grown by 5.5% in 2007, making it the fastest growth in the populations since the collection of statistics in 1871. Singapore's population had hit 4.84 million by end June 2008. This comprised 3.16 million citizens, 478,000 permanent residents (PRs) and 1.2 million foreign nationals working or studying in Singapore. The 1.2 million foreign nationals are defined as the 'non-resident population'. This segment accounted fully for 24.8% or almost one-fifth of the total population. If PRs and non-residents are lumped together, totaling some 1,675,000, this non-citizen component would account for 34.6% of the entire population.

In 2009, Singapore's population profile consisted of 3.2 million citizens, 533,000 PRs and 1.25 million foreign nationals. As a result, prices across the board started to rise and Singaporeans became more resentful. And with the issuance of the White Paper (2013), it was inflammatory. As has been shown in earlier chapters, the issue of institutional reflexivity may be moving ahead at a faster pace than individual reflexivity.

Abstention as a Dimension of Political Consumerism

A number of features about the Singapore situation overlap with the studies of political consumerism and reflexive citizenship discussed earlier. There is a reliance on reflexivity in that the state has made it very clear to both

Singaporeans as well as the casino operators that the primary market for the casinos must be foreigners rather than locals. In this discourse, subject categories such as 'foreigner', 'tourist' and 'citizen' are highly salient, with implications for the concomitant ease of access they may enjoy to the casinos. There is an appeal as well to the interests and values of citizens. In this case, the state's argument is that it is in the larger national interest to legalize casinos, since there are significant economic benefits in terms of revenue from tourism and job creation. At the same time, the state has argued that it is not in the personal interests of citizens to patronize the casinos. And it is on the basis of protecting their personal interests that the state has justified the implementation of various measures.

However, the Singapore situation is also interestingly different because it presents us with a case of abstention as a dimension of political consumerism. As we saw earlier, typical cases of political consumerism involve boycotts or buycotts, and these activities usually target specific organizations. A typical boycott or buycott in Singapore might then involve a specific casino operator being targeted because it is considered to have institutional practices that various individuals or groups find objectionable, such as racism or sexism. In contrast, the abstention called for by the Singapore state does not target a specific casino operator. Rather, it targets a generalized activity, that of casino gambling.

Calling for abstention in relation to an activity is not uncommon, of course. Many states, including the state in Singapore, discourage smoking, for example, on health grounds and even increasingly ban smoking from a number of public spaces. However, such enjoinments to refrain from smoking are based on health grounds that presumably apply to all human beings. It is not as though foreigners are more immune than citizens to the health problems associated with smoking. As a consequence, there is no specific attempt to link smoking to citizen status. In contrast, we have seen that the issue of casino gambling very explicitly links abstention to citizenship status. The state in Singapore has successfully convinced its citizens that while it is in the country's (and ultimately their) economic interests to have casinos legalized, it is not in their specific social interests to actually patronize the casinos. That is, while foreigners are encouraged to enter, locals are not.

The distinction between foreigners and locals is invoked in a manner that suggests that the former can be free to 'ruin' themselves gambling if they wish to do so as long as the latter are protected. The latter, in contrast, should simply reap the economic benefits of boosts to the tourism industry that the casinos provide. The state's goal is therefore to subjectivize moral consumers who wish to protect their families, and this subjectivization is expected to apply to all Singaporeans regardless of their financial status. In this sense, when it comes to regulating casino gambling, there is nothing like the graduated sovereignty that Ong (2006a, 2006b; see above) observes in relation to the productive citizen. All citizens are enjoined to abstain from casino gambling, leaving it to foreigners. The citizen–foreigner distinction is therefore reinforced rather than dropped.

However, the very nature of abstention is such that it requires self-discipline. So, while external mechanisms can be introduced that make it more difficult for citizens to enter the casinos, it is ultimately up to the citizens themselves to decide if and whether they wish to abstain from casino gambling. This suggests that to the extent that citizens are increasingly seen as lacking in self-discipline, the state may be under greater pressure to either revisit and strengthen the regulatory mechanisms it has put in place or perhaps even rethink its legalization of casinos and return Singapore to its previous 'casino-free' status. This means that the present system is problematic in at least two ways. One, for financially well-off Singaporeans, the entrance fee presents no obstacle and these individuals will therefore remain relatively unrestrained. Two, as we now illustrate, it is extremely difficult to stop the determined consumer. Some citizens have managed to circumvent the regulatory mechanisms by sending in 'proxy gamblers' who are noncitizens. Thus, foreign workers were reported to have been to the casinos to gamble on behalf of their employers (Soh 2011):

> Five bosses – some with exclusion orders against them – told The Straits Times that they have been handing workers cash, notebooks and mobile phones, then dispatching them to the casino. They claimed to know several other employers doing the same thing. The 'proxy gamblers', dressed mostly in company polo T-shirts and jeans, get a cut of the winnings, but if they lose too much, their pay is docked.

Following this report, the Ministry of Manpower and the Ministry of Community Development, Youth and Sports jointly announced that government authorities had met with the operators of Singapore's two IRs, 'and they had agreed to step up checks at their premises. MOM is also checking if the contractors involved may have committed any offences' (Soh 2011). Thus, the state is forced to continually monitor the behavior of its citizens, in order to be alert to any attempt by 'undisciplined' consumers to evade the regulatory mechanisms that have been instituted, and where necessary, fine tune these mechanisms.

Conclusion

The Singapore case alerts us to a different configuration of citizen, one where consumption is inflected with abstention. The focus is on national (economic) interests over individual (consumption) rights, with individual responsibility taking the form of self-discipline to refrain from gambling. While this particular configuration is by no means common, we want to close this chapter by suggesting in general terms what kind of economic condition might favor such a notion of citizenship.

It therefore seems to us that any consumer good (i.e., product or activity) that the state is keen to encourage foreign consumption of while discouraging domestic consumption might favor a tying of citizenship status to appeals for abstention plus the implementation of regulatory mechanisms.[4] Moreover, the reason given by the state for encouraging foreign consumption while asking locals to abstain/reduce their own consumption activity must be convincingly linked to the issue of national interests in order for the argument to gain traction. This line of argument is clearly non-neoliberal, since as Harvey (2005, 28) reminds us, 'Opposition within the rules of the neo-liberal state is typically confined to questions of individual human rights.' Thus, assuming Ong (2006a) is right about the exceptional status of neoliberalism in Asian states, it is a line of argument that might be easier to pursue in Asia than in, say, the US.

Nevertheless, it is still not an easy argument to make or sustain since it calls for self-discipline in the consumption of a good that is non-morally problematic. And clearly what counts as problematic from the state's perspective need not count as such from the individual's perspective. And of course, even those citizens who do accept the national interest argument may still be unwilling or unable to forego their own personal acts of consumption. Thus, even in Singapore, despite the fact that the casinos have indeed been an undoubted economic success, the state continues to deal with public expressions of misgivings about the legalizing of casinos and their potentially damaging social consequences.

---

4 The opposite situation, where the state wants to encourage domestic consumption over foreign consumption, is less interesting because states do not normally find it difficult or contentious to exclude foreigners from accessing a consumer good while providing their own citizens with access. There might be some regional or international backlash, but such effects are not especially significant for the study of citizenship.

Chapter 8

REGULATING CONSUMPTION AND THE 'PINK DOLLAR'

Introduction

This chapter considers a second case study, one that highlights the significance of discreet consumption as analytically relevant to our understanding of political consumerism. This second case study focuses on broadening the understanding of consumption across a range of heterogeneous populations in different cities. O'Connor and Kong (2009) put this in the broader context of the rise of the cultural and creative industries and their recognition in national and global city agendas. As they note: 'The increasing importance of cultural and creative industries in national and city policy agendas is evident in Hong Kong, Singapore, Taiwan, South Korea, Beijing, Shanghai and Guangzhou, and Wuhan. Much of the thinking in these cities has derived from the European and North American policy landscapes' (2009, 1).

This idea of the growth of 'creative clusters' (see Kong 2009 for the development of this concept in the context of Singapore) is linked to the notion of the 'creative class' (Florida 2005), described by O'Connor and Kong as 'one of the most significant forms of direct policy transfer seen in the last few years. From its use by US academic Richard Florida as a form of statistical civic boosterism tacked onto some loose claims about the ending of the industrial society, it has gone on to enthuse urban politicians and planners across the globe' (2009, 3). We are not claiming that heterogeneity is purely a feature of the growth of the 'creative classes' or the creative industries. Nevertheless, it is clear that the impact of the concepts for global city policy agendas has contributed to a greater hybridity and heterogeneity in the kinds of populations attracted to global cities. Mok (2009), for example, looks at the concept when applied to Hong Kong and Macau, whose governments have been attracted by the idea of the 'creative class', although he notes that development in these cities has not followed the 'Florida thesis'. Li and Hua (2009) show how Shanghai's strategic vision has been significantly influenced by the notion of the creative industries that have become a central plank in Shanghai's aspirations to become a global city.

One of the important dimensions in the recognition of heterogeneous populations in different global cities has been the rise in importance of the gay community and recognition of its value in terms of consumption. In this chapter we consider 'the pink dollar' and intersection with the regulation of consumption:

> The pink dollar or pink money describes the purchasing power of the gay community, often especially with respect to (but not necessarily limited to) political donations. With the rise of the gay rights movement in many cities, pink money has gone from being a fringe or marginalized market to a thriving industry in many parts of the Western world. For example, in the US, estimates of the LGBT market put its value at approximately $790 billion in the year 2012, and in addition 28 per cent of gay households in the US report as having an income in an excess of $50,000 a year. (*Wikipedia* 2014)

Florida (2012, ix) notes that, in recognizing and encouraging diversity, he was the subject of criticism:

> I caught a lot of flak for proposing that diversity – an openness to all kinds of people, no matter their gender, race, nationality, sexual orientation, or just plain geekiness – was not a private virtue but an economic necessity. I earned a certain measure of notoriety for suggesting a visible gay presence in a city can be seen as a leading indicator for rising housing values and high tech [Authors note: as has indeed been the case in San Francisco and parts of Southern California]. Some were outraged at the very suggestion. [...] Popular opinion now favors gay marriage, and a growing body of research notes the connection between diversity, innovation and economic growth.

Additionally, Florida (2012, xi) shows the link between diversity and creativity as follows:

> It's not just that diversity and inclusion are moral imperatives, which of course they are. They are economic necessities. Creativity *requires* diversity: it is the great leveler, annihilating the social categories we have imposed on ourselves, from gender to race and sexual orientation. This is why the places that are the most open-minded gain the deepest economic advantages. The key is not to limit or reverse the gains that the Creative Class has made but to extend them across the board, to build a more

open, more diverse, more inclusive Creative Society that can harness its members' – *all* of its members' – capacities.

Unlike the identity of a gambler, as seen in Chapter 7, sexual orientation – in this case, homosexuality – is not seen as an aspect of identity that an individual inhabits on a short-term or ephemeral basis. Our interest here is with the sociopolitical construction of homosexuality, and as far as this is concerned, a person's decision to buy a car or to enter a casino (and the concomitant consumer identity that the individual occupies as a motorist or a gambler) is clearly not seen in the same light as a person's decision to embrace a specific sexual orientation.

The pink dollar is about lifestyle, companionship and a sense of community, as we show below. In this regard, abstention is not an option when the activities in question could be as innocuous or nondescript as dancing, having drinks or shopping for clothes. Indeed, calling for abstention here would be economically counterproductive, since the very attraction of the pink dollar is its perceived affluence. The key issue here instead is whether individuals who share a specific sexual orientation feel welcome or comfortable engaging in such activities in the context of a particular city, such as Singapore.

We will see that the state in Singapore has been quite willing to adopt a more pragmatic attitude toward the gay community, because it appreciates that the 'pink dollar' can make a significant contribution to Singapore's economic growth. We will see that gay tourists (and gay locals) are encouraged to enjoy themselves in Singapore so long as this is done in a discreet manner that does not make the more conservative segments of society uncomfortable. In both these cases – that of the casinos and that of the pink dollar – the state is therefore attempting to regulate consumer behavior, albeit in different ways: Locals are encouraged to exercise restraint in the case of the casinos, leaving these as far as possible to foreigners. In the case of the pink dollar, however, both locals and foreigners are asked to pursue their activities with consideration for the more conservative elements of Singaporean society.

Thus, according to Lim (2004):

Despite the need to upkeep the social cohesion ideology, the Government's desire to reposition itself as a lifestyle capital necessitates the shedding of its strait-laced image. This necessitates the establishment of a new gay-friendly (or at least, gay-tolerant) image. To that end, the government has turned a blind eye to the establishment of gay-friendly shops and entertainment outlets at highly visible locations in Singapore. Whereas the 1980s and early 1990s saw regular police clampdowns on gay-cruising activities, such cases have been unheard of in recent times despite such increased visibility of homosexuality in the public realm.

In regulating consumption vis-à-vis the pink dollar, the state cannot appeal to the local/foreigner dichotomy, unlike in the case of regulating access to the casinos. To do so would lead to a counter-productive (at least from the standpoint of branding Singapore as a global city) situation where gay 'enclaves' such as bars or nightclubs or even shops are not open to locals in the same way as they would be to foreigners, analogous to the restrictions that were put in place for the casinos. To do so would also be to assume implausibly that the straight/gay distinction falls along the same lines as the local/foreigner divide, and this would be a fiction that would be hard to maintain (even if the state wanted to) not least because there are signs of increasing gay activism among locals (see below). This means that, unlike the case of the casinos, we are not looking at a situation involving the citizen-consumer. That is, this is not a situation where the state, in its attempt to regulate consumption, is hailing individuals in their combined identities as citizen and consumer.

Asian Values, Conservatism and Gay Activism in Asia

There has been much debate in the last decade as to what extent 'Asian values' still resonate with young Asians. The concept of Asian values as traditionally understood is based around the concept of 'shared values'. There were traditionally understood to be five proposed shared values: nation before community and society above self; family as the basic unit of society; regard and community support for the individual; consensus instead of contention; and racial and religious harmony. It is not clear just how distinctively Asian these values are, and skepticism over any state's motives in proposing these values meant that they were ultimately never fully constitutionalized. Nevertheless, as Chua (1995, 33) points out:

> Lacking legal status does not automatically preclude Shared Values from having institutional and ideological significance. As a publicly promoted and politically sanctioned document, it is now available to the government and its supporters as rational grounds for action, while constraining those who oppose it to debate issues within the parameters specified by the Shared Values themselves.

Chua is undoubtedly correct. But the institutional force of the shared values cuts both ways because these values – notwithstanding arguments over their specifics – have to be understood 'against the background of previous attempts to articulate core values' (Hill and Lian 1995, 219), such as meritocracy, multiracialism and even Confucianism. What this means is that a state like Singapore is itself all too aware that it has to be seen as upholding some notion of Asian/Singaporean values, and politically this often means being careful not to upset the more conservative segments of society.

Bearing in mind the foregoing, it is perhaps understandable why the state needs to tread even more carefully with regard to the issue of gay lifestyles than with regard to the legalizing of casinos. If we look at the state in Singapore we can see that it has perhaps been somewhat 'schizophrenic' in how it positions itself in relation to gays. For example, in 2003, it was reported (Agence France Presse, 14 September 2003) that 'although homosexual acts are still outlawed, Prime Minister Goh Chok Tong signaled his government's increasingly tolerant approach to the issue by announcing this year that gays are allowed to work in the civil service'. The same report noted that Singapore was

> slowly emerging as Asia's gay entertainment hub, with a slew of gay-friendly clubs, saunas, restaurants and fashion outlets appearing in the city-state over the past three years.
>
> The conservative country, better known for the government's tight rein on social values, is now the focus of 'enormous buzz and excitement' for Asia's gay community, said Stuart Koe, the chief executive of leading regional gay website Fridae.com.
>
> Koe told *AFP* Singapore's reputation as a shopping haven, combined with a burgeoning club scene and the proliferation of entertainment venues catering for gays contributed to the lure of Singapore.

The report also described the Nation party, essentially Singapore's version of a gay parade, which draws large crowds of celebrants from other parts of Asia:

> One event that is fast becoming a signature celebration for gays in Singapore and elsewhere in the region is the Nation party.
>
> Held on the eve of the city-state's national day holiday in August, it is increasingly being regarded as Asia's answer to the gay Mardi Gras events in Western countries.
>
> Only in its third year, Nation03 attracted 5000 revellers last month, twice as many as Nation02, including 1200 foreigners who were mostly from Asian countries.

'Those that came to Nation had a good time. They were from places like Taiwan, Japan, Korea and knew about the event through word-of-mouth', Koe said.

However, just two years later in 2005, the optimism and celebration about Singapore's status as a 'gay capital' appeared to have faded significantly. The Nation party was banned and had to be held in Phuket, Thailand, instead of Singapore (Agence France Presse, 12 June 2005):

> 'We are disappointed that the authorities have deemed a National Day celebration by Singapore's gay citizens as being 'contrary to public interest', when it had previously been approved four years without incident', said fridae.com chief executive Stuart Koe.
>
> 'This is a direct contradiction to previous calls for embracing of diversity.'
>
> Discrimination against homosexuals appeared to be easing after then Prime Minister Goh Chok Tong said in July 2003 that gays were already allowed to hold civil service positions, remarking that 'they are like you and me'.
>
> Taking their cue from Goh, gay groups became bolder and businesses began courting what was perceived to be a hip and affluent gay market – the so-called 'pink dollar' – as well as gay tourists from across Asia.
>
> However, after Goh stepped down in August 2004, his successor Lee Hsien Loong made it clear there were limits to what gays can do in public.
>
> A planned Christmas Day party also organized by fridae.com last December was banned because it was deemed to be 'contrary to public interest'.
>
> 'It does seem that there has been a change in policy and it doesn't look very heartening', said Alex Au, a co-founder of gay rights advocacy group *People Like Us*.

As we have pointed out, a key reason for this apparent flip-flopping has to do with the state's awareness that many Singaporeans are still conservative and are uneasy, to say the least, with accepting gay lifestyles as a public and mainstream component of Singapore society. Thus, according to Agence France Press (12 June 2005):

> But there are cultural and political reasons for the government's refusal to allow an openly gay festival to flourish here.
>
> Singapore officials have maintained that despite rapid economic progress and the impact of cultural globalisation, most ordinary

Singaporeans – popularly known as the 'heartlanders' – remain conservative.

A study by researchers at a local university supports this view.

'Singapore's government is in touch with the majority of Singaporeans', said Mark Cenite, an assistant professor at the communication school of Singapore's Nanyang Technological University.

'The majority of Singaporeans hold negative attitudes toward gay men and lesbians', said Cenite, who was part of the research team.

Telephone interviews of some 1000 respondents showed 68.6 percent of Singaporeans had a negative attitude toward gay men and lesbians, 22.9 percent had a positive attitude and 8.5 percent were neutral, he said.

We have emphasized throughout this book the importance of institutional reflexivity and, relatedly, second-order reflexivity. What the foregoing extracts point to, then, is the state's awareness that it has to be seen – by citizens as well as the world 'outside' – as relatively tolerant and open (in order to be consistent with the global city thrust); at the same time, it has to also be seen – mainly by citizens – as staying true to Asian values rather than jettisoning them. Second-order reflexivity comes into play here because the state is clearly required to manage the difficult balancing act of trying to accommodate the concerns of both the more conservative and the more liberal segments of Singapore society, requiring the state to reconcile how it wants to be perceived (as simultaneously progressive and traditional) with how different Singaporeans want their society to be perceived.

The sensitivities involved and political costs to the state can be highly consequential if it is seen to be either too liberal or too conservative. Especially since in the era of late modernity, many gay Singaporeans, along with their supporters, are becoming more open about supporting gay rights. Here are two recent examples. In April 2013, the Singapore High Court heard, and ultimately dismissed, a legal challenge brought about by a gay couple concerning the constitutionality of section 377A of the Penal Code, a throwback to when Singapore was still under British colonial rule. Section 377A criminalizes sex between men (but not women) (Channel News Asia, 9 April 2013):

In his 92-page judgment, Justice Quentin Loh said that in Singapore's legal system, whether a social norm that has 'yet to gain currency' should be discarded or retained is decided by Parliament. Parliament voted in 2007 to retain Section 377A.

'To my mind, defining moral issues needs time to evolve and is best left to the legislature to resolve', said Justice Loh, noting that Singapore society is 'in the midst of change'.

In January 2013, the law minister, K. Shanmugam, met with Sayoni (a gay rights group) to explain the concerns that the state faces in managing LGBT issues, and to assure the group that there is no intention to actively enforce the law that criminalizes sex between men (Wong 2013a). Once news of the meeting became public, the law minister had to meet with representatives of a group of churches, who were concerned that his meeting with Sayoni might have signaled a 'high-level endorsement of their agenda' (Wong 2013b). The churches pointed to the state's track record of 'being pro-family' and were therefore concerned about threats to 'this basic building block of our conservative society' (ibid.).

Given all these tensions arising from different attitudes toward the gay lifestyle, the state, even as it aims to court the pink dollar, has to rely on tolerance and compromise among all the parties involved, including, particularly, religious leaders who claim to represent a conservative position and gay activists who are seeking to push for social change and, increasingly, positioning the call for such change in relation to the discourse of rights. In the case of consumption, then, it is no wonder that the same strategies that were put in place when legalizing the casinos (assurances that potential social problems would be mitigated by imposing restrictions on access to casinos for locals, as well as calls for abstention) are not viable here. Instead, there is reliance on discretion, where those who wish to pursue a gay lifestyle and its concomitant activities are allowed to do so, as long as this is all done without drawing too much public attention.

The Risk Society and the Politics of Consumption

While the discussion in this book is not focused on the sociology of risk, the issue of risk has in fact been raised with regard to gambling. However, as we argue in this section, risk arises with greater pertinence – given our interest in state–society relations – when it comes to the pink dollar. We begin, however, with a brief consideration of the relation between risk and gambling.

The establishment of 'risk' as a sociological 'field' is of course attributed to the work of Ulrich Beck's (Beck 1992; Beck et al. 1994) formulation of 'reflexive modernization' in late modernity. Essentially Beck establishes the relationship between autonomy of the self and the 'world risk society' (Beck 1992). While Beck did not focus on gambling per se, the implications for a broader economic and political analysis are clear, as noted by Cosgrave (2006, 5):

Gambling is a global growth industry (McMillen 1996, 2003; Eaddington and Cornelius 1997) where a form of risk-taking is rationalized, capitalized, and marketed as a form of leisure, entertainment, and 'excitement' – in short, colonized by the gaming industry as well as by states. From a sociological perspective, the shift in gambling practices from local to global conditions, through the pressures of commercial colonization (Cosgrave and Klassen 2001; Reith 2002; McMillen 2003) raises questions not only about the meaning of gambling activities for participants in rationalized, commercial and anonymous gambling environments, but also about the larger cultural contexts within which legalized gambling enterprises are found.

The issue of gambling and risk has therefore not surprisingly been of great interest to contemporary sociologists including Beck (1992), Beck et al. (1994), Kingma (2004) and Reith (2002). As Cosgrave (2006, 1) comments: 'While legalized gambling is often represented now in terms of the "leisure" activity of individuals, such a focus tends to neglect the larger questions concerning the social organization of gambling, which must be considered in relation to political, economic and globalizing processes (McMillen 1996, 2003).' Cosgrave (2006, 3) shows how framing the debate around gambling within the sociology of risk contextualizes it within a neoliberal agenda: 'The sociology of risk can also contribute to the institutional analysis of gambling activity. Large scale commercial casinos for example, may be considered risk institutions since here we find nothing left to chance, and the management of risk is essential for economic success.'

One of the aspects of the link between neoliberalism and risk is the transference of risk from the state to the individual and the exposure of the individual in the process to greater risk (see Shiller 2000, 2005). This is particularly evident in Singapore but can be seen more generally in 'gambling behavior in markets' (Shiller 2005). As Cosgrave (2006, 1) shows:

> Legal gambling is acceptable, but one is enjoined by official state gambling agencies to be a 'responsible' gambler (Cosgrave and Klassen 2001; Campbell and Smith 2003). This neo-liberal moral discourse then raises the issue of the state's relationship to citizens, and since states promote and capitalize on gambling, critics draw attention to the increased accessibility to gambling, the creation of new problem gamblers and gambling-related suicides (Branswell 2002; Williams and Wood 2004).

The notion of risk, then, concerns the risk that the gambler accepts in his/her attempts to enjoy financial gains. And indeed, it could be argued that for at least some gamblers, it is the very riskiness of the activity that provides them with some form of adrenalin rush, and in this way contributes to the enjoyment and perhaps addictive nature of the activity. Likewise, for the casinos themselves, risk takes the form of a large-scale financial investment. That is, balancing the attractiveness of the gambling facilities (including its location and branding) against the possibility of cheats and the emergence of competing casinos are all part of the risk calculations that the casinos, much like any other businesses, need to consider. Thus, in so far as risk is considered as either the individual gambler's responsibility or part of the business calculations that the casinos need to bear in mind, there is nothing specifically significant being raised in relation to state–society relations.

Things become more interesting when we consider the pink dollar in Singapore. We have seen that the state is reluctant to ban establishments serving a gay clientele. At the same time, it is unable to be seen as directly encouraging such establishments. This ambivalence is crystallized in the status of section 377A of the Penal Code, which remains in legal force but which, according to the state, is unlikely to be actually enforced. That is, members of the gay community acknowledge that the state seems willing to 'turn a blind eye', but nevertheless worry that (Liang 2013)

> the law's presence is felt indirectly, particularly in instances where emergency services might be required.
>
> 'Many fear calling the police in situations of domestic violence, theft or rape because they may be charged' for being gay, said Lim.
>
> 'This creates a group that is unable and fearful of tapping upon essential public services.'

According to Liang (2013):

> Government officials, while openly promising that gays would not be hounded under the law, maintain that Section 377A must stay in the books because most Singaporeans are still conservative and do not accept homosexuality.
>
> Legal experts say the government's position of not enforcing the provision but leaving it intact is intended to send a social message.
>
> 'Keeping 377A in the books is a message that being gay is still not what the mainstream norms are', said Lynette Chua, assistant professor of law at the National University of Singapore (NUS).
>
> Michael Hor, a criminal law professor at NUS, said 'the government probably sees the non-repeal of an unenforced 377A as a political compromise – giving both contending lobbies something to take home'.

What all this points to is the need for members of the gay community to trust that the state will not prosecute even though it is legally able and perhaps obligated to do so. This, in turn, means that individuals pursuing a gay lifestyle, particularly sexually active gay men, are putting themselves at risk of prosecution. They have to rely on assurances from agents of the state that they really have nothing to worry about. In this regard, even as gay activists and other similar coalitions continue to petition the state for formal recognition of their particular vision of emancipatory 'life-politics' (Giddens 1991, 214), the pursuit of leisure and pleasure activities has to adopt lower profiles if the goodwill and cooperation of the state is to be sustained. That is, there must be some implicit appreciation that the state, too, is in a difficult position and too blatant an expression of the gay lifestyle in Singapore society would most likely be counterproductive in producing a backlash from the more conservative segments, possibly forcing the state to then adopt a strong 'pro-family' stance. According to Lim (2004):

As a means of not alienating itself from the mainstream population, there has been a strategy on the part of leaders in the gay community to steer clear of a confrontational gay-rights advocacy strategy. Energy and efforts seem more directed towards the accumulation of soft-power capital: empowerment through networking and the establishment of a resource base.

Precisely because gays in Singapore – in particular, sexually active gay men – are at risk of potentially being charged with the commission of a crime, the current situation requires that they trust the state to exercise restraint when the opportunity and basis for criminal prosecution arises. But of course ruling political parties may come and go. And even where the same party stays in power, the specific individual who assumes the position of the prime minister will change, and each individual may have a somewhat different view of just how tolerant (if at all) the state ought to be toward gay lifestyles. Trust, then, is based on assumptions regarding the likelihood (or not) of the status quo changing or remaining the same. As social and political conditions change, levels of trust can rise or decline.

As a consequence, one direct effect of the trust–risk dynamic that informs the relationship between the gay community in Singapore and the state is discreet consumption on the part of the former. Discreet consumption is a prudent response given the ever-present risk of prosecution and the concomitant reliance on trust in the state. What this means in practice is that the lively and active gay scene in Singapore is largely 'underground' (Eveland 2011, 163). Specifically, while there are specific locales that are known to be gay oriented, such knowledge is often gleaned only informally via word of mouth or the Internet. As Lim (2004) points out:

> Besides services for posting online personals, the existence of online gay forums allowed for the emergence of a community. The availability of gay-specific information on the internet is also particularly helpful not only for gays, but also youths in the process of questioning their sexuality. For the Singaporean gay, the internet is in essence a medium for the dissemination of information, a platform for networking, a means of creating a community, and most importantly, a source of empowerment.

In Ong's (2006a) terminology, these locales can be considered zones of technology. But unlike the IRs that contain the casinos, which have been explicitly carved out by the state's regulatory agencies, the locales catering to the gay community are informally set up, highly mobile and fast changing. Here are some examples, taken from an online list of various 'Singapore gay venues' (*SgWiki*, 2013):

(i) Art venues, such as the Substation and Utterly Art. These do not necessarily focus solely on works by LGBT artists or only on LGBT themes. But they do have exhibitions, performances and seminars that deal with such themes.

(ii) Bars, pubs and karaoke joints. Most of the gay bars in Singapore are located around the Tanjong Pagar area. But the website also notes that some of these have closed and newer ones have opened along Neil Road.

(iii) Also listed are saunas and discos. Some of the saunas even have 'nude nights'. One of the saunas is described by the website as 'the first to have an *al fresco* swimming pool, which later had to be covered up, as office workers in the neighbouring building could have a bird's-eye view of the frequently naked men lounging around the poolside'.

Related to the discreet consumption is deniability arising from ambiguity. Specifically, what this means is that many of the venues are not formally or officially exclusive to a gay clientele, even if this kind of exclusivity informs actual practice. Some good examples include the art venues, and even the bars and pubs, mentioned above. Those 'in the know' can assume that these venues will tend to be patronized by a predominantly or perhaps even exclusively gay clientele. And uninformed patrons might find themselves surprised if they were to enter the venues unsuspectingly. But such ambiguity is critical to the discreet nature of the consumption activities because it provides the relevant individuals involved (usually the venue's management and, to a lesser extent, the patrons themselves) with the opportunity to deny, if necessary, that the venue in question is 'really/truly' a gay scene.

But despite the attempts at discretion, ambiguity and deniability – or perhaps precisely because of the nebulous nature of these attributes – there will be instances when gay consumption activities appear to test the boundaries of what might be considered acceptable to the state. In the next section, we touch upon of some of these instances.

Testing the Boundaries of Discreet Consumption

We have indicated throughout this book that 'the consumer is an economic construct: a key figure in the liberal social imaginary of Western capitalist democracies' (Clarke et al. 2007, 2). However, beyond the economic relationship, the relationship between the citizen and the state is also an important one. As Clarke et al. (2007, 2) note: 'It is the consent of the citizen that empowers the state; while the state provides and secures the conditions that enables citizens to lead their lives. In these very abstract terms, the citizen is a political construct.'

However not all citizens share equal access and rights, and access is often influenced by gender, race, age and a variety of criteria of 'competence' that have structured patterns of exclusion. Additionally, as Giddens (1994) and Beck (1992) have shown in their analyses of late modernity, the 'dynamics of individualization and reflexivity provide the conditions for "life politics" as projects in which individuals come to define themselves both individually and collectively' (Clarke et al. 2007, 10). However this area is a contested one, as Giddens (1994, 91) points out: 'Life politics is a politics of identity as well as of choice.' The implication of this is that the issue of consumer culture and the citizen is not a level playing field, and as Trentmann (2006, 2) has noted, 'both historical studies and contemporary sociology have neglected the subjectivities of the consumer'.

The construction of subjectivities is particularly pertinent when it comes to Singapore and for the purpose of our discussion here, and for constructions of the citizen qua consumer in relation to masculinity and for the gay community. Homosexuality, as we have observed, is still a crime in Singapore. But as we have also indicated, the state in Singapore has adopted a pragmatic attitude toward the gay community (both locals and tourists), in recognition of the consumer power of the 'pink dollar' (see above).

The issue of masculinity in Singapore has traditionally been seen as an aspect of national identity, which defines 'fatherhood' (Heng and Devan 1995) and national service as key manifestations of what counts as masculinity. As Pugsley (2010, 173) comments:

> The state's involvement in negotiating masculinity was first modeled in former Prime Minister Lee Kuan Yew's image of an idealised Singaporean male based on 'Victorian gentlemanly codes as well as neo-Confucian patriarchal ideals' leading to a privileging of ethnic Chinese on the island and a 'Sinicization of Singaporean masculinity' (Khoo 2004).

In fact, Khoo (2004, 2) notes that 'Mr Lee's claim to Singaporean nationality was based in his own words as a "half-Peranakan Chinese, middle-class English-colonial-educated man".'

The incorporation of masculinity within the concept of national identity is thus reflected in the fact that homosexuality is illegal in Singapore. Pugsley (2010, 175) maintains: 'Contemporary Singaporean nationalism is shaped by an almost unanimous quest to create and maintain the appearance of economic and cultural superiority in the region, reinforced by government campaigns such as those of pitching Singapore as a cosmopolitan "Renaissance City" (MITA 2000).'

One of the ways in which Singapore aimed to stay ahead in the growth of a neoliberal environment was what Ong (2004, 178) describes as an 'ecosystem of technical interconnectedness and intellectual capital'. This involved integrating foreign professionals and citizens so that the integration of talent could produce higher levels of creativity and productivity.

The Singapore state understood that 'foreign talent' expected a more liberal cultural environment in which to live and work, and began to craft one in response. Pugsley (2010, 176) shows how this process was implemented:

> The state's 2003 Censorship Review Committee recommended the adoption of a 'tripartite formula' that included regulators but signaled a shift in state attitudes. The CRC conceded that 'a greater leeway should be accorded to depiction of non-exploitative sex and nudity targeting adults' (CRC 2003, 53). Thus it called for a lifting of the longstanding bans on *Cosmopolitan* magazine and the controversial US TV program *Sex and the City* on the proviso that there were 'suitable distribution channels' put in place. This meant, respectively the sale of *Cosmopolitan* in a sealed plastic bag and the TV program being confined to late-night broadcasts. However this 'leeway' did not extend to publications such as *Playboy*, with the CRC stating that 'our community is not ready for the liberal use of sexually explicit photographs' (CRC 2003, 53).

Despite this, attitudes toward sex and sexuality were still 'prudish', as Pugsley (2010, 177) observes:

> The MDA's Content Guidelines for Imported Publications (2009) uses the category of 'Adult Interest Lifestyle Magazines' and under its ruling on magazine cover pages, section H (2), states that:
> 'Covers should be appropriate for public display and must not feature nudity, sexual positions or sexually-provocative texts. The following are not allowed:
>
> (i) Models in sexually suggestive poses that are excessively revealing e.g. appearing naked with breasts and/or genitals covered by hands.
> (ii) Models in see-through clothes which reveal pubic hair, genitalia or women's nipples.
> (iii) Promotion of alternative lifestyles or deviant sexual practices.'

More broadly the significance of Asian designers, models and fashion has given Asian subjectivities a much higher profile in terms of a neoliberal cosmopolitan culture. In particular, the use of ethnic Chinese male models in the fashion industry contributes to a more flexible attitude to masculinity, and as Chen (2002, 317) notes, it provides a more accurate picture of masculinity where 'meanings of masculinities have shifted to reflect the growing engagement with a market economy and consumer culture'.

Given the foregoing, there is little doubt that there are significant tensions involved, as Holden (2001, 403) notes, in the 'production of an Asian modernity which lives "uncomfortably" with capitalism'. This concept of modernity is linked to Lee Kuan Yew's vision of Singapore and the 'determination to avoid creating a "soft" society' (ibid., 410). As Ling (1999, 283–4) notes, this can result in a move toward 'hypermasculinity'.

Thus, despite a greater tolerance being shown by the state in Singapore toward sexuality and sexual diversity, particularly in acknowledging the importance of the 'pink dollar' in terms of consumption, Singapore and its baseline population remains a conservative, staid and somewhat homophobic society. And on occasion, this can lead to public outcries over what might be seen as the promotion of homosexuality.

A recent example of this was documented in an article in the *Straits Times* (Wong 2013c), which highlighted the ongoing prejudices. The article outlines the response of some in the Singapore community to a concert by the gay singer Adam Lambert that was held in a performing center owned by a local church. The National Council of Churches in Singapore (NCCS) received numerous complaints about Lambert's concert along the lines of: 'the gay lifestyle may be promoted at the concert, and that concert venue is owned by a church'. Lambert had previously performed at Resorts World Sentosa in 2010 and at the Formula One Grand Prix at the Padang in 2011 without any problems.

The issue is one, according to the authorities, of 'public decency' and falls under the remit of the Media Development Authority (MDA), who attempt to balance complaints from conservative society with a liberalization of the arts to reflect the requirements of a cosmopolitan population. As Wong (2013c, 25) comments:

> This is not the first time that 'Christians' have raised concerns about a pop concert in recent months. The MDA previously met with the NCCS and Live Singapore, a network of 100 churches, about Lady Gaga's concert in May last year. It is understood that they have raised concerns over how she may have insulted Christians and promoted homosexuality at her concert.

A spokesperson for the MDA (quoted in the article) stated that the agency frequently receives feedback that helps the MDA ensure events 'are in line with community standards and protect the young from undesirable content while allowing consumers to make more informed decisions' (Wong 2013c, 25). This statement begs the question of whether the MDA's regulatory policy is being determined by the more vocal and right-wing elements of Singapore society.

The Adam Lambert example can be seen as a case of relatively 'indiscreet' consumption not least because Lambert himself as a performer is openly gay and has been active in pushing for the advancement of gay rights. Thus, there was no ambiguity as to the fact that there was a 'gay element' involved, which meant that deniability was not an option. The only reasonable position open to those pushing for the concert was to argue that Lambert's sexuality was incidental to the concert. However, this was a rather difficult position to maintain for two reasons. One, some of the songs that he was going to perform were about his personal life. So, while the concert was allowed to go on, the MDA did issue an advisory (Salimat 2013): 'On Wednesday, the MDA gave the concert an advisory rating for those 16 and above. It also gave the advice that it will have "some mature content" as it will feature two songs of which the lyrics are based on the singer's personal experience and lifestyle.' Two, an Adam Lambert headline concert – already a highly public event – was therefore seen as endorsing not only the gay lifestyle but also catering to the local gay community, and perhaps even influencing those who might be as yet unsure about their sexuality. What added to the controversy was the fact that the concert was to be held at a venue owned by a church, albeit by the church's business arm. Nevertheless, this raised concerns among some individuals that the church was compromising its religious values, even as others saw this as a purely business decision (Salimat 2013).

In another example, Hirokazu Mizuhara, a former marketing manager at *Harper's Bazaar* in Beijing, decided to launch a magazine aimed at gay Asian males. The magazine, *Element*, is being published by Singapore-based independent media company Epic Media. According to Low (2013):

> A local publisher has launched a magazine solely targeting gay men and advertisers that are reaching for the pink dollar. *Element* magazine will cover topics such as fashion, fitness, sex and relationship as well as personality interviews which is aimed at being more relevant to them than other mainstream men's lifestyle journals, said a note in its press release. Current advertisers already on board are fashion brand Paul Smith, local nightspot Avalon, Small Luxury Hotel Group and underwear brand Private Structure.

Significantly, the magazine will only be available online in order to avoid licensing restrictions (Mahtani 2013):

> The bi-monthly magazine will only be available online through the Apple and Android application stores. The application is free, but each issue will cost US$1.99 [...]
>
> *Element* is working around media rules in Singapore. Print magazines distributed in the city-state require a license through the government's Media Development Authority, which regulates and censors media content. The online world, by comparison, is regulated with a 'light touch', circumventing many of the same license applications mandatory in printed content.
>
> The website is also hosted in the US, meaning it is not subject to Singapore's 'codes of practice' regulating locally hosted websites.

Element is somewhat different from the Lambert concert because there is an explicit interest in promoting and catering to the gay lifestyle. No issues of deniability or ambiguity arise here, and precisely because of this the founders of the magazine were all too aware that the odds were against them had they tried to establish the magazine by the 'traditional' route of mainstream media: the licensing authorities would have likely rejected the application and the backlash from society in general would have been difficult to avoid. The attempt to be relatively discreet motivated the strategy of founding the magazine online, since even its potential base of interested readers might be uncomfortable buying a hard copy of the magazine in the unlikely event that stores in Singapore actually agreed to carry such a magazine (Mahtani 2013):

> But social disapproval of homosexuality in Singapore – and the chilling effect that has on gay people – also plays a role in the magazine's decision to stick to online.
>
> 'Not many gay men would pick up a copy of a magazine like this on a newsstand – that's just the culture here', Mr Mizuhara said.

The difficulties faced by both the state as well as the gay community in negotiating appropriate levels and forms of discreet consumption make it useful to compare the situation in Singapore with a number of other cities where there is little or no need for discreet consumption, including San Francisco and Stockholm. We turn to this in the next section, but first we chart the history of gay culture and city life in a number of cities in the West and Asia.

Gay Culture and City Life

Some writers have maintained that urbanization is 'a precondition to the emergence of a significant gay subculture' (Sibalis 1999, 2001). Sibalis traces their emergence in Paris and shows that it has in fact been a gay capital since the 1700s (see also Merrick and Ragan 1996; Merrick and Sibalis 2001). A number of other writers have also highlighted the relationship between homosexuality and city life. Kenney's (2001) book on urban development in Los Angeles, entitled *Mapping Gay LA: The Intersection of Place and Politics*, focuses on what she argues is 'the greatest hidden chapter in American gay and lesbian history' (7). She maintains that a combination of factors – including among others the pronounced impact of Hollywood, the influence of West Hollywood in particular as a largely gay area, and the provision of gay-related social services – contribute to LA as a gay city.

Sydney has long been seen as a gay city, and Aldrich (2004, 1729) maintains that, based on a heritage of male colonial and criminal migration, by the 1980s Sydney was seen as something of a gay mecca. Aldrich cites Faro's (2000) book *Street Seen: A History of Oxford Street*, which focuses on the gay precinct as significant in Sydney's cultural and historical development:

> First an Aboriginal pathway, Oxford Street became the main conduit from the colonial city centre to the Pacific Ocean. A thoroughfare by the mid 19th century, it was also the location of a jail and a barracks, and a developing reputation for dissident groups. The opening of department stores attracted shoppers, while busy commercial activities and inexpensive housing brought in office-workers, labourers and bohemians, as well as

Mediterraneans, Chinese and other 'ethnic' residents. Already at the end of the 1800s, numerous pubs catered for male drinkers, a Turkish *hammam* hosted homoerotic dalliances and newspapers caricatured 'sissy' shop assistants. In the 1970s, with sex-on-premises venues and gay emporia, Oxford Street remained Sydney's 'golden gay mile' (Aldrich 2004, 1729).

Apart from Sydney, South American – particularly Brazilian – cities have also been popular gay cultural sites (see Higgs 1999). Green (1999) traces an identifiable gay culture in Rio back to the late nineteenth century, showing how homosexuals have invested in the city and how its gay carnival has become the benchmark for those in other cities. Gay life has also been combined with other cultural traditions in South Africa, particularly in Cape Town.

Aldrich also shows that it is not only Western but also Asian cities that provide a distinctive cultural environment for gay culture. He identifies Bangkok as particularly tolerant of gay culture for tourists who frequent 'boybars', gay cabarets and saunas. Within cities such as Bangkok, Buddhism provides a tolerant environment of sexual desire for homosexuals; Thai law is liberal and does not criminalize same-sex acts, unlike Singapore, which has had a far less open attitude historically to gay culture. As Aldrich (2004, 1729) shows:

> In the 1950s, transvestite prostitutes frequented the infamous Bugis Street, but with its transformation into the powerhouse of south-east Asia, Singapore exchanged a reputation as a city of sin for a button-down image. The first gay bar in Singapore opened in the late 1970s. [...] Homosexual acts remain criminal, and a 'don't ask, don't tell' rule prevails but Singaporeans have developed a quietly active gay culture.

We explore some of these developments in the next section.

Singapore, San Francisco and Stockholm

In this section we draw comparisons between three cities that provide interesting contrasts in terms of the politics of inclusivity. Singapore's 'Pink Dot' movement is just 5 years old and clearly popular with the young in Singapore. Nevertheless, there are still significant differences in the approaches of Singapore, San Francisco and Stockholm to gay politics and lifestyle.

We have seen how in Singapore there is a need for discreet consumption, ambiguity and deniability, given the political and social sensitivities that have to be respected despite the push for global city status. San Francisco, of course, represents a significant contrast given that city's proud status as a gay mecca, a status that is socially, culturally and politically embraced. But precisely because of the strong and open support for a gay lifestyle, we find little to none of the trust–risk dynamic that might otherwise inform the relationship between the residents of San Francisco and that of the local city government. Likewise, consumption activities in San Francisco, unlike Singapore, have no need to be concerned with discretion, ambiguity or deniability. However, we will also see that San Francisco is not without problems of its own. Most notably, it is trying hard not to lose its identity as a 'gay mecca', especially since the demise of DOMA (Defense of Marriage Act) and of Proposition 8 (a California ballot proposition, ultimately ruled unconstitutional, created by opponents of same-sex marriage) in June 2013. From the perspective of second-order reflexivity, Singapore and San Francisco make for interesting comparisons. This is because, whereas the former is trying to inch its way toward a reputation as a city that is 'gay friendly', the latter is struggling to maintain its reputation as a 'gay mecca'.

We have noted in the case of Singapore that gay tourists and gay locals are encouraged to enjoy themselves in Singapore so long as this is done in a discreet manner that does not make the more conservative segments of society uncomfortable. In both these cases – casinos and attitudes to the gay community – the state is therefore attempting to regulate consumer behavior, albeit in different ways. Locals are encouraged to exercise restraint in the case of the casinos, leaving these as far as possible to foreigners. In the case of the 'pink dollar', both locals and foreigners are asked to pursue their activities with consideration for more conservative elements.

By contrast, California – San Francisco in particular – has long been a focal point for gay lifestyles and consumers. In fact San Francisco is sometimes considered 'the gay capital of the world'. Much has been written about gay culture in San Francisco (see Stryker and van Kuskirk 1996; Leyland 2002). Boyd (2003) charts the history of 'queer' San Francisco to the nineteenth century and maintains that San Francisco was a 'queer town' because sex and lawlessness were part of the city's history, a product of the city's location on the Pacific frontier as well as the 1849 Gold Rush and the process of migration and explosion of wealth that followed.

Armstrong (2002; cited in Aldrich 2004, 1727) looks at the interrelationship of gay culture and politics in San Francisco, particularly in the election of the openly gay Harvey Milk to the city council in 1977. She charts 'the transformation of an underground sub-culture into a culturally vibrant, politically ambitious, organizationally complex gay identity movement'. The Castro district of San Francisco is a largely gay area and is seen as an important element of diversity in the city and state's policies on gay lifestyles and rights. Gays have always held prominent positions on the city legislature. For example, San Francisco supervisor Harvey Milk, a longtime gay activist in the Castro, was assassinated by fellow supervisor Dan White, who also shot and killed Mayor George Moscone on

27 November 1978. The city of San Francisco continues to have various services and organizations all devoted to gay issues. There are also openly gay politicians serving on the city's Board of Supervisors. Moreover, in 2011 the state senate approved legislation that would require California's public schools to include gay history in social studies lessons. The legislation leaves it up to local school districts to decide what to include in the lessons and at what grade students would receive them. In addition, the annual gay pride parade – a proud San Franciscan tradition – continues to attract thousands of people to the city.

Nevertheless, the high costs of living, especially housing, have made it almost impossible for San Francisco to continue to be a viable destination for many gays, especially those from other parts of America or from migrant populations (see Brooks and Simpson 2012). Precisely because of this, and given the increasingly middle-class nature of the gay community in San Francisco, the issue of the extent to which San Francisco can continue to legitimately and plausibly lay claim to the label 'gay mecca' or 'gay haven' has been fully acknowledged by both the city's government and its highly vocal and educated residents, and the implications for the identity of the city as 'gay friendly' have been widely debated. The recent decision challenging Proposition 8 in California is key to understanding the economic and political value of the 'pink dollar'. It was somewhat surprising that California's Proposition 8 ban on same-sex marriage was ever raised let alone passed. Proposition 8 has just been challenged in the Supreme Court and the challenge is supported by President Obama and the federal government. The case being brought to the Supreme Court goes further than simply challenging Proposition 8 and asserts a claim for full equality for gay and lesbian Americans. Proposition 8 is being overthrown as we complete this book, and this will have significant impact on lifestyle issues in San Francisco, which is likely to become even more popular among the gay community. In fact, the overthrowing of DOMA and the demise of Proposition 8 has been followed by a series of high-profile marriages among gays in San Francisco and Los Angeles. While there is no direct request for constitutional change in the marriage laws, this is a significant step in challenging equal rights under the constitution (Socarides 2013). Again, from the perspective of second-order reflexivity, the public image of California, and San Francisco in particular, as 'gay friendly' is taking a beating when compared with other states in the US that have already legalized same-sex marriages, such as Connecticut, Iowa, Maine, Maryland, New York, Vermont and Washington, as well as the District of Columbia (Sherman 2013).

Given the rising level of gay activism in Singapore that we noted above, we can expect that many gay Singaporeans will undoubtedly follow the US government's case with interest. As things stand, Singapore's former chief justice Chan Sek Keong has noted that the 'global growth of lesbian, gay, bisexual and transgender (LGBT) communities has not left Singapore untouched and this is a new challenge the country must face. […] The needs and interests of this community must be addressed' (Vijayan 2013). The growth of gay activism in Singapore might even be expected to gain momentum if a recent study is correct in suggesting that Singaporeans and permanent residents are becoming more tolerant of gays and lesbians. According to a study conducted by the Nanyang Technological University in Singapore, 'while attitudes remain sharply polarized, they have shifted slightly to become a little more favorable over a five-year period from 2005' (Channel News Asia 2013). These developments have the potential, in the medium-to-long term, to make it easier for the state to become even more open in its tolerance of the gay community and its lifestyle and consumption activities. Although highly unlikely, it may be possible to even imagine Singapore one day posing a serious alternative to San Francisco for 'gay haven' status – a possibility that as recently as ten years ago would have been completely unimaginable.

Perhaps occupying a position somewhere between Singapore and San Francisco is Stockholm. Stockholm certainly veers closer to San Francisco in being gay friendly, and since 1998 it has hosted Stockholm Pride, which is often considered Scandinavia's largest pride festival. But unlike San Francisco's Castro district, Stockholm has no gay-specific enclave, even though many gay-friendly bars and restaurants can be found in the districts of Sodermalm and Gamla Stan (Old Town). Stockholm's gay scene has also been described as being 'not a heaven for cruising in saunas or clubs, but it is a relaxed and pleasant place for socializing in tasteful gay and gay-friendly cafes, restaurants and clubs' (Patroc 2013). This relatively low-key approach arguably places Stockholm closer to Singapore's preference for discreet consumption, although of course the hotels and bars in Stockholm are much more open about being gay friendly than those in Singapore. Significantly, in what is clearly a competitive city-scale attempt to bring in the pink dollar, Stockholm has been holding a 'Pink Christmas Week' in addition to Stockholm Pride, which is held during the summer. For the 2013 iteration of Pink Christmas Week, the Stockholm Visitors Board and Visit Sweden have been working together with Pink Christmas to organize a contest in order to 'attract even more international LGBT visitors to Sweden's capital city' (Thompson 2013).

Competition for the pink dollar would appear to be intensifying. It thus remains to be seen what further initiatives and collaborations other cities around the world – Singapore and San Francisco included – might introduce and what implications for the regulation of consumption such introductions might have. In other words, as cities around the world aim to turn pink, the trick lies in ensuring that their more conservative residents do not see red.

Chapter 9

STATES AS 'MIDWIVES' TO CITIES: COSMOPOLITANISM, CITIZENSHIP AND CONSUMPTION IN THE MODERN STATE

Introduction

In this concluding chapter, we consider more generally the relationship between states and cities – not just global cities. Our discussion brings together the themes of cosmopolitanism, citizenship and consumption that have been the organizing rubrics in the preceding chapters, and highlights at least one important way that the state continues to function as an important 'midwife' to globalization (as per Sassen's remarks; see Chapter 1). As different cities attempt to establish their own identities in ways that make them attractive not just to their own residents but to potential future residents and investments, it becomes useful to ask just what kinds of roles states can or should play in facilitating these goals. In this way, our concluding discussion fills an important gap in current debates in urban studies concerning the roles played by cities, creative classes and dispersion models (Florida 2005; Kotkin 2010; Sassen 2001a, 2001b), which have not given sufficient attention to the dialectical relationship between cities and states.

As we have already noted, Singapore is fortunate in that, as a city-state, the state faces relatively fewer problems in being a 'midwife' to the city, at least where problems of scale are concerned. But more often than not this is clearly not the case, and states and cities are not generally coterminous. Therefore, by placing our discussion of Singapore in a comparative perspective with data from other cities, a more nuanced appreciation of the relationship between cities and states emerges. In developing this comparison, we take as our point of departure Wright's (2009) notion of 'real utopias'. All city or state planning is utopian to the extent that some vision of the 'good society' is involved. We suggest that a consideration of value ecology, unit scale and developmental trajectory can help to distinguish realistic utopias from unrealistic ones.

By value ecology, we refer to the fact that utopian thinking necessarily involves highlighting particular values that social actors are committed to (such as the desire to eradicate poverty, or to eliminate racial or sexual discrimination). Any attempt to effect social change based on these highlighted values will need to address their relationships to other values (e.g., the relationship between poverty and capitalism or between sexual diversity and more conservative mores). By unit scale, we refer to the unit of planning. This can in principle range in size from the relatively small (e.g., the family) to something intermediate (e.g., the neighborhood, the city) to something much larger (e.g., the nation, the world). Last but not least, by developmental trajectory, we refer to the question of how the utopian vision is to be achieved. Does some form of 'revolutionary transformation' (Wright 2009, i) have to be involved? Our key argument in this chapter is that it is at the city scale where social ideals about the kinds of society that ought to be aimed for can find the greatest purchase.

Distinguishing between Realistic and Unrealistic Utopias

A sociological investigation into 'real utopias' (Wright 2009) requires some means of distinguishing between realistic and unrealistic utopias. The anchoring in reality means that realistic utopias have to cope with the tensions that arise when there are competing visions of the 'good society'. Even assuming that there is some consensus about the substance of this vision, there is yet the question of how such a vision is to be realized. Finally, this entire enterprise is further complicated by the inevitability of social change, so that the utopian vision, if it is to remain grounded in reality, has to be constantly renegotiated in relation to a variety of dynamic factors that could include, among other things, the effects of social diversity (including migration and an ageing population), the scarcity of resources and changing social attitudes (including the potential loss of enchantment with the utopian vision itself).

Realistic utopias are therefore asymptotes. They are visions that are constantly and necessarily deferred. Even where alternatives to the status quo have been outlined, agreed upon and subsequently made manifest, newer alternatives (or at the very least minor adjustments) are always going to be needed because the status quo is never static. All of which make the identification of realistic utopias particularly challenging.

We mentioned above Wright's claim that the realization of utopian visions involves 'revolutionary transformation'. But just how revolutionary is 'revolutionary'? For individuals invested in the status quo, relatively minor changes might already be perceived as 'too much' and/or 'too fast'.

This question is critical, since only unrealistic utopias have the luxury of focusing exclusively on the desired end state. In contrast, realistic utopias have to ask how getting 'there' is possible given the constraints imposed by the existing state of affairs.

We illustrate the conceptual and empirical relevance of these notions – value ecology, unit scale and developmental trajectory – by returning to our discussion of the management of same-sex relations in Singapore, Stockholm and San Francisco, as well as other cities (see Chapter 8). We stress that we are by no means suggesting that Singapore, Stockholm or San Francisco are utopias, realistic or otherwise. Singapore is, however, interesting and relevant to our discussion because it is by and large recognized as a place where the quality of life is good (Mauzy and Milne 2002, 2), though it is markedly ambivalent in its attitudes toward homosexuality (see Chapter 8). The situation in Singapore contrasts usefully with that of Stockholm, where its LGBT festival has been described as 'the largest Pride celebration in Scandinavia' (Stockholm Visitors Board 2013), and that of San Francisco, a city that has been described as a 'gay mecca'. We also consider how the role of the Mardi Gras and Mardi Gras tourism in Sydney has contributed to making Sydney an international gay and lesbian city (Markwell 2002).

However, there are concerns, even in Stockholm, about hate crimes against gays (Tiby 2001). And in San Francisco there are concerns that the high cost of living is making it difficult for gays to live there (Rapaport 2011). But as we have seen, all three cities have reasons, albeit different ones, for wanting to be seen as 'gay friendly'. And each faces different problems in this regard.

We organize our discussion as follows. In the next section, we describe the situations in Singapore and San Francisco vis-à-vis the management of same-sex relations. This comparative approach allows us to discuss the notion of realistic utopias by concretely grounding the relevance of value ecology, unit scale and developmental trajectory. At the same time, an appreciation of the considerations involved requires that we move on toward a consideration of 'alternative institutions and structures' (Wright 2011), which we do toward the end of the chapter.

Managing Same-Sex Relations in Singapore, Sydney, Stockholm and San Francisco

As we have shown in this book, the Singapore state's attempt to re-present Singapore as a global city arises from its conviction that positioning Singapore as a major player as various cities compete for the attention of globally mobile individuals and major investors is the only way to ensure the city's continued economic growth. It is also motivated by the state's acceptance of the fact that many Singaporeans are traveling, working abroad and even emigrating. The state thus hopes to attract talented foreigners as potential new citizens, to replace those Singaporeans who may decide to emigrate permanently.

This rebranding has led to Singapore legalizing casinos (which had been banned for many years; see Chapters 6 and 7), mainly in order to make sure that it remains attractive to international tourism. The legalizing of casinos has already attracted some controversy, with claims that the state is putting the need for economic growth over and above the need to protect families from the problems associated with gambling addiction. Even more controversial is the potential liberalization of Singapore's attitude toward homosexuality, mainly in the name of pursuing the 'pink dollar' (Chapter 8). That is, Singapore 'wants to be seen as the kind of tolerant, vibrant, forward-thinking place that is attractive to professionals and entrepreneurs, regardless of their sexual preference, but, [gay] activists contend, its stance on gay sex sends a signal that it is a stilted environment' (Prystay 2007). For example, consensual sex between men still remains illegal, although the state has tried to downplay the possibility of actual prosecution. In fact, in 2003, the then prime minister Goh Chok Tong was quoted as saying that homosexuals 'are like you and me' and that gays are allowed to work in the civil service (Agence France Presse, 14 September 2003).

These apparent shows of tolerance are, however, mixed with events that continue to create wariness in the gay community. Thus, in 2004, Fridae.com (a gay-oriented company) was denied a license to hold a rave party because it was deemed to be against public interest. This was despite the fact that such parties had been allowed in the previous three years, attracting a large number of gay tourists. This means that even though there are many gay clubs and bars, these operate underground. A gay graduate student, Sam Chan, was quoted as saying (Agence France Presse, 14 September 2003):

'Being gay in Singapore is an underground business where things are spread by word of mouth, but with the proliferation of the Internet, you get to know about gay-friendly clubs and restaurants' […].
    He said he has many foreign friends 'who think it is getting exciting here' and locals can finally find shops that cater to their needs.

Thus, the main problem for Singapore in its pursuit of the pink dollar is the state's ambivalence about the gay lifestyle. And this ambivalence has in fact deterred some gay individuals and even companies from setting up businesses in Singapore. Perhaps most famously, Sir Ian McKellan was apparently distraught to learn about Singapore's antigay laws when he arrived in 2007 to perform in the Royal Shakespeare Company's production of *King Lear*. He was quoted as saying, 'Had I known what the law was, I would have said to the Royal Shakespeare Company "What are you doing sending me to a country that thinks my private behavior is a criminal activity?"' (Prystay 2007).

The problem for the state, as we have seen, is that there are more conservative citizens and religious groups who are uncomfortable with Singapore's cosmopolitanism, especially if this is seen to be undermining more traditional 'Asian values' and identity. It would therefore not be easy for the state to adopt an openly gay-friendly stance, since this would be seen as undermining a commitment to these 'Asian values' and would probably cause controversy and unease among the more conservative segments of the population. One example of this unease can be seen in the recent decision by the Singapore National Parks Board to honor the singer Elton John by naming an orchid after him (Toh 2011):

> He promptly asked his partner David Furnish and their baby boy Zachary up on stage to share the honour. [...] The musician joins a list of more than 100 heads of state, dignitaries and celebrities who have orchids named after them. The plants are housed in the VIP section of the National Orchid Garden at the Singapore Botanic Gardens.

This led to the following letter protesting the move (Tay 2011):

> I read with disappointment that Elton John has been given the honour of having an orchid named after him. [...] I am dismayed that his partner David Furnish and their adopted son Zachary [...] were also publicized to 'share his honour'. [...] Is homosexuality to be openly encouraged and endorsed by the Government?

Singapore, despite the ambivalence toward homosexuality, has an enviable reputation for safety. In this regard, hate crimes are rare to nonexistent. Stockholm, too, is a generally safe city and is also clearly much more gay friendly than Singapore. But despite this, gays in Stockholm do worry that an open approach toward pursuing their lifestyle can lead them to being targeted for violence. Thus, Tiby (2001) notes that there are different rates of victimization that correlate with being open about one's sexual identity and frequenting nightlife activities that are clearly associated with the pursuit of a gay lifestyle. For example, in 2008, a gay couple was attacked by three men, with one of them being stabbed in the stomach. The Stockholm police investigated the attack as a hate crime (*Pink News*, 28 July 2008).

Hate crimes, too, are a cause for concern in San Francisco. But more recently, unlike Singapore, which is trying to inch its way toward a city that is 'gay friendly', San Francisco has been struggling to maintain its reputation as a 'gay mecca'. For example, the city has various services and organizations all devoted to gay issues (Rapaport 2011). These include a fertility center for 'alternative families', a center for gay youths, counseling services, centers for advancing transgender rights, and a professional development group for lesbians. There are also openly gay politicians serving on the city's Board of Supervisors. Nevertheless, the high costs of living, especially housing, have made it almost impossible for San Francisco to continue to be a viable destination for gays hoping to sink roots. Rapaport quotes Jeff Sheehy, a gay activist, as saying:

> I do worry because of the affordability issue, that we're losing the regeneration of the more dynamic elements of the queer community: the young, the marginalized, and the disenfranchised, for which San Francisco was always a beacon. [...] The economy is not diverse enough to support people just showing up here to try and make a go of it. There's not a lot of lower-middle-income jobs in San Francisco. Housing – off the charts. So the economics have robbed the city of that.

Echoing a similar concern, Doan (2011, 1) observes that:

> Although the Castro District in San Francisco remains a big visible gay neighborhood (gayborhood) for those who can afford to live there, high property values and rents have made living, working, and organizing in the area difficult for many in the LGBT community. In addition, the desirability of this gentrified space means many upper middle class people who do not identify as gay are moving into the neighborhood.

Sydney also has a history of gay culture (see Chapter 8) as well as some dark aspects of past repressive tendencies that have seemingly been overcome in the aggressive marketing of the city as a center of gay tourism, particularly through the role of the Mardi Gras. As Markwell (2002, 94) comments:

> The changes in the nature of the Mardi Gras parade and in its social and political milieu are evident in the relations between the state and Mardi Gras. [...] In recent years members of the Police Service have marched in the parade along with the boys' and girls' marching bands, the leather queens, and a multitude of other individuals and groups.

This change in relations can also be seen in promotion of Mardi Gras by tourism marketing boards at both the federal and state levels of government.

In fact the role of the Mardi Gras has grown well beyond being just a gay tourist attraction, and attracts more tourists than any other event as well as attracting significant corporate and government sponsorship. It has significantly contributed toward the identification of Sydney as a world-class gay and lesbian city with an economy based on consumption and leisure.

The identification of the Mardi Gras as an international festival and of Sydney as a gay and lesbian city can be seen in the way the Mardi Gras is marketed overseas. Mardi Gras packages are advertised in the gay and lesbian press in European and North American cities. In terms of the implications for consumption locally, some maintain that the 'professionalization' of the Mardi Gras board has led to the disenfranchisement of working-class, suburban gays as well as gays and lesbians of color.

Beyond the corporate dimension of the role of the Mardi Gras in consumption is the iconography afforded by the Mardi Gras for the gay community in Sydney. As Markwell (2002, 85) states: 'Mardi Gras has been pivotal in the increasing visibility of gay and lesbian imagery and cultures in Australia, as well as playing a significant role in the social construction of gay and lesbian identities. Mardi Gras today occupies a central position in Australian popular culture.' Thus, despite the corporatization of gay tourism in Sydney, and while homosexuals have been actively engaged in 'place making' in Sydney since the late nineteenth century (see Wotherspoon 1991), the Mardi Gras has been important in the internationalization of Sydney as a gay city.

Singapore, Sydney, Stockholm and San Francisco all have reasons for wanting to be seen as friendly to homosexuals, the former as part of its admittedly more pragmatic strategy to be recognized as a global city so as to sustain economic growth, the latter two because they take pride in their heritage as cities that do not discriminate against homosexuals and in fact actively welcome them. At the same time, Singapore, Stockholm and San Francisco face rather different kinds of problems in their respective attempts to achieve their goals. This leads us to the notion of value ecology.

Value Ecology

Because utopian visions involve some notion of the 'good society', there is an ethical dimension that is being appealed to here, a belief that things can and should be done differently from the status quo. This points to the influence of what Ong (2006, 22; emphasis added) has described as 'ethical regimes' (see also Chapter 1):

> An ethical regime can therefore be construed as a style of living guided by given values for *constituting oneself* in line with a particular ethical goal. Religions – and, I would argue, feminism, humanitarianism, and other schemes of virtue – are ethical regimes fostering particular forms of self-conduct and visions of the good life.

In addition to the ethical regimes mentioned by Ong, other examples might include concerns for the environment, animal welfare and respect for sexual diversity. Thus, to the extent that individuals identify with specific ethical regimes, they are likely to want to be able to pursue a style of living that is consistent with these regimes. Ethical regimes are relevant to the study of utopias because it is clear that individuals will have significant differences of opinion as to what specific ethical regimes are worth valorizing. Even when there is agreement on which ethical regimes are important, there may still be disagreements about how to prioritize different ethical regimes in the face of limited resources. However, utopian visions not only involve a sense of how the self ought to live, but also expectations about the conduct and values of surrounding others as well. Hence, it is important to understand ethical regimes as one part of what we mean by value ecology, which more broadly corresponds to the extent to which value expectations regarding various dimensions of social life are shared or not.

Most people are concerned with redressing specific dimensions rather than wanting the society they live in to change wholesale. That is, there are likely to be aspects of the status quo that they want to preserve while still hoping to see changes to other aspects. But different people will have in mind different values. And this brings up the question of which aspect(s) of the status quo to keep and which to change, and also how to reconcile the relationships between different values. For Singapore, the problem lies in reconciling greater tolerance of homosexuality with Asian conservatism. Singapore's tolerance of the gay community arises from a more pragmatic or instrumental orientation – that is, the desire to be seen as a global city in order to ensure continued economic growth. But while its citizens are generally keen for economic growth to continue, a more conservative segment is concerned that this comes at a price, where traditional values are compromised and homosexuality encouraged. In contrast, a more liberal and even activist segment sees the greater tolerance of homosexuality as a positive development.

For Stockholm, the problem lies in maintaining its image as a liberal and welcoming city that does not discriminate against different ethnicities or sexual orientations. The difficulty for Stockholm is exacerbated because it also wants to be seen as welcoming of migrants, especially those seeking asylum from human rights abuses in their home countries. And for at least members of the gay community, the Stockholm police are seen as 'queerphobic', partly because they play key roles in identifying and deporting 'queer refugees' and partly because their interactions with members of the gay community seem to display a lack of sensitivity toward gender identification preferences – for example, addressing some transgendered individuals as 'girls' when the preference of these individuals is for the male gender (*Struggles in Sweden*, 8 August 2013). The issue of migration and its intersection with discrimination against sexual identities/orientations is one that can be expected gain in significance, not just for Stockholm but for other cities and states within the European Union. This is because of a recent ruling by the European Court of Justice that a 'credible threat of imprisonment for homosexuality' constituted grounds for asylum (Eyal 2013):

> The verdict will have an immediate effect on asylum applications from mainly African citizens now before the national immigration authorities of the EU's 28 member states, with the exception of Denmark which has opted out of the justice mechanism. But, over time, it may also affect asylum applications from all nations where homosexuality is still deemed a criminal act.

For San Francisco, in contrast, the problem lies in reconciling its desire to continue to be welcoming to gays while also remaining business friendly. The first goal requires making sure that even those individuals who are not financially affluent, particularly young people from other parts of America who identify as gay, will find the city an affordable place in which to live. The second goal, on the other hand, requires being open to the vagaries of the free market and acknowledging that, if left unchecked, this may result in the city having a social demographic of predominantly financially affluent and established individuals, who may or may not identify as gay. This would arguably leave San Francisco's (historical) commitment to the gay community either considerably diluted or lost entirely.

Unit Scale

By unit scale, we refer to the particular unit that is the object of utopian thinking. Smaller units tend to understand that the success of realizing their utopian visions depends on the ability to segment themselves away from other units, whether at the same or different scale. For example, in M. Night

Shyamalan's movie *The Village* (2004), the founders of a village attempt to sustain its preindustrial lifestyle by relying on the presence of a large forest to keep the world 'outside' at bay. As the scale of the unit grows to become more all-encompassing, the issue of boundary maintenance may be less of a concern. Rather, proponents of a utopian vision that is larger in scale may then be engaged in trying to break down the boundaries set up by those whose interests lie with units that are smaller in scale.

The fact that individuals have different value commitments means that conflicts are unavoidable, although some of these conflicts become more pressing depending on the scale involved. We suggest that it is at the level of the city where the need to manage the normative demands of different value ecologies becomes not only most salient but also perhaps most tractable. In short, given the complexities of today's world, the most realistic scale at which utopian thinking ought to be geared is that of the city, including even the so-called megacity (Mitlin and Satterthwaite 1994; see also Liddle and Moavenzadeh 2002, 2). As Amen et al. (2011, 3; emphasis added) observe:

> Cities are one site where formal government occurs – where the reins and instruments of public policy are held. But they are also sites for the intersection of governance and government in the everyday lives of *people who employ their ideas about ways of seeing the world to move beyond the possible outcomes established by formal governance mechanisms.*

From a slightly different perspective, but making largely the same point, Kotkin (1993, 32, 43) points out that 'global tribes' (i.e., transnational groups that form overseas communities based on ethnic or national affiliation) have typically had to rely on themselves to provide aid and resources to their members rather than depend on the host state, and he goes on to suggest that such tribes fare best when they supplant the power of the state with the more localized authority of the city (257). It is at the city scale, then, that the expectations and hopes of individuals and communities come into contact with the constraints and effects of 'real world' forces such as migration, changing demographics, ageing population, and the need to carefully manage the commitment of resources (manpower, economic capital, fuel, etc.) (Bollens 2007, 233–4). That is, for value ecologies to be sustainable, there is not only a need to balance the (horizontal) relationships between values, but also to manage the (vertical) relationship between values and available resources.

Admittedly, the imperative to attend to the relationships between values and resources is also operative at levels other than the city. But at these other levels, some of the effects are either more easily ignored, and can thus be 'offloaded' to other units, or they are less within the control and management of the unit itself. Consider, for example, a scale below the city, such as that of the neighborhood. Neighborhoods lack sufficient economic clout and independence to realistically sustain a utopian vision. Thus, in Chicago, the neighborhood of Provincetown has relatively affluent and young social preservationists who valorize the idea of local employment and independence from global networks as markers of authenticity about the neighborhood's character and history. But there is a degree of misrecognition going on here, since the preservationists' own ability to romanticize such localized independence is made possible because of their own participation in resources and networks that exist beyond the neighborhood. As Brown-Saracino (2009, 160; emphasis original) observes:

> They romanticize the struggling merchant, the undiscovered artist, and the yeoman farmer. However, they dismiss those who achieve success because their appreciation for independence is rooted in esteem for those *unlike* them and for the mutual in-group *dependence* required of those who face financial struggle, which they take as an indicator of strong ties.

The idea of social preservation constitutes a value where aspects of a place that are considered particularly 'authentic' might be seen as in need of protection from change. But at the level of the neighborhood, such social preservation is achieved by offloading the less 'authentic' features of social life to the levels up the scale – namely, the city and beyond.

Returning to the management of sexual diversity, the issue of an 'authentic' gay neighborhood is certainly pertinent in the case of San Francisco, given that the Castro remains a significant emblem of San Francisco's gay culture. But as we saw earlier, the Castro's increasing gentrification also means that it is in danger of losing its gay identity. More relevant to the issue of unit scale, however, is whether it is necessarily desirable to aim to preserve a specifically gay neighborhood. As Muller Myrdahl (2011, 161–2; citing Fincher and Iveson 2008; and Rankin 2009) points out, while establishing a separate district like a gay village can 'celebrate' marginalized identities, it also does 'little to disrupt existing structural norms and policies that perpetuate enduring inequalities'. In fact, it seems clear that what makes San Francisco a 'gay mecca' goes beyond the Castro itself. It is that the city in general treats homosexuality as a normalized aspect of life so that gay advertisements are relatively unmarked and the celebration of, say, Father's Day routinely acknowledges the diversity of family structures in establishments such as Macy's or the Body Shop.

In the case of Singapore, establishing a specific gay enclave or neighborhood is obviously not an option at all. Such a move would undoubtedly be seen as licensing, if not 'celebrating', the homosexual lifestyle. Singapore itself needs to remain at the relevant scale at which diverse sexual identities are tolerated if not welcomed.

Consider now a scale above the city – say, the nation-state, the region or even the world. The region or the world might be the relevant scale at which Stockholm has to grapple with issue of migration and homosexuality. As we have seen in the discussion above about the European Union's ruling, the issue extends beyond the city and even the Swedish state, covering as it does potentially all members of the EU. And because many of the migrants currently come from Africa, the scale of the issue is really more than just regional. Nation building, however, is a fraught process, and attempts at realizing a societal vision that might even be considered vaguely utopian are confounded by marked disparities in socioeconomic incomes, internal migration from rural to urban areas, and (in some cases) the desire of smaller states/provinces to secede. At the level of the region and beyond, attempts to promote human rights or combat climate change are problematized by an international arrangement where supranational organizations such as the United Nations and other supragovernmental organizations are relatively weak, despite being charged with ensuring that individual states live up to human rights obligations or take active steps to deal with climate change. It would be interesting therefore to see to how well the European Court of Justice's ruling is received and implemented by the member states of the EU in time to come. For now, there is no denying that supragovernmental organizations have had mixed success in getting individual states to deal with human rights issues (Brysk 2002; Mutua 2002). And in the case of climate change, Hoornweg (2011, 93–4) has observed:

> Cities are the most tangible level of government for mediation between the rights of an individual and the aspirations of society. Cities are therefore the essential element of democracy. For example, in most nations over the last decade, the introduction and application of same-sex marriage legislation was catalyzed by cities through issuance of marriage certificates. Well before the Federal Government of the US adopted any formal response to climate change, about 1000 cities signed onto binding legislation for the Kyoto Protocol. Without cities to generate ideals and promote debate, it would be difficult to visualize a democratic society.

It is at the city scale, then, where social ideals about the kinds of society that ought to be aimed for can find greatest purchase. In the construction of realistic utopias, we need to understand 'cities as the place where the business of modern society gets done' (Holston and Appadurai 1999, 3). This by no means suggests that no problems arise at all at the level of the city. To get a better sense of the nature of such problems and how they might be addressed, we need to bring in the notion of developmental trajectory.

Developmental Trajectory

The issue of developmental trajectory highlights the ways in which the utopian vision is to be attained. Utopian visions are of course motivated by a sense of dissatisfaction with the status quo. But moving from the status quo toward the utopian goal presents significant problems, and here it is useful to compare the 'clean slate' approach with one that is more incremental in nature. The former simply aims to eliminate all traces of the status quo in order that things may begin from a 'Year Zero'. An example of this would be the Khmer Rouge, and needless to say, the social and human costs involved are huge and the effects brutal. The latter in contrast takes the status quo as an unavoidable given, and accepts that any trajectory toward the utopian vision may have to be more graduated.

In the case of Singapore, the developmental trajectory – at least where the state is concerned – involves the desire for the city to be seen as cosmopolitan and welcoming of diverse talents (and to a lesser extent, lifestyles). This, Yue (2007, 368) suggests, stems from the government's acceptance of Florida's creative cities thesis, which treats 'diversity of populations' as an indicator of economic productivity (Muller Myrdahl 2011, 158). Under this approach to city planning, 'sexuality becomes "a technology for cultural policy in the creative city": it is a policy from which the city is intended to benefit economically under the guise of an embrace of diversity' (159; citing Yue 2007, 366). Sexual diversity is thus treated simply as the means toward an end, with the assumption that the end will justify the means.

There are two problems here. The first problem is that, from a city planning perspective, the issue of sexual diversity is not properly taken into consideration, due in no small part to the state's own ambivalence. The second problem is that there has been insufficient public discussion between the state and the inhabitants about whether there might be any reservations about the ends and the means. These two problems are related because proper city planning – that is, planning that is sensitive to the needs and aspirations of the inhabitants – requires input from the inhabitants themselves (Kornberger 2012). Doan (2011, 4) gives a good example of how the omission of women from voting rights in the last century and the belief that planning was considered an unsuitable career for women led to the city being constructed as primarily a male space: 'Urban reformers (who at the time happened to be exclusively male) viewed the presence of unaccompanied women in the city as a sign of moral turpitude and a cause of urban disorder.'

It took the later involvement of feminist planners to bring into relief the 'sexist nature of cities and the planners who shaped them', and subsequently to highlight the importance of a more sensitive consideration of issues 'such as universal childcare, transportation solutions that relieve the double burden of home-making and paid labor, and housing design that makes life easier for families' (Doan 2011, 4–5). But as Doan points out, while city planning activities have now started to actively take into consideration issues raised by differences in gender and ethnicity, there is still 'resistance to planning for the LGBT community' (7). The main problem is that there is still a prevalent and influential assumption that 'good planners should only be planning for people, and not promoting "lifestyle choices", [that] planning should only promote the status quo for people who are "normal"' (8).

To a lesser extent, this lack of sufficient planning for 'lifestyle choices' is also a problem in Stockholm and San Francisco. While both cities are quite explicit about wanting to embrace diversity, there has been a lack of careful discussion about what can be done to keep the entire city safe against hate crimes as well as from becoming far too expensive a place to life in. High costs of living – increasingly a concern in Stockholm as well as San Francisco – can have the consequence of creating a population that, while differing in gender, ethnicity and sexual preferences, is largely unified in attitudes concerning consumption so that 'the city becomes an increasingly exclusionary space for those deprived of economic and cultural capital' (Leslie 2005, 404; quoted in Muller Myrdahl 2011, 160).

This can be seen in the case of Toronto, which has embraced the creative cities thesis with some enthusiasm. Muller Myrdahl (2011, 160) presents the following extract from strategic planning documents proposed for Toronto by the Creative City Planning Framework: 'Returns from creative policies, partnerships or projects can be calculated in greater asset and property value, higher revenues, stronger quality of place […] and more inclusive social practices and outcomes.'

As Muller Myrdahl (2011, 161) observes, the 'lip service to inclusivity, while perhaps well-intentioned, is drowned out by the focus on increased property values and higher revenues, which often are joined by an increase in the sanitization and privatization of public spaces'. Something like this is already happening in San Francisco, and not just in the Castro. Consider the Polk Gulch neighborhood, one of the city's original gay neighborhoods, which has recently also become the subject of highly controversial gentrification (Fulbright, 2005):

Gay Shame, an activist group that champions the rights of 'radical queers', says gentrification is pushing out 'hookers, hustlers, drug addicts, homeless people, trannies, needle exchange services, working-class queers and other social deviants'.

'Polk Street is one of the last remaining places where there has been cross-class, cross-gender and cross-sexuality, an interaction between street cultures', said one member of the group who identified himself as Mary. (Gay Shame members have a policy of not using their real names when speaking with the news media). 'To see that steadily replaced by high-end destinations for partying suburbanites is really heartbreaking and very intolerant.'

A recent swell of bars has replaced Polk Street's hustler watering holes of the past. The Polk Gulch Saloon, a renowned place for drag queens and transsexuals, is now the chic Lush Lounge, which serves bright-colored cocktails and caters to the happy-hour crowd. Reflections, a place where johns were known to drink, is now a dance club called Vertigo that brings in DJs and young clubbers. The Hemlock, a hangout with live bands and lots of local hipsters, replaced the historic gay bar The Giraffe. Rendezvous, the last male hustler bar in the neighborhood, closed about six months ago, and a wine bar called SNOB opened a few doors down.

The point, of course, is that utopian planning is about lifestyle choices. It involves initiating discussions about what kind of city 'we' want and what 'we' are prepared to do to attain this. This means that greater voice needs to be given to marginalized individuals and groups. This is not an easy task, for at least two reasons. One, all too often, city planning tends to ignore or leave out marginalized voices, with the consequence that rather than taking advantage of the opportunity to redress social inequalities, it ends up reinscribing such power asymmetries into the construct of the city. Thus, as an alternative to the creative cities thesis, there have been calls for a 'just cities' approach (Fainstein 2010; Healy 1997). According to Fincher and Iveson (2008, 5; cited in Muller Myrdahl 2011, 161; emphasis original): 'To create more just cities, planners need a framework for *making judgments between* different claims in the planning process, as well as for *facilitating* them. That is to say, planning frameworks must enable planners to make calculations about "what should be done", not just about "how it is done".' But realizing the concept of 'just cities' requires that greater attention be given to the more challenging question of making judgments between different claims, which leads us to the 'elaboration of alternative institutions and structures' (Wright 2011).

Two, as we noted in Chapter 5 in our discussions of Malaysia and Hong Kong, there are often tensions between visions articulated at the city level and those expounded at the state level. Reconciling such tensions is certainly no easy task. Zoning technologies represent one option in reconciling city and state visions (Ong 2006; see also Chapters 6 and 7). In the case of China, for example, special economic zones and special administrative zones are set up to allow for spaces where economic and political activities can be treated as 'exceptional' and thus explicitly divergent from any national or state-level vision. Malaysia, arguably, is attempting something similar with the Iskandar Malaysia project. This is envisioned as an economic zone encompassing multiple cities and towns, where commercial, residential and entertainment activities are expected to grow by capitalizing on the region's proximity to Singapore.

Another option might involve reconstituting the populace into different communities, though as Kornberger (2012, 100) points out:

> Politically speaking, assembling the public as communities has two effects. First, it homogenizes parts of the population and glosses over the differences between them by labeling them as a community. Does the gay community, for example, not portray a false unity among a rather diverse set of subcultures? Second, it undermines the building of solidarity between diverse groups. By dividing the population into communities, it stops them from engaging with each other and discovering common platforms for joint action.

There is of course no magic formula, but if different cities (within a larger state) are to indeed be allowed to pursue diverse utopian visions, then some combination of division into communities with zoning technologies might be the most feasible option. This is notwithstanding Kornberger's cautionary remarks about creating a false sense of homogeneity and undermining solidarity. But we need to bear in mind that Kornberger's comments are about governance within a city rather than allowing different cities to flourish in different ways.

On Institutions of Public Deliberation

Our discussion of value ecology, unit scale and developmental trajectory has highlighted the critical importance of public and inclusive discussions to realistic utopian visions.

In the case of Singapore, as Chua (1995, 184–5) observes, the state 'is both thoroughly skeptical regarding the rationality of the ordinary citizen and unapologetically anti-liberal'. As a consequence, the state believes that 'only a few of the best and the brightest are capable of leading well' (Mauzy and Milne 2002, 53). But as was made clear in the 2011 general elections, the state has had to come to terms with the possibility that, despite its successes, many

Singaporeans feel that it is too authoritarian and insufficiently consultative. Indeed, as Singh (2012, 240) points out, 'It is clear that the 2011 General Elections were a "wake-up call" for the ruling party, making the PAP see that the electorate can "speak loudly".' In the case of San Francisco, public views are freely aired. But all too often, rather than resolving differences, it seems as though the point is to 'keep alive those differences which are (i) fertile of edifying forms of controversy, and (ii) expressive of the irresolvable plurality of views, frameworks and "life-styles" in any decently "free" and moderately diverse community' (D'Agostino and Gaus 1998, xxii).

Both situations are of course clearly problematic. Without the engagement of the general community, estrangement becomes a risk. Without the resolution of differences, however temporary, no policy can be pursued in a sustained enough manner for its benefits or weaknesses to be properly assessed. It seems clear that what is currently missing are institution structures that are dedicated to cultivating and facilitating the public deliberation of sometimes difficult and even sensitive issues. By deliberation here, we mean not simply the airing of differences but the willingness to arrive at some kind of agreement, even if temporary. What this demonstrates is that even realistic utopias can only go so far in the absence of institutional structures that facilitate public deliberation.

At this point, we note – not without a sense of irony given the theme of the chapter – that there has been a tendency to idealize (or 'utopianize') the nature of such public deliberation. Thus, Hobbes, Rawls and Habermas have all in one way or another suggested that legitimate public deliberation depends on the rationality of the participants, with the notion of rationality narrowly understood here to mean that once private judgments and interests are set aside, participants will be 'naturally/logically' led to arrive at shared conclusions (Hobbes 1948; Habermas 1984; Rawls 1993). In this regard, the theory of deliberative democracy (Benhabib 1996, 98; Bohman 1995, 99; Dryzek 1990) proves relevant since, as Benhabib (1998, 101) observes:

It is incoherent to assume that individuals can start a process of public deliberation with a level of conceptual clarity about their choices and preferences that can actually result only from a successful process of deliberation. Likewise, the formation of coherent preferences cannot precede deliberation; it can only succeed it. Very often individuals' wishes as well as views and opinions conflict with one another. In the course of deliberation and the exchange of views with others, individuals become more aware of such conflicts and feel compelled to undertake a coherent ordering.

One suggestion for how deliberative democracy can be institutionally realized comes from Dryzek, who defines a 'discursive design' as (1990, 43) a social institution around which the expectations of a number of actors converge. It therefore has a place in their conscious awareness as a site for recurrent communicative interaction among them. Individuals should participate as citizens, not as representatives of the state or any other corporate and hierarchical body. No concerned individuals should be excluded. [...] There should be no hierarchy of formal rules, though debate may be governed by informal canons of discourse.

One institutional design that has been proposed to facilitate informed public deliberation is that of a deliberative poll (Goodin 2008, 17):

Deliberative Polls gather a random sample of between 250 and 500 citizens. They hear evidence from experts, break up into smaller groups (around 15 people each) to frame questions to put to the experts, and then reassemble in plenary session to pose these questions to panels of experts. Before-and-after surveys of participants are taken to measure both information acquisition and opinion change over the course of the event.

Deliberative polls are therefore useful because they encourage citizens to interact with experts as well as one another under conditions that encourage mutual engagement and accommodation. The deliberative poll can be modified to include key policy makers among the participants, and not just ordinary citizens, so that influential policy makers participate alongside their fellow citizens in listening to experts and posing questions. Alternatively, policy makers need not actually participate in such a poll, but can instead make a prior commitment to implementing whatever recommendations might emerge as a result of the polls. The latter situation has been exemplified in the People's Republic of China (Goodin 2008, 19; emphasis added):

Perhaps the most surprising success story along these lines is the 2005 Chinese Deliberative Poll in Zeguo. Participants were asked how the township should allocate funds across some thirty proposed public infrastructure projects, *and the government committed in advance to implementing recommendations of the Deliberative Poll.* The results of their deliberation surprised the leadership, but their recommendations were indeed faithfully implemented.

Perhaps most importantly, participants are encouraged to compromise and cooperate – recognizing that trade-offs and the balancing of interests are necessary when conflicts are deep – and to do so while engaged in informed dialogue with one another (Bohman 1995, 268–9).

One interesting question that has arisen with regard to deliberative democracy and institutional designs concerns the relationship with social complexity – that is, 'whether complex societies are still capable of democratic rule' (Benhabib 1998, 84). The institutional designs suggested by Dryzek and Goodin indicate that the answer is 'yes', and in the context of our discussion, this 'yes' is perhaps most importantly realized at the scale of the city. As Holston and Appadurai (1999, 9) point out:

> As nowhere else, the world's major cities make manifest these reconstitutions of citizenship. The compaction and reterritorialization of so many different kinds of groups within them grind away at citizenship's assumptions. They compel it to bend to the recognition that contemporary urban life comprises multiple and diverse cultural identities, modes of life, and forms of appropriating urban space.

Conclusion

Realistic utopias give careful attention to the constraints of the status quo while unrealistic ones focus overly on the desired end state, perhaps to the point where that end state must be achieved whatever the cost. It is therefore obvious that in plotting developmental trajectories, realistic utopias have to aim for incremental changes to the status quo rather than hoping for a clean slate. As regards unit scale, too small a scale would require an unrealistic level of isolation and autonomy from society at large or the world itself, whereas too ambitious a scale would mean either riding roughshod over the visions of small units or imposing a vision that has little 'buy-in', so that the final result is nothing more than a loose confederation of units, some of which may even chafe at being co-opted into a larger unit. An appreciation of the constraints imposed by the status quo also means that realistic utopias tend to be fairly selective in the kinds of sociocultural dimensions that are being addressed, so that the issue of value ecology is made more manageable as well. As we pointed out, most people in fact are concerned with redressing specific dimensions rather than wanting the society they live in to 'start from scratch'. The problem lies in balancing these different dimensions since not everyone is concerned with making the same kinds of changes and conversely, there are different things about the status quo that different individuals would like to retain. Finally, there is a need to cultivate institutions that foster public deliberation so as to manage the tensions that might arise.

REFERENCES

Abercrombie, N. 1991. 'The Privilege of the Producer'. In *Enterprise Culture*, edited by R. Keat and N. Abercrombie, 171–85. London/New York: Routledge.

Adams, M. 2006. 'Hybridizing Habitus and Reflexivity: Towards an Understanding of Contemporary Identity?' *Sociology* 40 (3): 511–28.

Adkins, L. 2002. *Revisions: Gender and Sexuality in Late Modernity*. Buckingham: Open University Press.

_____. 2003. 'Reflexivity: Freedom or Habit of Gender?' *Theory, Culture and Society* 20 (6): 21–42.

Agence France Presse. 2003. 'Singapore Is Asia's New Gay Capital', 14 September. Online: http://www.singapore-window.org/sw03/030914af.htm (accessed 8 May 2013).

_____. 2005. 'Singapore's Pink Capital Image Fades after Gay Festival Ban', 12 June. Online: http://www.singapore-window.org/sw05/050612af.htm (accessed 8 May 2013).

Aldrich, R. 2004. 'Homosexuality and the City: An Historical Overview'. *Urban Studies* 41 (9): 1719–37.

Alexander, J. 2006. *The Civil Sphere*. Oxford: Oxford University Press.

Amen, M., N. J. Toly, P. L. McCarney and K. Segbers. 2011. Introduction to *Cities and Global Governance*, edited by M. Amen, N. J. Toly, P. L. McCarney and K. Segbers, 1–12. Surrey: Ashgate.

Amery, D., and M. Kibbe. 2010. *Give Us Liberty: A Tea Party Manifesto*. New York: HarperCollins.

Amin, A., and N. Thrift. 1992. 'Neo-Marshallian Nodes in Global Networks'. *International Journal of Urban and Regional Research* 16 (4): 571–87.

_____. 2008. *Cities: Reimagining the Urban*. Cambridge: Polity.

Anderson, B. 1983. *Imagined Communities: Reflections on the Origins and Spread of Nationalism*. London: Verso.

Appadurai, A. 1996. *Modernity at Large: Cultural Dimensions of Globalization*. Minneapolis: University of Minnesota Press.

Archer, M. 2012. *The Reflexive Imperative in Late Modernity*. Cambridge: Cambridge University Press.

Armstrong, E. A. 2002. *Forging Gay Identities: Organizing Sexualities in San Francisco 1950–1994*. Chicago: University of Chicago Press.

Arnold, W. 2007. 'In Singapore, a Local Switzerland for Asia's Wealthy'. *International Herald Tribune*, 24 April.

Ataguba, J. E. 2012. 'Alcohol Policy and Taxation in South Africa: An Examination of the Economic Burden of Alcohol Tax'. *Applied Health Economics and Health Policy* 10 (1): 65–76.

Austrin, T., and J. West. 2005. 'Casino Gaming: Work, Consumption and Regulation'. *Work, Employment and Society* 19 (2): 305–26.

Balakrishnan, V. 2010. 'Singapore Discontinues Casino Shuttle Bus Services'. thegovmonitor. com, 15 September. Online: http://www.thegovmonitor.com/world_news/asia/ singapore-discontinues-casino-shuttle-bus-services-38636.html (accessed 25 March 2011).

Barnett, R. 2010. 'Top 10: Modern Femme Fatales', *Askmen*. Online: http://www.askmen.com/ top_10/entertainment/top-10-modern-femme-fatales.html (accessed 28 March 2010).

Bauman, Z. 1992. *Institutions of Post-modernity*. London: Routledge.

_____. 1998. *Work, Consumerism and the New Poor*. Buckingham: Open University Press.

_____. 2005. *Work, Consumerism and the New Poor*, 2nd edition. Buckingham: Open University Press.

Beck, U. 1992. *Risk Society*. London: Sage.

_____. 1994. 'The Reinvention of Politics: Towards a Theory of Reflexive Modernization'. In *Reflexive Modernization: Politics, Tradition and Aesthetics in the Modern Social Order*, edited by U. Beck, A. Giddens and S. Lash, 1–55. Cambridge: Polity.

_____. 2000. 'The Cosmopolitan Perspective: Sociology of the Second Age of Modernity'. *British Journal of Sociology* 51 (1): 79–105.

Beck, U., and E. Beck-Gernsheim. 1996. *The Normal Chaos of Love*. Cambridge: Polity.

Beck, U., A. Giddens and S. Lash. 1994. *Reflexive Modernization: Politics, Tradition and Aesthetics in the Modern Social Order*. Stanford: Stanford University Press.

Benhabib, S. 1996. 'Toward a Deliberative Model of Democracy'. In *Democracy and Difference: Contesting the Boundaries of the Political*, edited by S. Benhabib, 67–94. Princeton, NJ: Princeton University Press.

_____. 1998. 'Toward a Deliberative Model of Democratic Legitimacy'. In *Public Reason*, edited by F. D'Agostino and G. F. Gaus, 97–124. Aldershot: Ashgate.

Benjamin, G. 1976. 'The Cultural Logic of Singapore's "Multiracialism"'. In *Singapore: Society in Transition*, edited by R. Hassan, 115–33. Kuala Lumpur: Oxford University Press.

Berking, H. 2004. '"Ethnicity Is Everywhere": On Globalization and the Transformation of Cultural Identity'. In *Global Forces and Local Life-Worlds*, edited by U. Schuerkens, 51–66. London: Sage.

Blommaert, J. 2005. *Discourse*. Cambridge: Cambridge University Press.

_____. 2006. 'The Sociolinguistics of Scales'. *Working Papers in Urban Language and Literacies*. London: Institute of Education. Online: https://www.academia.edu/1410324/ Sociolinguistic_scales (accessed 12 March 2014).

Bohman, J. 1995. 'Public Reason and Cultural Pluralism: Political Liberalism and the Problem of Moral Conflict'. *Political Theory* 23: 253–79.

_____. 1999. 'Practical Reason and Cultural Constraint: Agency in Bourdieu's Theory of Practice'. In *Bourdieu: A Critical Reader*, edited by R. Shusterman, 129–52. Oxford: Blackwell.

Bokhorst-Heng, W. D. 1998. 'Language and Imagining the Nation in Singapore'. PhD dissertation, University of Toronto.

Bollens, S. A. 2007. *Cities, Nationalism and Democratization*. London: Routledge.

Bourdieu, P. 1977. *Outline of a Theory of Practice*. Cambridge: Cambridge University Press.

_____. 1984. *Distinction: A Social Critique of the Judgement of Taste*. Cambridge, MA: Harvard University Press

_____. 1990. *The Logic of Practice*. Translated by R. Nice. Cambridge: Polity.

Bourdieu, P., and J. Passeron. 1979. *The Inheritors: French Students and Their Relation to Culture*. Chicago: University of Chicago Press.

Boyd, N. A. 2003. *Wide Open Town: A History of Queer San Francisco to 1965*. Berkeley: University of California Press.

Branswell, B. 2002. 'Gamblers Try to Collect a Debt to Society'. *Toronto Star*, 13 July.

Brooks, A. 2008. 'Reconceptualising Reflexivity and Dissonance in Professional and Personal Domains'. *British Journal of Sociology* 59 (3): 539–59.

_____. 2010a. *Social Theory in Contemporary Asia: Intimacy, Reflexivity and Identity*. London/New York: Routledge.

_____. 2010b. 'Citizenship, "Moral Economies" and "Biopolitical Otherness": The Politics of Inclusion and Rights in Southeast Asia'. Paper presented at the 105th ASA Annual Meeting, 'Towards a Sociology of Citizenship: Inclusion, Participation and Rights', Atlanta, 14–17 August (ASA Archives 2010).

Brooks, A., and L. Wee. 2008. 'Reflexivity and the Transformation of Gender Identity: Reviewing the Potential for Change in a Cosmopolitan City'. *Sociology* 42 (3): 503–21.

_____. 2010. '"Sexual Citizenship" and the Regulation of Intimacy: Citizenship as an Ethical Regime in Cosmopolitan Asia'. Paper presented at the 105th ASA Annual Meeting, 'Towards a Sociology of Citizenship: Inclusion, Participation and Rights', Atlanta, 14–17 August (ASA Archives 2010).

Brown-Saracino, J. 2009. *A Neighborhood that Never Changes*. Chicago: University of Chicago Press.

Brysk, A. 2002. Introduction to *Globalization and Human Rights*, edited by A. Brysk, 1–16. Berkeley: University of California Press.

Bucholtz, M., and K. Hall. 2004. 'Language and Identity'. In *The Blackwell Companion to Linguistic Anthropology*, edited by A. Duranti, 369–94. Oxford: Blackwell.

Cai, H. 2011. 'From Dialect to Mandarin and English'. *Straits Times*, 15 January 2011.

Calhoun, C. 1993. 'Habitus, Field and Capital: The Question of Historical Specificity'. In *Bourdieu: Critical Perspectives*, edited by C. Calhoun, E. LiPuma and M. Postone, 61–88. Chicago: University of Chicago Press.

Cameron, D. 2000. 'Styling the Worker: Gender and the Commodification of Language in the Globalized Service Economy'. *Journal of Sociolinguistics* 4: 323–47.

Carmichael, B. A. 1998. 'Foxwood's Resort Casino: Who Wants It? Who Benefits?' In *Casino Gambling in North America: Origins, Trends and Impacts*, edited by K. Meyer-Arendt and R. Hartmann, 67–75. New York: Cognizant Communications.

Carter, B., and A. Sealey. 2000. 'Language, Structure and Agency: What Can Realist Social Theory Offer to Sociolinguistics?' *Journal of Sociolinguistics* 4: 3–20.

Carver, T. 1998. 'Sexual Citizenship: Gendered and De-gendered Narratives'. In *Politics of Sexuality: Identity, Gender, Citizenship*, edited by T. Carver and V. Mottier, 13–24. London: Routledge.

Carver, T., and V. Mottier. 1998. Introduction to *Politics of Sexuality: Identity, Gender, Citizenship*, edited by T. Carver and V. Mottier, 1–12. London: Routledge.

Castells, M. 1996. *The Rise of the Network Society*. Oxford: Blackwell.

_____. 1997. *The Power of Identity*. Oxford: Blackwell.

Chang, R. 2012. 'Framing THE Singapore Conversation'. *News Clips* (blog), 26 September. Online: http://heresthenews.blogspot.sg/2012/09/framing-singapore-conversation.html (accessed 23 October 2012).

Channel NewsAsia. 2013. 'Singapore High Court Upholds Criminalization of Homosexuality', 9 April. Online: http://www.channelnewsasia.com/news/singapore/singapore-high-court/633188.html (accessed 8 May 2013).

Channel NewsAsia, with E. Neubronner. 2013. 'NTU Study: "Slightly More Tolerance" Now towards Homosexuals Here'. *Today*, 10 January.

Chen, N. N. 2002. 'Embodying Qi and Masculinities in Post-Mao China'. In *Chinese Femininities/Chinese Masculinities*, edited by S. Brownell and J. N. Wasserstrom, 315–29. Berkeley: University of California Press.

Chen, T.-P. 2012. 'Hong Kong Cracks Down on Mainland Mothers'. *Wall Street Journal*, 28 October. Online: http://online.wsj.com/article/SB10001424052970204005004578080521695217696.html (accessed 17 May 2013).

Chen, Z. 2013. 'Hong Kong's New Milk Powder Restriction Sparks Complications between Mainland and Hong Kong'. *Neon Tommy*, 13 March. Online: http://www.neontommy.com/news/2013/03/hong-kongs-new-milk-powder-restriction-inflaming-friction-between-mainland-and-hong-kon (accessed 17 May 2013).

Cheong S.-W. 2013. 'The Merits of an Unfinished City'. *Straits Times*, 19 February.

Chua B. H. 1995. *Communitarian Ideology and Democracy in Singapore*. London/New York: Routledge.

_____. 2011. 'Singapore as Model: Planning Innovations, Knowledge Experts'. In *Worlding Cities: Asian Experiments and the Art of Being Global*, edited by A. Roy and A. Ong, 29–54. Oxford: Blackwell.

Clarke, P. 1996. *Deep Citizenship*. London: Pluto Press.

Clarke, J., J. Newman, N. Smith, E. Vidler and L. Westmarland. 2007. *Creating Citizen-Consumers*. London/Thousand Oaks: Sage.

Clifford, J. 1994. Diasporas. *Cultural Anthropology* (summer): 1–50.

_____. 1997. *Routes: Travel and Translation in the Late Twentieth Century*. Cambridge, MA: Harvard University Press.

Cohen, M. 2010. 'Singapore Wins, for Now'. *Asia Times*, 1 July. Online: http://www.atimes.com/atimes/Southeast_Asia/LG01Ae02.html (accessed 23 December 2010).

Coll, K. 2010. *Remaking Citizenship: Latina Immigrants and New American Politics*. Stanford: Stanford University Press.

Collins, J. 1993. 'Determination and Contradiction: An Appreciation and Critique of the Work of Pierre Bourdieu On Language and Education'. In *Bourdieu: Critical Perspectives*, edited by C. Calhoun, E. LiPuma and M. Postone, 116–38. Chicago: University of Chicago Press.

Cortright, J., and H. Mayer. 2004. 'Increasingly Rank: The Use and Misuse of Rankings in Economic Development'. *Economic Development Quarterly* 18 (1): 34–9.

Cosgrave, J., ed. 2006. *The Sociology of Risk and Gambling Reader*. London/New York: Routledge.

Cosgrave, J., and T. R. Klassen. 2001. 'Gambling against the State: The State and the Legitimation of Gambling'. *Current Sociology* 49 (5): 1–22.

Cox, R. W. 1987. *Production, Power and World Order*. New York: Columbia University Press.

Censorship Review Committee. 2003. *Report of the Censorship Review Committee*. Singapore: Singapore Ministry of Information, Communications and the Arts.

Cremin, C. S. 2003. 'Self-Starters, Can-Doers and Mobile Phoneys: Situations Vacant Columns and Personality Culture in Employment'. *Sociological Review* 51 (1): 109–28.

D'Agostino, F., and G. F. Gaus. 1998. Introduction to *Public Reason*, edited by F. D'Agostino and G. F. Gaus, xi–xxiii. Aldershot: Ashgate.

Da Cunha, D. 2010. *Singapore Places Its Bets: Casinos, Foreign Talent and Remaking a City-State*. Singapore: Straits Times Press.

DiMaggio, P. J., and W. W. Powell. 1983. 'The Iron Cage Revisited: Institutional Isomorphism and Collective Rationality in Organizational Fields'. *American Sociological Review* 48 (2): 147–60.

_____. 1991. Introduction to *The New Institutionalism in Organizational Analysis*, edited by W. W. Powell and P. J. DiMaggio, 1–38. Chicago: University of Chicago Press.

Dinkelspiel, F. 2012. 'Tom Bates and Loni Hancock Visit Sister City in Cuba'. *Berkeleyside*, 31 December. Online: http://www.berkeleyside.com/2012/12/31/tom-bates-and-loni-hancock-visit-sister-city-in-cuba/ (accessed 17 July 2013).

Doan, P. L. 2011. 'Why Question Planning Assumptions and Practices about Queer Spaces'. In *Queering Planning*, edited by Petra L. Doan, 1–18. Surrey: Ashgate.

Du Gay, P. 1996. *Consumption and Identity at Work*. London: Sage.

———.1997. 'Organizing Identity: Making Up People at Work'. In *Production of Culture, Cultures of Production*, edited by P. du Gay, 285–344. London: Sage.

Du Plessis, Henri. 2013. 'Africa Has a Drinking Problem'. IOL News, 18 September. Online: http://www.iol.co.za/news/africa/africa-has-a-drinking-problem-1.1579131#. Uo6wGesyAXw (accessed 22 November 2013).

Dryzek, J. 1990. *Discursive Democracy: Politics, Policy and Political Science*. New York: Cambridge University Press.

Eaddington, W. R., and J. Cornelius, eds. 1997. *Gambling: Public Policies and the Social Science*. Reno: University of Nevada.

Earley, P. 2001. *Super Casino: Inside the New Las Vegas*. New York: Bantam.

Elder, R. W., B. Lawrence, A. Ferguson, T. S. Naimi, R. D. Brewer, S. K. Chattopadhyay, T. L. Toomey, J. E. Fielding; Task Force on Community Preventive Services. 2010. 'The Effectiveness of Tax Policy Interventions for Reducing Excessive Alcohol Consumption and Related Harms'. *American Journal of Preventative Medicine* 38 (2): 217–29.

Elliott, A., and C. Lemert. 2006. *The New Individualism: The Emotional Costs of Globalization*. New York/London: Routledge.

Ellison, N. 1997. 'Towards a New Social Politics: Citizenship and Reflexivity in Late Modernity'. *Sociology* 31 (4): 697–717.

Eveland, J. 2011. *Frommer's Singapore and Malaysia*. Oxford: John Wiley.

Eyal, J. 2013. 'Easier for Gay Refugees to Get EU Asylum Now'. *Straits Times*, 14 November.

Fainstein, S. 2010. *The Just City*. Ithaca: Cornell University Press.

Fals Borda, O. 2000. 'Peoples' SpaceTimes in Global Processes: The Response of the Local'. *Journal of World Systems Research* 6 (3): 624–34.

Faro, C., and G. Wotherspoon. 2000. *Street Seen: A History of Oxford Street*. Melbourne: Melbourne University Press.

Faulks, K. 2000. *Citizenship*. London/New York: Routledge.

Featherstone, M. 2002. 'Cosmopolis: An Introduction'. *Theory, Culture, Society* 19 (1–2): 1–16.

Fincher, R., and K. Iveson. 2008. *Planning and Diversity in the City: Redistribution, Recognition and Encounter*. Basingstoke: Palgrave Macmillan.

Fisiy, C. 1995. 'Chieftaincy in the Modern State: an Institution At the Crossroads of Democratic Change'. *Paideuma* 41: 49–62.

Florida, R. 2005. *Cities and the Creative Class*. London: Routledge.

———. 2012. *The Rise of the Creative Class: Revisited*. New York: Basic Books.

Foucault, M. 1977. *Discipline and Punish*, trans. Alan Sheridan. New York: Pantheon.

———. 1980. *Power/Knowledge*. Brighton: Harvester Wheatsheaf.

———. 2000. *Power: Essential Works of Foucault, 1954–1984*, vol. 3. Edited by James Faubion. New York: New York Press.

Fowler, B. 1997. *Pierre Bourdieu and Cultural Theory: Critical Investigations*. London: Sage.

Frankfurt, H. 1988. *The Importance of What We Care About*. Cambridge: Cambridge University Press.

———. 2004. *The Reasons of Love*. Princeton, NJ: Princeton University Press.

Fu, G. 2012. National Day speech to Singaporean community in Seoul, Korea. Online: http://app.mewr.gov.sg/web/contents/contents.aspx?contid=1703 (accessed 26 October 2012).

Fujita, J., and N. Layne. 2013. 'Japan's Biggest Property Developer Teams Up for Possible Tokyo Casino'. Reuters US, 8 November 2013. Online: http://www.

reuters.com/article/2013/11/08/us-japan-casino-idUSBRE9A70EC20131108 (accessed 13 November 2013).

Fulbright, L. 2005. 'Polk Gulch Cleanup Angers Some, Gentrification Pushing Out "Hookers, Hustlers"'. *SFGate*, 12 October. Online: http://www.sfgate.com/default/article/SAN-FRANCISCO-Polk-Gulch-cleanup-angers-some-2602990.php (accessed 5 December 2011).

Gee, J. P., G. Hull and C. Lankshear. 1996. *The New Work Order: Behind the Language of the New Capitalism*. Boulder: Westview Press.

Giddens, A. 1987. *Social Theory and Modern Sociology*. Cambridge: Polity.

_____. 1990. *The Consequences of Modernity*. Cambridge: Polity.

_____. 1991. *Modernity and Self-Identity*. Cambridge: Polity.

_____. 1992. *The Transformation of Intimacy*. Cambridge: Polity.

_____. 1994. 'Replies and Critiques'. In *Reflexive Modernization*, edited by U. Beck, A. Giddens and S. Lash, 174–215. Cambridge: Polity.

_____. 2002. *Runaway World: How Globalization Is Reshaping Our Lives*, 2nd edition. London: Profile Books.

Glenn, E. N. 2002. *Unequal Freedom: How Race and Gender Shaped American Citizenship and Labor*. Cambridge: Harvard University Press.

_____. 2011. 'Constructing Citizenship: Exclusion, Subordination and Resistance'. *American Sociological Review* 76 (1): 1–24.

Globalization and World Cities Research Network, Loughborough University. 'Cities Globalization Index'. Online: http://www.lboro.ac.uk/gawc/projects/projec71.html (accessed 18 July 2013).

Goffman, E. 1981. *Forms of Talk*. Oxford: Blackwell.

Goh, C. T. 1999. 'First-World Economy, World-Class Home' (National Day Rally speech). Online: http://www.moe.gov.sg/media/speeches/1999/sp270899.htm (accessed 20 October 2012).

Goodin, R. E. 2008. *Innovating Democracy: Democratic Theory and Practice after the Deliberative Turn*. Oxford: Oxford University Press.

Goodwin, C., and M. H. Goodwin. 2004. 'Participation'. In *A Companion to Linguistic Anthropology*, edited by A. Duranti, 222–44. Oxford: Blackwell.

Gopalakrishnan, R., and K. Lim. 2011. 'Singapore PM Makes Rare Apology as Election Campaign Heats Up', Reuters India, 4 May. Online: http://in.reuters.com/article/2011/05/04/idINIndia-56766220110504 (accessed 24 October 2012).

Green, J. M. 1999. *Male Homosexuality in Twentieth-Century Brazil*. Chicago: University of Chicago Press.

Greenwood, R., C. Oliver, K. Sahlin and R. Suddaby, eds. 2008. *The Sage Handbook of Organizational Institutionalism*. London: Sage.

Gu, Z., and J. Z. Gao. 2006. 'Financial Competitiveness of Macao in Comparison with Other Gaming Destinations'. *UNLV Gaming Research and Review Journal* 10 (2): 1–12.

Habermas, J. 1984. *The Theory of Communicative Action*, vols 1 and 2. Translated by T. McCarthy. Boston: Beacon Press.

Hardt, M., and A. Negri. *Empire*. Cambridge, MA: Harvard University Press.

Harvey, D. 2005. *A Brief History of Neoliberalism*. Oxford: Oxford University Press.

Healey, P. 1997. *Collaborative Planning: Shaping Places in Fragmented Societies*. London: Macmillan.

Heelas, P. 1996. 'Detraditionalization and Its Rivals'. In *Detraditionalization*, edited by P. Heelas, S. Lash and P. Morris, 1–20. Oxford: Blackwell.

Heller, M. 1999. 'Alternative Ideologies of *la francophonie*'. *Journal of Sociolinguistics* 3: 336–59.

Heng, G., and J. Devan. 1995. 'State Fatherhood: The Politics of Nationalism, Sexuality and Race in Singapore'. In *Bewitching Women, Pious Men: Gender and Body Politics in Southeast Asia*, edited by A. Ong and M. G. Peletz, 195–205. Oakland, CA: University of California Press.

Herod, A., and M. Wright. 2002. 'Placing Scale: An Introduction'. In *Geographies of Power: Placing Scale*, edited by A. Herod and M. Wright, 1–14. Oxford: Blackwell.

Higgs, D., ed. 1999. *Queer Sites: Gay Urban Histories Since 1600*. London: Routledge.

Hill, M., and K. F. Lian. 1995. *The Politics of Nation Building and Citizenship in Singapore*. London: Routledge.

Hobbes, T. 1948. *Leviathan*. Edited by M. Oakeshott. Oxford: Blackwell.

Hochschild, A. R. 1983. *The Managed Heart: Commercialization of Human Feeling*. Berkeley: University of California Press.

Holden, P. 2001. 'A Man and an Island: Gender and Nation in Lee Kuan Yew's *The Singapore Story*'. *Biography* 24 (2): 401–24.

Holston, J., and A. Appadurai. 1999. 'Introduction: Cities and Citizenship'. In *Cities and Citizenship*, edited by J. Holston, 1–18. Durham, NC: Duke University Press.

Hoornweg, D. 2011. 'The Evolution of City Indicators: Challenges and Progress'. In *Cities and Global Governance*, edited by M. Amen, N. J. Toly, P. L. McCarney and K. Segbers, 91–109. Surrey: Ashgate.

Hussain, Z. 2011. 'More English in Malay, Tamil Homes'. *Straits Times*, 15 January.

Johnstone, B. 2004. 'Place, Globalization, and Linguistic Variation'. In *Sociolinguistic Variation: Critical Reflections*, edited by C. Fought, 65–83. New York: Oxford University Press.

Joppke, C. 2010. *Citizenship and Immigration*. London: Polity.

Jordan, A., R. K. W. Wurzel, A. R. Zito and Brückner, L. 2004. 'Consumer Responsibility-Taking and Eco-Labeling Schemes in Europe'. In *Politics, Products and Markets: Exploring Political Consumerism Past and Present*, edited by M. Micheletti, A. Follesdal and D. Stolle, 161–80. London: Transaction.

Keat, R. 1991. Introduction. In *Enterprise Culture*, edited by R. Keat and N. Abercrombie, 1–17. London: Routledge.

Kennedy, P. 2001. 'Introduction: Globalization and the Crisis of Identities'. In *Globalization and National Identities: Crisis or Opportunity?*, edited by P. Kennedy and C. Danks, 1–28. New York: Palgrave.

Kenney, M. R. 2001. *Mapping Gay LA: The Intersection of Place and Politics*. Philadelphia: Temple University Press.

Khoo, G. C. 2004. 'The Asian Male Spectacle in Glen Goei's Film *That's the Way I Like It* (a.k.a. Forever Fever)'. Working Paper Series 26, Asia Research Institute, National University of Singapore, June. Online: http://www.ari.nus.edu.sg/docs/wps/wps04_026.pdf (accessed 23 April 2013).

Kingma, S. 2004. 'Gambling and the Risk Society: The Liberalisation and Legitimation Crisis of Gambling in the Netherlands'. *International Gambling Studies* 4 (1): 47–67.

Ko, V. 2012. 'Trouble Down South: Why Hong Kong and Mainland Chinese Aren't Getting Along'. *Time World*, 24 January. Online: http://world.time.com/2012/01/24/trouble-down-south-why-hong-kong-and-mainland-chinese-arent-getting-along/ (accessed 30 September 2012).

Kong, L. 1999. 'Globalization and Singaporean Transmigration: Re-imagining and Negotiating National Identity'. *Political Geography* 18 (5): 563–89.

——. 2009. 'Beyond Networks and Relations: Towards Rethinking Creative Cluster Theory'. In *Creative Economics, Creative Cities: Asian-European Perspectives*, edited by L. Kong and J. O'Connor, 61–75. New York: Springer.

Kong, L., and J. O'Connor, eds. 2009. *Creative Economies, Creative Cities: Asian-European Perspectives*. New York: Springer.

Kornberger, M. 2012. 'Governing the City: From Planning to Urban Strategy'. *Theory, Culture and Society* 29 (2): 84–106.

Kotkin, J. 1992. *Tribes: How Race, Religion and Identity determine Success in the New Global Economy*. New York: Random House.

_____. 2010. 'Urban Legends: Why Suburbs, Not Dense Cities, Are the Future'. *Joel Kotkin* (blog), 16 August. Online: http://www.joelkotkin.com/content/00276-urban-legends-why-suburbs-not-dense-cities-are-future (accessed 18 December 2010).

Kymlicka, W. 1995. *Multicultural Citizenship*. Oxford: Oxford University Press.

Lareau, A. 2003. *Unequal Childhoods: Class, Race, and Family Life*. Berkeley: University of California Press.

Lash, S. 1993. 'Pierre Bourdieu: Cultural Economy and Social Change'. In *Bourdieu: Critical Perspectives*, edited by C. Calhoun, E. LiPuma and M. Postone, 193–211. Chicago: University of Chicago Press.

_____. 1994. 'Reflexivity and Its Doubles: Structure, Aesthetics, Community'. In *Reflexive Modernization*, edited by U. Beck, A. Giddens and S. Lash, 110–73. Cambridge: Polity.

Lash, S., and J. Urry. 1994. *Economies of Sign and Space*. London: Sage.

Latour, B. 1996. 'On Actor-Network Theory: A Few Clarifications'. *Soziale Welt* 47: 369–81.

Lee, H. L. 2005. 'Ministerial Statement on the "Proposal to Develop Integrated Resorts"'. Singapore government press release, 18 April. Online: https://www.mti.gov.sg/MTIInsights/Documents/PM%20Lee%20Hsien%20Loong-Parliament-18Apr2005.pdf (accessed 12 March 2014).

_____. 2011. National Day Rally Speech. http://www.pmo.gov.sg/content/pmosite/mediacentre/speechesninterviews/primeminister/2011/August/Prime_Minister_Lee_Hsien_Loongs_National_Day_Rally_2011_Speech_in_English.html#.Uyj_PesyAXw (accessed 15 March 2014).

Lee, S. M., G. Alvarez and J. Palen. 1991. 'Fertility Decline and Pronatalist Policy in Singapore'. *International Family Planning Perspectives and Digest* 17 (2): 65–9.

Lee, T. 2002. 'The Politics of Civil Society in Singapore'. *Asian Studies Review* 26 (1): 97–116.

Lee, V. 2010. 'From the Heartlands to the IR'. Resorts World, Singapore, 9 September. Online: http://resortsworld-singapore.com (accessed 25 March 2011).

Leidner, R. 1993. *Fast Food, Fast Talk: Service Work and the Routinization of Everyday Life*. Berkeley: University of California Press.

Lewin, A. Y., C. B. Weigelt and J. D. Emery. 2004. 'Adaptation and Selection in Strategy and Change: Perspectives on Strategic Change in Organizations'. In *Handbook of Organizational Change and Innovation*, edited by M. S. Poole, 108–60. Oxford: Oxford University Press.

Leyland, W. 2002 *Out in the Castro: Desire, Promise, Activism*. San Francisco: Leyland.

Li, W. W. and Hua J. 2009. 'Shanghai's Emergence into the Global Creative Economy'. In *Creative Economics, Creative Cities: Asian-European Perspectives*, edited by L. Kong and J. O'Connor, 167–71. New York: Springer.

Liang, A. 2013. 'Modern Singapore Grapples with Archaic Sex Law'. *Borneo Bulletin*, 30 April 2013. Online: http://borneobulletin.com.bn/index.php/2013/04/30/modern-singapore-grapples-with-archaic-sex-law/ (accessed 8 May 2013).

Liddle, B., and F. Moavenzadeh. 2002. 'Cities: Challenges and Opportunities for Sustainability. In *Future Cities: Dynamics and Sustainability*, edited by F. Moavenzadeh, K. Hanaki and P. Baccini, 1–16. Dordrecht: Kluwer.

Lim, R. 2004. 'A Military Intelligence Report'. *Yawning Bread*, January. Online: http://www.yawningbread.org/guest_2004/guw-089.htm#return9 (accessed 9 May 2013).

Lim, W. Y., Fong C. W., Chan J. M., Heng D., Bhalla V. and Chew S. K. 2007. 'Trends in Alcohol Consumption in Singapore 1992–2004'. *Alcohol and Alcoholism* 42 (4): 354–61.

Ling, L. H. M. 1999. 'Sex Machine: Global Hypermasculinity and Images of the Asian Woman in Modernity'. *Positions: East Asia Cultures Critiques* 7 (2): 277–306.

Li, W., V. Saravanan and Ng L. H. J. 1997. 'Language Shift in the Teochew Community in Singapore: A Family Domain Analysis'. *Journal of Multilingual and Multicultural Development* 18 (5): 364–84.

Lister, R. 1997 *Citizenship: Feminist Perspectives*. Basingstoke: Macmillan.

———. 2002. 'Sexual Citizenship'. In *Handbook of Citizenship Studies*, edited by E. F. Isin and B. S. Turner, 191–207. London: Sage.

Liu, J. 2012. 'Surge in Anti-China Sentiment in Hong Kong'. BBC News, 8 February. Online: http://www.bbc.co.uk/news/world-asia-china-16941652 (accessed 17 May 2013).

Local. 2012. 'Booze Home Delivery Kicks Off Near Stockholm'. 3 October. Online: http://www.thelocal.se/20121003/43586 (accessed 22 November 2013).

Loi, K.-L. and Kim W. G. 2010. 'Macau's Casinos Industry: Reinventing Las Vegas in Asia'. *Cornell Hospitality Quarterly* 51 (2): 268–83

Low, E. 2013. 'Magazine for Gay Men Launched'. *Marketing*, 28 March. Online: http://www.marketing-interactive.com/news/39231 (accessed 10 May 2013).

Lui, J. 2009. 'Aw Shucks, Jeanette'. *Straits Times*, 12 January 2009.

Mahathir, M. 1970. *The Malay Dilemma*. Singapore: Times Books International.

Mahtani, S. 2013. 'Singapore Gay Magazine Finds a Safe Space'. *Wall Street Journal*, 1 April. Online: http://blogs.wsj.com/searealtime/2013/04/01/singapore-gay-magazine-finds-a-safe-space (accessed 10 May 2013).

Malaysian Insider. 2013. 'Reform or Lose Next Elections, Bloomberg Tells Najib and BN', 7 May. Online: http://www.themalaysianinsider.com/malaysia/article/reform-or-lose-next-elections-bloomberg-tells-najib-and-bn (accessed 14 May 2013).

Maregele, B. 2012. 'Cape Town Dubbed "Drinking Capital of SA"'. IOL News, 15 March. Online: http://www.iol.co.za/news/south-africa/western-cape/cape-town-dubbed-drinking-capital-of-sa-1.1257273#.Uo6xnOsyAXw (accessed 22 November 2013).

Massey, D. 1994. *Space, Place and Gender*. Minneapolis: University of Minnesota Press.

———. 1999. 'Imagining Globalization: Power-Geometries of Time Space'. In *Global Futures: Migration, Environment, and Globalization*, edited by A. Brah, M. Hickman and M. Mac an Ghail, 27–44. Basingstoke: Macmillan.

Markwell, K. 2002. 'Mardi Gras Tourism and the Construction of Sydney as an International Gay and Lesbian City'. *GLQ: A Journal of Lesbian and Gay Studies* 8 (1–2) 81–99.

Marshall, T. H. 1963. *Class, Citizenship and Social Class*. New York: Doubleday.

———. 1992. 'Citizenship and Social Class'. In *Citizenship and Social Class*, edited by T. H. Marshall and T. Bottomore, 3–51. London: Pluto Press.

Maupin, A. 1978. *Tales of the City*. New York: Harper and Row (originally serialized in the *San Francisco Chronicle*).

Mauzy, D. K., and Milne, R. S. 2002. *Singapore Politics under the People's Action Party*. London: Routledge.

McCartney, G. J. 2005. 'Casinos as a Tourism Redevelopment Strategy: The Case of Macao'. *Journal of Macau Gaming Research Association* 2: 40–54.

McClure, K. 1992. 'On the Subject of Rights: Pluralism, Plurality and Political Identity'. In *Dimensions of Radical Democracy: Pluralism, Citizenship, Community*, edited by C. Mouffe, 108–25. London: Verso.

McMillen, J., ed. 1996. *Gambling Cultures: Studies in History and Interpretation*. London: Routledge.

_____. 2003. 'From Local to Global Gambling Cultures'. In *Gambling: Who Wins? Who Loses?*, edited by G. Reith, 49–63. Amhearts: Prometheus Books.

McNay, L. 1999. 'Gender, Habitus and the Field: Pierre Bourdieu and the Limits of Reflexivity'. *Theory, Culture and Society* 16 (1): 95–117.

_____. 2000. *Gender and Agency: Reconfiguring the Subject in Feminist and Social Theory*. Cambridge: Polity.

Merrick, J., and B. T. Ragan, eds. 1996. *Homosexuality in Modern France*. Oxford: Oxford University Press.

Merrick, J., and M. Sibalis, eds. 2001. *Homosexuality in French History and Culture*. New York: Harrington Press.

Micheletti, M., A. Follesdal and D. Stolle. 2004. Introduction to *Politics, Products and Markets: Exploring Political Consumerism Past and Present*, edited by M. Micheletti, A. Follesdal and D. Stolle, ix–xxvi. London: Transaction.

Miller, D. 1989. *Market State and Community: Theoretical Foundations of Market Socialism*. Oxford: Clarendon.

Miller, M., and L. Kroll. 2010. 'Bill Gates No Longer World's Richest Man'. *Forbes*, 10 March. Online: http://www.forbes.com/2010/03/09/worlds-richest-people-slim-gates-buffett-billionaires-2010-intro.html (accessed 14 September 2010).

Mir, A., B. Mathew and R. Mir. 2000. 'The Codes of Migration: Contours of the Global Software Labor Market'. *Cultural Dynamics* 12: 5–33.

Mitlin, D., and D. Satterthwaite. 1994. 'Cities and Sustainable Development'. Background paper for Global Forum '94. Manchester: International Institute for Environment and Development.

Mok, P. 2009. 'Asian Cities and Limits to Creative Capital Theory'. In *Creative Economics, Creative Cities: Asian-European Perspectives*, edited by L. Kong and J. O'Connor, 135–50. New York: Springer.

Mouffe, C. 1993. *The Return of the Political*. London: Verso.

Mouzelis, N. 2009. *Modern and Postmodern Social Theorizing: Bridging the Divide*. Cambridge: Cambridge University Press.

Mukherjee, A. 2005. 'Can Singapore Rediscover Itself as a Fun City?' *Bloomberg News*, 21 April. Online: http://www.singapore-window.org/sw05/050421bl.htm (accessed 28 October 2012).

Muller Myrdahl, T. 2011. 'Queerying Creative Cities'. In *Queerying Planning*, edited by P. L. Doan, 157–66. Farnham, Surrey: Ashgate.

Musfirah, H. 2010. 'Rise in Self-Exclusion Applications since RWS Opened: NCPG'. Channel NewsAsia, 23 February. Online: http://www.channelnewsasia.com/stories/singaporelocalnews (accessed 24 December 2010).

Mutua, M. 2002. *Human Rights: A Political and Cultural Critique*. Philadelphia: University of Pennsylvania Press.

National Library Singapore. 2012. 'Remaking Singapore'. Online: http://was.nl.sg/details/www.remakingsingapore.gov.sg.html (accessed 20 October 2012).

Nash, K. 2010. 'Between Citizenship and Human Rights'. *Sociology* 43 (6): 1067–83.

Nasri, G. 2012. 'The World's Most Business-Friendly Countries'. Reuters, 30 January. Online: http://www.reuters.com/article/2012/01/30/uk-the-worlds-most-business-friendly-idUSLNE80T02K20120130 (accessed 23 June 2012).

NLB Singapore. 1997. 'Singapore 21: Vision for a New Era'. Online: http://www.nlb.gov.sg/annualreport/fy97/htm/vision.htm (accessed 23 October 2012).

Nonini, D. M. 2004. 'Spheres of Speculation and Middling Migrants: Chinese Indonesians in the Asia-Pacific'. In *State/Nation/Transnation: Transnationalism in the Asia-Pacific*, edited by B. Yeoh and K. Willis, 37–66. London: Routledge.

O'Hara, K. 2008. 'Identity, Privacy and Technology in Singapore'. University of Southampton. Paper presented at the 'Identity and the Information Society' conference, Arona, Italy, 28–30 May. Online: http://eprints.soton.ac.uk/265992 (accessed 12 March 2014).

Ohmae, K. 1996. *The End of the Nation-State: The Rise of the Regional Economies*. New York: Touchstone.

Ong, A. 1999. *Flexible Citizenship*. Durham, NC: Duke University Press.

_____. 2000. Graduated sovereignty in Southeast Asia. *Theory, Culture and Society* 17 (4): 55–75.

_____. 2004. 'Intelligent Island, Baroque Ecology'. In *Beyond Description; Singapore, Space, Historicity*, edited by R. Bishop, J. Phillips and W. W. Yeo, 176–89. London/New York: Routledge.

_____. 2006a. *Neoliberalism as Exception: Mutations in Citizenship and Sovereignty*. Durham, NC: Duke University Press.

_____. 2006b. 'Mutations in Citizenship'. *Theory, Culture and Society* 23 (2–3): 499–531.

Overseas Singapore Unit (OSU). 'Singapore Day'. Online: http://www.overseassingaporean.sg/c-event#sgday (accessed 28 October 2012).

Pakir, A. 1992. 'English-Knowing Bilingualism in Singapore'. In *Imagining Singapore*, edited by K. C. Ban, A. Pakir and C. K. Tong. 234–62. Singapore: Times Academic Press.

_____. 2000. 'Singapore'. In *Language Policies and Language Education: The Impact in East Asian Countries in the Next Decade*, edited by W. K. Ho and R. Y. L. Wong, 259–84. Singapore: Times Academic Press.

Patroc. 2013. 'Stockholm Gay Travel Guide'. Online: http://www.patroc.com/stockholm (accessed 13 November 2013).

Pennycook, A. 1994. *The Cultural Politics of English as an International Language*. London: Longman.

Perrons, D. 2004. *Globalization and Social Change: People and Places in a Divided World*. London/New York: Routledge.

Pessanaha, I. 2008. 'Gaming Taxation in Macau'. *Gaming Law Review and Economics* 12 (4): 344–8.

Pink News. 2008. 'Stockholm Police Confirm Stabbing of Gay Man Was a Hate Crime', 28 July. Online: http://www.pinknews.co.uk/2008/07/28/stockholm-police-confirm-stabbing-at-europride-is-a-hate-crime/ (accessed 14 November 2013).

Plummer, K. 'Inventing Intimate Citizenship'. Paper presented at the *Rethinking Citizenship* conference, University of Leeds, June 1999.

_____. 2003. *Intimate Citizenship*. Seattle: University of Washington Press.

PMO Singapore. 2004. 'Prime Minister Lee Hsien Loong's National Day Rally 2004 Speech'. Online: http://www.pmo.gov.sg/content/pmosite/home.html (accessed 11 March 2014).

Portmann, K. 2010. 'Despite Success, Singapore Casinos Face Political Risks'. *Malaysian Mirror*, 7 October. Online: http://www.malaysianmirror.com/featuredetail/ (accessed 23 December 2010).

Poster, M. 1991. *The Mode of Information*. Cambridge: Polity.

Prystay, C. 2007. 'Singapore Swing: The City's Gay Balancing Act'. *Straits Times*, 10 August.

Pugsley, P. 2010. '*Singapore FHM*: State Values and the Construction of Singaporean Masculinity in a Syndicated Men's Magazine'. *Asian Studies Review* 34: 171–90.

Rabinow, P. 1996. *The Anthropology of Reason*. Princeton, NJ: Princeton University Press.

Ramesh, S. 2006. 'Feedback Unit to Be Renamed REACH'. Channel NewsAsia, 12 October. Online: http://www.wildsingapore.com/news (accessed 19 October 2012).

———. 2010. 'More than One Million Visits by Locals to Casinos in IRs'. 15 September. Online: http://www.asiaplate.com/blog.php?blog_id=599 (accessed 24 March 2011).

Rampton, B. 2006. *Language in Late Modernity*. Cambridge: Cambridge University Press.

Rankin, K. 2009. 'Critical Development Studies and the Praxis of Planning'. *City* 13: 219–29.

Rapaport, L. 2011. 'Is San Francisco Still a Gay Mecca?' *San Francisco Bay Guardian*, n.d. Online: http://www.sfbg.com/39/38/cover_gay_mecca.html (accessed 19 October 2011).

Rappa, A., and L. Wee. 2006. *Language Policy and Modernity in Southeast Asia: Malaysia, the Philippines, Singapore, Thailand*. New York: Springer.

Rawls, J. 1993. *Political Liberation*. New York: Columbia University Press.

REACH. 'Overview'. Online: http://www.reach.gov.sg/AboutREACH/Overview.aspx (accessed 20 October 2012).

Reith, G. 2002. *The Age of Change: Gambling and Western Culture*. London: Routledge.

Richey, L., and S. Ponte. *Brand Aid: Shopping Well to Save the World*. Minneapolis: Quadrant.

Ritzer, G. 2010. *Enchanting a Disenchanted World*, 3rd edition. California/London: Sage.

Rivera, D. O. 2013. 'Melco Crown Fosters Big Time Dreams for Manila Casino'. GMA News, 9 October. Online: http://www.gmanetwork.com/news/story/330139/economy/companies/melco-crown-fosters-big-time-dreams-for-manila-casino (accessed 13 November 2013).

Robbins, B. 1992. 'Comparative Cosmopolitanisms'. *Social Text* 31/32: 169–86.

Rose, N. 1990 *Governing the Soul: The Shaping of the Private Self*. London: Routledge.

RSC (Remaking Singapore Committee). 2003. *Changing Mindsets, Deepening Relationships: Report of the Remaking Singapore Committee*. Singapore: Ministry of Community Development and Sports.

Salimat, S. 2013. 'Churchgoers Dismiss Controversy over Adam Lambert's Singapore Gig'. Yahoo! News, 7 March. Online: http://sg.news.yahoo.com/churches-council-receives-complaint-over-upcoming-adam-lambert-gig-192455264.html (accessed 10 May 2013).

Sanyal, S. 2005. 'Asian Global City in the Making'. *Business Times Weekend*, 19–20 March.

Saravanan, V. 1998. 'Language Maintenance and Language Shift in the Tamil-English Community'. In *Language, Society and Education in Singapore*, edited by S. Gopinathan, A. Pakir, Ho W. K. and V. Saravanan, 155–78. Singapore: Times Academic Press.

Sarjent, D. 2008. 'Alcoholism in Swedish Women Increases by 50pc'. *Telegraph* 2 September. Online: http://www.telegraph.co.uk/news/worldnews/europe/sweden/2668332/Alcoholism-in-Swedish-women-increases-by-50pc.html (accessed 22 November 2013).

Sassen, S. 1999. 'Whose City Is It? Globalization and the Formation of New Claims'. In *Cities and Citizenship*, edited by J. Holston, 177–94. Durham, NC: Duke University Press.

———. (1991) 2001a. *The Global City: New York, London, Tokyo*, 2nd edition. Princeton, NJ: Princeton University Press.

———. 2001b. 'Global Cities and Global City-Regions: A Comparison'. In *Global City-Regions*, edited by A. J. Scott, 78–95. New York: Oxford University Press.

_____. 2006. *Territory, Authority, Rights: From Medieval to Global Assemblages*. Princeton, NJ: Princeton University Press.

Sassoon, A. S. 1991. 'Equality and Difference: the Emergence of a New Concept of Citizenship'. In *Socialism and Democracy*, edited by D. McLellan and S. Sayers, 87–105. London: Macmillan.

Sayson, I., and V. Chan. 2013. 'Melco to Boost Budget for Manila Casino, to Add Gaming Tables'. Bloomberg, 9 October. Online: http://www.bloomberg.com/news/2013-10-09/melco-to-boost-budget-for-manila-casino-to-add-gaming-ta.html (accessed 13 November 2013).

Scott, W. R. 2008. *Institutions and Organizations*, 2nd edition. London: Sage.

Seggie, Janet. 2012. 'Alcohol and South Africa's Youth'. *South African Medical Journal* 102 (7): 587.

Sennett, R. 1998. *The Corrosion of Character*. New York: Norton.

SgWiki. 2013. 'Singapore Gay Venues: Contemporary'. Online: http://sgwiki.com/wiki/Singapore_gay_venues:_contemporary (accessed 9 May 2013).

Sherman, M. 2013. 'Proposition 8: California Gay Marriage Argument at High Court Tuesday'. *Huffington Post*, 26 March. Online: http://www.huffingtonpost.com/2013/03/26/proposition-8_n_2952595.html (accessed 11 May 2013).

Shiller, R. J. 2000. *Irrational Exuberance*. Princeton, NJ: Princeton University Press.

_____. 2005. 'American Casino: The Promise and Perils of Bush's "Ownership Society"'. *Atlantic Monthly* (March): 33–44.

Shklar, J. H. 1998a. *Redeeming American Political Thought*. Chicago: University of Chicago Press.

_____. 1998b. *Political Thought and Political Thinkers*. Chicago: University of Chicago Press.

Sibalis, M. 1999. 'Paris-Babylone/Paris-Sodome: Images of Homosexuality in the Nineteenth-Century City'. In *Images of the City in Nineteenth Century France*, edited by J. West-Sooby, 13–22. Mooroka: Boombana.

_____. 2001. 'The Palais-Royal and the Homosexual Subculture of Nineteenth-Century Paris'. In *Homosexuality in French History and Culture*, edited by J. Merrick and M. Sibalis. New York: Harrington Press.

Silverstein, M. 2004. Cultural concepts and the language-culture nexus. *Current Anthropology* 45: 621–52.

Singapore Department of Statistics. 2010. 'Census of Population'. Singapore: Ministry of Trade and Industry.

Singapore Government. 1991. *Shared Values*. Singapore: Singapore National Printers.

Singh, B. 2012. *Politics and Governance in Singapore: An Introduction*, 2nd edition. Singapore: McGraw-Hill.

Siswo, S. 2012. 'Eat Less Rice, Indonesians Urged'. Channel NewsAsia, 19 January. Online: http://www.channelnewsasia.com/stories/southeastasia/view/1177841/1/.html (accessed 20 March 2012).

Skeggs, B. 1997. *Formations of Class and Gender: Becoming Respectable*. London: Sage.

_____. 2002. 'Techniques for Telling the Reflexive Self'. In *Qualitative Research in Action*, edited by T. May, 349–75. London: Sage.

_____. 2004. 'Context and Background: Pierre Bourdieu's Analysis of Class, Gender and Sexuality'. In *Feminism after Bourdieu*, edited by L. Adkins and B. Skeggs, 19–33. Oxford: Blackwell.

_____. 2005. 'The Making of Class and Gender through Visualizing Moral Subject Formation'. *Sociology* 39 (5): 965–82.

Skocpol, T. 2003. *Diminished Democracy: From Membership to Management in American Civic Life*. Norman: University of Oklahoma Press.

Smale, W. 2004. 'Singapore Signs Up to Global Casino Club'. BBC News, 23 August. Online: http://news.bbc.co.uk/1/hi/business/3590184.stm (accessed 17 February 2014).

Socarides, R. 2013. 'Obama's Brief against Proposition 8 Goes Far'. *New Yorker*, 1 March. Online: http://www.newyorker.com/online/blogs/newsdesk/2013/03/socarides-on-prop-8.html (accessed 21 March 2013).

Soh, E. 2011. 'Bosses Send Foreign Workers to Gamble'. *Straits Times*, 4 November. Online: http://www.straitstimes.com/BreakingNews/Singapore/Story/STIStory_730424.html (accessed 11 March 2012).

Sowell, T. 2004. *Affirmative Action around the World: An Empirical Study*. New Haven: Yale University Press.

Stevenson, D. 2013. *The City*. Cambridge: Polity.

Stockholm Visitors Board. 2013. 'Gay and Lesbian Stockholm'. Visitstockholm.com. Online: http://www.visitstockholm.com/en/Dine/Tips/Gay--Stockholm (accessed 14 November 2013).

Straits Times. 2010. 'Banning Foreign Workers from Casinos: We Don't Have the Right'. 17 November.

———. 1983. 'Speech on Radio'. 15 August. Online: http://newspapers.nl.sg/Digitised/Article/straitstimes19830815.2.32.1.aspx (accessed 11 March 2014).

Stroud, C., and L. Wee. 2010. 'Language Policy and Planning in Singaporean Late Modernity'. In *English in Singapore: Unity and Utility*, edited by L. Lim, A. Pakir and L. Wee, 181–204. Hong Kong: Hong Kong University Press.

———. 2012. *Style, Identity and Literacy: English in Singapore*. Clevedon: Multilingual Matters.

Struggles in Sweden (blog). 2013. 'Police Attack Queers during the Stockholm Pride Parade', 8 August. Online: http://libcom.org/blog/police-attack-queers-during-stockholm-pride-parade-08082013 (accessed 14 November 2013).

Stryker, S., and J. Van Kuskirk. 1996. *Gay by the Bay: A History of Queer Culture in the San Francisco Bay Area*. San Francisco: Chronicle Books.

Sullivan, A. 2001. 'Cultural Capital and Educational Attainment'. *Sociology* 35 (4): 893–912.

Swales, J. M. 1990. *Genre Analysis: English in Academic and Research Settings*. Cambridge: Cambridge University Press.

Sweetman, P. 2003. 'Twenty-First Century Dis-ease? Habitual Reflexivity or the Reflexive Habitus'. *Sociological Review* 51 (4): 528–49.

Tai, J., and Lim Y. H. 2013. 'New Curbs to Limit Monthly Gambling Visits: Rules Target the Financially Vulnerable'. *Straits Times*, 29 May.

Tan, E. S. 2005. 'Globalization, Nation-Building and Emigration: The Singapore Case'. In *Asian Migrations*, edited by B. P. Lorente, N. Piper, H. H. Shen and B. Yeoh, 87–98. Singapore: Asia Research Institute, Singapore University Press.

Tan, K. P. 2001. '"Civic Society" and the "New Economy" in Patriarchal Singapore'. *Crossroads* 15 (2): 95–124.

Tay, J. 2011. 'Why Orchid for Elton?' *Straits Times*, 26 November.

Teh, J. L., and M. Kok. 2010. 'Easier Casino Exclusion for Foreign Workers'. *Straits Times*, 6 November.

Teo, X. 2012. 'Building a Home with Hope and Heart: Prime Minister Lee Spells Out What the Next Chapter of the Singapore Story Should Be About'. *Today*, 27 August. Online: http://www.todayonline.com/Singapore (accessed 23 October 2012).

Thang, L. L. 2005. 'Private Matters, Public Concern: Procreation Issues in Singapore'. *Japanese Journal of Population* 3 (1): 76–108.

Thompson, J. 1991. Introduction to *Pierre Bourdieu, Language and Symbolic Power*, 1–42. Cambridge, MA: Harvard University Press.

Thompson, M. 2013. '"Pink Christmas" Contest Attracts LGBT Travelers to Stockholm'. *Examiner.com*, 31 October. Online: http://www.examiner.com/article/pink-christmas-contest-attracts-lgbt-travelers-to-stockholm (accessed 13 November 2013).

Tiby, E. 2001. 'Victimization and Fear among Lesbians and Gay Men in Stockholm'. *International Review of Victimology* 8 (2): 217–43.

Toh, E. 2011. 'Orchid Named after Elton John', *Straits Times*, 19 November.

Toh, Y. C. 2012. 'Civil Servants Can Take Part in Dialogues with Gag Order Lifted'. *Straits Times*, 16 October. Online: http://www.straitstimes.com/breaking-news/singapore/story/civil-servants-can-take-part-dialogues-gag-order-lifted-20121016 (accessed 24 October 2012).

Tor, C. L. 2006. 'Reaching Out Better'. *Today*, 13 October. Online: http://www.wildsingapore.com/news/20060910/061013-1.htm (accessed 24 September 2012).

Touraine, A. 1995. *Critique of Modernity*. Translated by David Macey. Cambridge: Blackwell.

Trentmann, F. 2006. 'Knowing Consumers: Histories, Identities, Practices: An Introduction'. In *The Making of the Consumer: Knowledge, Power and Identity in the Modern World*, edited by F. Trentmann, 1–27. Oxford: Berg.

Turner, B. S. 1993. 'Contemporary Problems in the Theory of Citizenship'. In *Citizenship and Social Theory*, edited by B. S. Turner, 1–18. London: Sage.

_____. 2011. 'Judith N. Shklar and American Citizenship'. *Citizenship Studies* 15 (6–7): 933–43.

Vidal, G. 1948. *The City and the Pillar*. New York: E. P. Dutton.

Vijayan, K. C. 2013. 'Growth of Gay Groups "a Challenge": Singapore Will Have to Address Their Needs and Interests, Says Former Chief Justice'. *Straits Times*, 13 April 2013.

Vogel, D. 2004. 'Tracing the American Roots of Political Consumerism'. In *Politics, Products and Markets: Exploring Political Consumerism Past and Present*, edited by M. Micheletti, A. Follesdal and D. Stolle, 83–100. London: Transaction.

Vong, C. K. 2004. 'Gambling Attitudes and Gambling Behavior of Residents in Macao: The Monte Carlo of the Orient'. *Journal of Travel Research* 42 (3): 271–8.

Wade, R. 2001. 'Is Globalization Making World Income Distribution More Equal?' DESTIN Working Paper 01-01, London School of Economics. Online: mercury.ethz.ch/serviceengine/Files/ISN/137944/.../en/WP10.pdf (accessed 12 March 2014).

Wallerstein, I. 1996. 'The National and the Universal: Can There Be Such a Thing as World Culture?' In *Culture, Globalization and the World-System*, edited by A. D. King, 91–106. Minneapolis: University of Minnesota Press.

_____. 1997. *The Time of Space and the Space of Time: The Future of Social Science*. Online: http://www2.binghamton.edu/fbc/archive/iwtynesi.htm (accessed 20 February 2014).

Warde, A. 1994. 'Consumption, Identity-Formation and Uncertainty'. *Sociology* 28 (4): 877–98.

Webb, J. 2004. 'Organizations, Self-Identities and the New Economy'. *Sociology* 38 (4): 719–38.

West, J., and T. Austrin 2011. 'States, Markets and New Media: The Contemporary Politics of Gambling'. In *The New Politics of Leisure and Pleasure*, edited by P. Bramham and S. Wagg, 119–35. London: Palgrave.

Wee, L. 2007. 'Linguistic Human Rights and Mobility'. *Journal of Multilingual and Multicultural Development* 28 (4): 325–38.

———. 2008. 'The Technologization of Discourse and Authenticity in English Language Teaching'. *International Journal of Applied Linguistics* 18 (3): 256–73.

———. 2011. 'The Ranked List as Panopticon in Enterprise Culture'. *Pragmatics and Society* 2 (1): 37–56.

———. 2012. 'Prescribing Pastoral and Pragmatic Orientations: Challenges for Language Policy'. In *The Languages of Nation*, edited by C. Percy and M. C. Davidson, 63–82. Clevedon: Multilingual Matters.

Wee, L., and W. Bokhorst-Heng. 2005. 'Language Policy and Nationalist Ideology: Statal Narratives in Singapore'. *Multilingua* 24: 159–83.

Wee, L., and A. Brooks. 2010. 'Personal Branding and the Commodification of Reflexivity'. *Cultural Sociology* 4 (1): 45–62.

Williams, R., and R. Wood. 2004. *The Demographic Sources of Ontario Gaming Revenue: Final Report.* Guelph: Ontario Problem Gambling Research Center.

Wikipedia. 2013a. 'Right of Abode in Hong Kong'. Online: http://en.wikipedia.org/wiki/Right_of_abode_in_Hong_Kong (accessed 17 May 2013).

———. 2013b. 'Early 2012 Hong Kong Protests'. Online: http://en.wikipedia.org/wiki/Early_2012_Hong_Kong_protests (accessed 18 May 2013).

———. 2014. 'Pink Money'. Online: http://en.wikipedia.org/wiki/Pink_money (accessed 20 February 2014).

Wong, K. S. 2006. 'Launch of the Overseas Singaporean Portal'. Ministry of Home Affairs (Singapore), 26 August. Online: http://www.mha.gov.sg/news_details.aspx?nid=MzIy-WzpmKhqwnZs%3D (accessed 26 October 2012).

Wong, T. 2013a. 'Shanmugam Meets Gay Activists: Discussion with Women Gay Rights Group Part of Ongoing Engagement'. *Straits Times*, 5 January 2013.

———. 2013b. 'Minister to Meet Church Group over Gay Issues: Churches Worried about Govt's Stand on Homosexuality Send E-mail to Shanmugam'. *Straits Times*, 20 January.

———. 2013c. 'Church Feels the Heat over Gay Singer's Gig'. *Straits Times*, 2 March.

World Airport Awards. 2009. 'Incheon International Airport Is Named as the World's Best Airport for 2009'. 9 June. Online: http://www.worldairportawards.com/Awards_2009/Airport2009.htm (accessed 22 March 2010).

Wotherspoon, G. 1991. *City of the Plain: History of a Gay Sub-culture.* Sydney: Hale and Ironmonger.

Wright, E. O. 2009. 'Envisioning Real Utopias'. Author's website: http://www.ssc.wisc.edu/~wright/ERU.htm (accessed 10 November 2011).

———. 2011. 'Real Utopias for a Global Sociology'. *Global Dialogue*, 18 July. Online: http://www.isa-sociology.org/global-dialogue (accessed 10 November 2011).

Yeo, G. 2004. Speech by minister of trade and industry George Yeo at the Committee of Supply Debate, Ministry of Trade and Industry, Singapore, 12 March.

Young, I. M. 1989. 'Polity and Group Difference: A Critique of the Ideal of Universal Citizenship'. *Ethics* 99: 250–74.

Yue, A. 2007. 'Hawking in the Creative City: *Rice Rhapsody*, Sexuality and the Cultural Politics of New Asia in Singapore'. *Feminist Media Studies* 7 (4): 365–80.

INDEX

www.ingramcontent.com/pod-product-compliance
Lightning Source LLC
Chambersburg PA
CBHW022358280326
41935CB00007B/226